Shusaku Endo

FOREIGN STUDIES

British Library C.I.P.

Endo, Shusaku, *1923–*
  Foreign studies.
  I. Title
  895.635[F]

  ISBN 0-340-53084-7

Printed and bound in Great Britain for Hodder and Stoughton Paperbacks, a division of Hodder and Stoughton Ltd., Mill Road, Dunton Green, Sevenoaks, Kent TN13 2YA. (Editorial Office: 47 Bedford Square, London WC1B 3DP) by Clays Ltd., St Ives plc.

Introduction

The reader of *Foreign Studies* may be surprised that the novel comprises three separate parts. But, as the author of the work, I believe that a common motif underlies these three seemingly unrelated narratives.

Kudo, the Oriental protagonist in Part One, 'A Summer in Rouen', never feels totally at ease during this his first experience of living abroad. Encountering the warm and friendly reception extended to him by the French Christian family who offer him lodgings and the kindness of the people of Rouen in general, Kudo withdraws into himself and feels a certain nervous tension. Whilst seeking to respond to the well-intentioned overtures of his French hosts, he becomes aware of the gap that exists between their feelings and his. Every Japanese student who has had the opportunity of studying abroad in this way should be able to empathize with such feelings. But there can be no doubt that these would have been particularly acute in the case of the poor student sent to study in France so soon after Japan's defeat in the Pacific war.

(Needless to say, this protagonist is not myself; neither are his experiences mine. Indeed, I subsequently came to look on the husband, wife and children of the 'R' family who actually looked after me during my own stay in Rouen as my French family. Since then I have on occasion felt unhappy with the French colonial policy, but even so I have never lost my love for the people of France – and I see this as a result of the friendships I developed with this family and with the students in Lyon.)

In subsequent years I have acted as proxy parent for several students from South-East Asia whilst they pursued their studies in Japan; and all admitted to having experienced this same sense of uneasiness during the initial months of their stay. This sense of uneasiness stems from the differences in daily life, customs, social mores and ways of thinking, and the same theme is carried over into the third part of the novel, 'And You, Too'.

The chief protagonist of Part Two, 'Araki Thomas', is a figure from Japan's distant past, one of several young Japanese students who travelled to Europe to study as early as the seventeenth century. Confronted by Western Christianity, Araki Thomas also suffers from a sense of uneasiness, a painful awareness of the distance between himself and European culture. Like the hero of 'A Summer in Rouen', this protagonist of three hundred years ago owes his chance of studying abroad to the Christian Church, but he senses a contradiction between the true spirit of Christianity and the aggressive penetration into the Orient being perpetrated by the Christian Church in Europe at that time. As he heads towards Europe, he is increasingly aware that the Christian Church to which he planned to devote the rest of his life was seeking to pursue the propagation of the Gospel in the Orient fully aware of the aggression being perpetrated to this end. He was also painfully aware of the numerous poor Japanese who were dying as a result of the Church's determination to proceed with this policy.

Of course I do not empathize with him unreservedly. Rather, it was my wish as a Japanese novelist to write a short story highlighting the existence of Japanese men, women and children who suffered during the seventeenth century as a result of this attempt by the Christian Church to spread the Gospel in the Orient.

Clearly the same motif can be detected in both 'A Summer in Rouen' and 'Araki Thomas'. Regardless of the age, there will always be a great difference between the Oriental student who travels to Europe to pursue his studies and the French student who goes to Italy. It is my belief that, if we ignore this difference, we shall never be able to achieve a true dialogue between East and West, a genuine harmony between Eastern wisdom and Western ideas.

The central character of Part Three, 'And You, Too', is a young Japanese scholar who is given an opportunity to study in France. The reader can assume that the events occur in about 1965.

In the fifth year after the cessation of hostilities in the Pacific war, I myself travelled to France to study. At the time, the Western world looked on Japan as a nation guilty of aggression in the war, but, with a few companions, I secured a fourth-class berth in a French ship and arrived in Marseille following a six-weeks' voyage. During the period I was in France there was only a handful of Japanese even in Paris, and the three of us at the university where I was studying were the first Japanese students to come there after the war.

The student life of Tanaka, the hero of this novel, is relatively relaxed when compared with my own personal experiences. By 1965 there was a thriving Japanese community in Paris and a Japanese embassy to cater for their needs. (In my day, since Japan had yet to renew her peace treaties, there was no embassy.) In this sense, the conditions under which Tanaka found himself studying in France were much more advantageous than those I experienced. Nevertheless, for all the superficial differences between the two life-styles, I have woven much of my own experience of studying abroad into the personality of Tanaka.

Speaking from personal experience, for about the first year of my stay in Europe I felt as though I were making good progress in my attempt to understand France. During the long war years it is little exaggeration to say that the only news to reach Japan from Europe concerned the progress of the German army, as a result of which the Japanese remained ignorant of the Resistance movement and the holocaust of the Nazi concentration camps, about which the Europeans knew only too well.

During the first year of my studies there I was able to experience at first hand everyday life in post-war France and made some progress in my study of the language. I devoted all my time to my subject of study, twentieth-century Christian authors (focusing in particular on some of the *grands écrivains* of French literature like Mauriac, Bernanos and Julien Green). I was also able to establish several friendships with some of the French students at my university. Optimistically I began to believe I had taken the first steps towards acquiring an understanding of Europe.

And yet, in about the middle of my second year, I learnt that towering beyond the hill I had scaled lay an enormous mountain. Further on lay an even more imposing mountain. I now found myself wondering whether there was any way that a visitor from the

Far East could ever truly comprehend France. As a Japanese confronted with the tradition, rich cultural heritage and confidence of Europe, I came to sense a certain unfathomable distance.

The Japanese scholars who studied in Europe before me appear to have been fortunate enough to have managed to avoid this sense of distance. Following the reopening of the country in 1868 after the more than two and a half centuries during which Japan effectively isolated herself from all contact with the outside world, many scholars were sent to study in Europe. It seems they returned confident in a belief that it is indeed possible for the Japanese to reach a full understanding of Europe. I believe that this is the great difference between my own experience and that of those who preceded me to Europe.

In my opinion there are two reasons for this.

The first of these involves the failure of my predecessors to distinguish between civilization and culture. They confused study of the technological aspects of European civilization with study of European culture *per se*. Even today it is not too difficult for students from the developing nations to acquire technological knowledge of a foreign civilization. But there is a difference between an understanding of the technology of a civilization and the culture itself. Those Japanese who travelled to Europe to study art and music remain optimistic. I still occasionally hear the music of young Japanese musicians who have returned from a period of study abroad, and they are clearly superior to their predecessors in terms of technique. But I remain convinced that the difference is one of technique, not an indication of genuine understanding.

The same holds true for the artists who travel to the West to study. Unfortunately I detect in much of their work mere imitation of the techniques of Western artists. With a few notable exceptions, it is extremely difficult to discern much that is unique to the Japanese artist.

In all this I am certainly not seeking to detract from the experiences of those Japanese who, whilst studying abroad, ignored the distance between European and Japanese culture. But, in my case, things did not work out so smoothly.

Some time during the second year of my stay in France I gradually became more conscious of my identity as a Japanese. The more I came into contact with European art and culture, the more aware did I become that they derived from emotions and a sensibility which remained alien to me. As I have already mentioned, my depiction of the daily life of Tanaka is not intended as a portrayal of my own experiences as a foreign student. Apart from anything else, Tanaka studied in Paris whereas I attended the University of Lyon. But for all that, as he becomes increasingly aware of this sense of distance, Tanaka experiences the same mental anguish which I felt. He travels to Sade's château and the blood that he spits up there is the blood of this suffering. (I too coughed up blood during my stay in Lyon.)

This same sense of distance is evidenced in my novel *Silence*. One of the main themes of *Silence* concerns the question of whether Christianity, a religion that developed largely out of European ways of thinking, can ever take root in Japan. In that novel, one of the characters tells the missionary, Rodrigues, 'Japan is a mudswamp'. This is a reflection of my own doubts formed during my stay in France as to whether Western culture (not civilization) can ever truly take root when planted in Japan.

In this sense 'And You, Too' can be described as a prelude to *Silence*. But whereas *Silence* deals with events that occurred in Japan some three hundred years ago, 'And You, Too' is set mainly in Paris in the mid-1960s. It is no coincidence that Tanaka chose to study the life and works of the Marquis de Sade. In France during the 1950s there was a renewed interest in Sade and his philosophy. Intellectuals like Sartre and Simone de Beauvoir wrote about Sade. And I still remember the works of Gilbert Lely and other Sade specialists which attracted my attention as I sat in my cheap lodgings in Lyon.

I was intrigued as to why the originator of 'Sadism' should be the focus of such attention. Part of the answer lies in a consideration of the war and the concentration camps. Massacre and torture were not perpetrated only in the concentration camps; the city of Lyon where I lived was the scene of similar atrocities. The building in which the Nazis tortured members of the French Resistance still stood in the centre of Lyon and one could see into the underground chamber from the pavement. Often, on my way to and from the university, I would peer into that underground chamber. It was dark and I was unable to distinguish anything clearly. But on such occasions I would say to myself, 'This is like the inner recesses of the human soul – dark and unfathomable.'

I do not believe that this instinct was mistaken. The impulse towards sadistic behaviour lies hidden in man's deep psyche, transcending all considerations of intellect, rationality and morality. That deep psyche is dark, like that underground chamber.

The Second World War exposed the dark recesses of the human soul. To the logical and disciplined French mind, the existence of this impenetrable deep psyche within man must have appeared quite bizarre. It was this that led Sartre, de Beauvoir and others to attempt a rational analysis of the phenomenon. Although still a student at the time, I too realized that an exploration of this reality in the depth of the human soul, this phenomenon that lurked beneath the conscious, could represent a major theme for literature of the future. In other words, I was interested in the problem of the unconscious. It was for this reason that I portrayed Tanaka as interested in the works of Sade.

The theme of the unconscious was prominent in Eastern writing long before it was taken up in Western literature. Since about the fifth century AD one of the sects of Buddhism divided the human soul into several levels, drawing a sharp distinction between the conscious and unconscious worlds. In contrast to this, Western Christianity has tended to view the world of the unconscious as belonging to the realm of evil (a belief that has influenced the works of Freud) and, as such, heretical. Even the Spanish mystics, who touched on the concept of the unconscious world, failed to treat it seriously, and it was left to Buddhism to claim that it is the unconscious which lies at the heart of man.

Whilst he is involved in the study of Sade, Tanaka grows gradually more and more aware of the distance between himself and the West. This occurs as he stands at the parting of the ways, forced to make a choice between the view of Sade as a perceptive rationalist on the one hand and that which saw him as a pioneer of the study of the unconscious world on the other. Simone de Beauvoir saw Sade as extremely perceptive. But, confronted with that conclusion, the Japanese student can feel only that this is 'Western, so Western'.

Tanaka's experiences whilst studying abroad offer constant reminders of this sense of distance between himself and the culture of the West. Most of the other Japanese studying in the West appear content to ignore this gap, but, as a sincere student, he is unable to deceive himself on this score. It is this that leads to his pain and suffering.

Twenty years have passed since I wrote *Foreign Studies*, and I now find myself viewing my former self struggling with that sense of distance between East and West as in the nature of a pitiful younger brother. Over the past twenty years – especially since the writing of *Silence* – my thoughts on the subject have slowly changed. As a result of continuous consideration of the concept of 'the unconscious' in my literature, I am now convinced that meaningful communication between East and West is possible. I have gradually come to realize that, despite the mutual distance and the cultural and linguistic differences that clearly exist in the conscious sphere, the two hold much in common at the unconscious level. It is for this reason that the hero of 'And You, Too' does not represent my present self. Rather, I should like him to be seen as a reflection of my former self.

Finally I should like to express my sincere appreciation to Mark Williams, who completed the English translation of this novel. Without his effort, this work would not have become available to a wider, foreign readership.

Shusaku Endo

Part One

A Summer in Rouen

Kudo had never seen such a mirror in Japan. There was nothing wrong with its oval shape, but the arabesque pattern around the edge had been daubed with a garish gold. It seemed like an imitation baroque piece, yet in no way could it be considered a fine work of art. And to make matters worse, a copper band bearing the words *Use this mirror to change your appearance* had been affixed to it.

Reflected in this mirror was the sweat-covered face of one just woken from an afternoon nap. It was still less than a month since his arrival in France; and yet, either as a result of travel fatigue or of the nervous tension that inevitably accompanies a visit to a new culture, his cheeks appeared to have hollowed somewhat. And then, for some reason or other, there were times when he felt a dull pain in his back. It was still only 2.30 and a great quiet reigned over the house. The oppressive sun could be seen beating down mercilessly on the garden fence which was visible from the window. It was brilliant white. Inside the house it seemed that everyone was still asleep.

As Kudo slipped stealthily downstairs, his nostrils were assailed by the smell of fruit used for jam-making, which emanated from the kitchen. And there in the kitchen stood the elderly maid, her back towards him. Her dark shadow was etched in bold relief on the stone floor, yet it was not clear what she was doing. He politely indicated that he was just off for a walk, but as the maid was hard of hearing, she made no response.

By 2.30 on a summer afternoon the average Frenchman has only just finished lunch – unlike his Japanese counterpart. This day was no exception. The stone pavement shone like a dried-up river-bed. There were no signs of life in the square. The fountains had stopped, and a couple of deserted taxi-cabs were parked under the roadside trees. There was a chemist with a sign that read *Pharmacie* and an antique dealer announced himself with the word *Antiquités* painted in the window, but both would remain closed until the heat of the midday sun had relented slightly.

Sitting on the edge of the dried-up fountain, Kudo fell to wondering where to go next. He had been in Rouen less·than a week, yet he had already covered most of the town on foot. Just to his left was the famous cathedral that Rodin is said to have loved so much – but Kudo had already been there three times! All the picture postcards on sale in the local cafés and souvenir shops showed the old tower where Joan of Arc was held captive, yet he had lost count of the number of times he had been there. He could even remember the grave tone of voice adopted by the guide as he showed visitors the well and the dank room where apparently she was held. Apart from that, there was nothing but Flaubert's house down by the station and the site where Joan of Arc was burnt at the stake. Flaubert's house was open only in the morning, and the place of execution had nothing more to offer than a statue of Joan dressed in white, her arms clasped to her breast. At this time of day the powerful rays of the sun reflected off the statue would be stifling.

A priest wearing the round cap of the Benedictine order crossed the road and came towards him. Seeing Kudo sitting by the fountain, he stopped in his tracks and a somewhat condescending smile formed in the centre of his large, chubby face.

'You're the Japanese student staying with the Vealeauxes, aren't you?'

Kudo was about to stand up, but the priest gestured to him to remain seated.

'I've heard about you from Madame Vealeaux. How do you like Rouen?'

'Very nice, thank you. It's the kind of place I'd like to settle down in.'

Kudo watched nonchalantly as the priest clad in black disappeared down an alley leading from the square to the rue St

Jacques. Since this was a small town, Kudo was already something of a local celebrity, and, two or three times whilst he had been out for a walk, he had been approached by smiling women who had addressed him in the same mannner as the priest. On such occasions, anxious to create the best possible impression, he would force a smile and bow his head respectfully.

He decided to visit the harbour. That was the one place in this windless town where he really felt able to breathe. He had been there once before, when the Vealeauxes had taken him in their car. Though the locals referred to it as the harbour, it was really no more than a wharf for the barges that plied up and down the Seine, and yet the labourers there, carrying boxes of vegetables and fruit on their shoulders, paid much less attention to Kudo than did the people in the town itself. He had heard that, if one followed the Seine far enough upstream, one eventually came to Paris. He felt convinced that Paris would provide him with more space to breathe in than Rouen.

And yet it was somehow irksome to have to walk to the harbour in the heat of the sun . . . and ultimately, he felt he had no choice but to give up the idea of going for a walk and return home. I must buy some cigarettes and airmail paper, he thought.

There was no one in the tobacconist next to the chemist. But the door was not locked. By pushing open the door, he activated the little bell hanging above it. It emitted a hollow sound. A youth with chestnut-coloured hair wearing a red sports shirt appeared and stared at Kudo intently.

'You're Japanese, aren't you?'

'That's right.'

'Hey, I read about you in the paper. It was in the church newsletter. They mentioned the Vealeauxes too.'

From behind the glass case he held out his hand. It was a stout hand, almost like a glove, and seemed totally to envelop Kudo's palm. It was covered in sweat.

'Well, how do you like Rouen?'

Kudo forced the same smile he had previously shown the priest, and replied, 'Nice. It's the kind of place I'd like to settle down in.'

'Don't you think the French are friendly?'

'Yes, they really are.'

The youth appeared content, bowed and turned to the shelf piled high with cigarettes. Getting a couple of packets, he said, 'Here, take these. They're on me.'

When he returned home, the sound of footsteps suggested that people were beginning to stir from their afternoon nap. Yet the floor and desk were still bathed in sunlight, shining down like molten tin. Sprawled across his bed, Kudo stared at the two packets of cigarettes. They were Gauloises, the most popular brand in the country. He gave me these for nothing, he thought.

He had been given these cigarettes. With his limited French, Kudo had not been able to produce the proper expression in order to be able to pay for things without upsetting the other person's feelings. Consequently he had merely expressed his thanks and left the shop. But it was not merely the sensation of the youth's sweaty hand which had remained with Kudo. An unpleasant feeling lingered there. It's not merely the cigarettes that are free. Everything's free in this house, he thought.

Kudo did not have to pay for either room or board in the Vealeauxes' house. This was because the Vealeauxes had agreed to take him in for the whole of the summer in accordance with the wishes of the Church. It had been two years previously that the Far Eastern mission of the Roman Catholic Church had devised the plan to invite students from the East to study in every European country. From Japan alone it had been decided to send one student respectively to Spain, Italy, Germany and France. Costs for the whole trip for each of the selected students were then to be defrayed by contributions from Christians in each of the countries involved in the programme.

It was less than five years since the end of the Second World War, and with Japan still to sign peace treaties with her former adversaries, Japanese embassies and consulates abroad remained closed. As such, the idea of travelling abroad remained little more than a dream for most Japanese. This was the only time that Kudo was glad he had been baptized as a child. The examination to select candidates for the programme had not been so difficult. The real difficulty had been in gaining permission to travel from the Japanese government and in obtaining a French visa.

On the day of departure Kudo had left Yokohama with his three colleagues aboard a sparkling white French ship. The subject of his research in France was to be Christian literature, but, more than that, he was excited at the thought of travelling to a part of the world about which he knew nothing. His friends were all jealous of his opportunity, and Kudo himself was elated. He was determined to take advantage of his rare good fortune and use it as a springboard for establishing his future career. For, to the Japanese youth of his day, the chance to study abroad was still considered a foothold on the ladder to success.

On arrival in Marseille following a journey of over a month, the group was met by some clergymen dressed in black and wearing wide-brimmed hats. Kudo was accompanied by one of these clerics on the train to Paris. An elderly, compassionate-looking man, he hardly spoke in the train, spending his time thumbing through a leather-bound prayer-book.

'Where am I going from here?'

There was a note of apprehension in his voice as Kudo spoke in faltering French, but the elderly priest, raising his head from his book, gave him a soothing smile.

'Don't worry. We've found a family who'll take care of you for the summer.'

That was the first the priest had mentioned of the Vealeauxes. A devout family living in Rouen, they had apparently come forward and offered to take Kudo in for the summer.

'How long will I stay there?'

'Until the end of the summer holiday. Once the university term begins, we'll look for another place for you.'

The priest explained how, when one has come to France, the only way to understand the culture properly was to experience real family life.

'With the Vealeauxes, not only will your French improve, but you'll be able to see for yourself what a true Christian home is like. They have great expectations of you.'

'What do you mean, "great expectations"?'

'I mean that what you learn here will ultimately contribute to the mission effort in Japan. That's why believers in France have been willing to give so generously and why the Vealeauxes are happy to take you in.'

Kudo tried to picture both this French family who were going to take him in, and the town of Rouen in which they lived. He had only the vaguest image of Rouen. It was where Corneille had lived, the little town for which Madame Bovary had held such an affection. The Vealeauxes had been landowners there for generations. Madame Vealeaux had a weak heart, and the couple had no children. Apparently they had had one son, but he had died in a motor accident just after the war, when he was a student at a seminary.

'He was born in the same year as you ... and wanted to go as a missionary to Japan. One of the reasons Madame Vealeaux wanted to take you in was presumably a means of trying to fulfil the dreams her son had cherished. Her weak heart is the direct result of her son's death. For a long time after his death she remained cooped up in her room and refused to venture outside. It was only after the Church had made this plan to invite a Japanese student into the house that she recovered her health. In short, by taking you into her home, Madame Vealeaux is trying to realize her son's ambitions.'

Before the train slipped into Paris, the priest produced a white envelope from his old brief-case.

'For the time being anyway, let me give you this. All right? Never forget that, imprinted on each of these notes, are the expectations of French Christians.'

To be on the safe side, Kudo attached the envelope to the inside pocket of his jacket with a safety-pin. Every time he moved, the tip of the safety-pin caught his chest. When he dwelt on the fact that the money contained in that envelope had been contributed for his sake by the faithful of this country, he felt a vague sense of pain in his chest.

He heard the sound of footsteps on the stairs. They were not those of Madame Vealeaux. Her footsteps would have been much slower and fainter because of her weak heart. These bustling steps belonged to Monsieur Vealeaux's younger sister, Anne, a spinster who always wore black clothes which made her look as though she were in mourning. She was a teacher at an elementary school in a place called Neufchâtel just outside Rouen, but she also managed the home on behalf of her invalid sister-in-law.

'May I open the door?'

Kudo got up hurriedly from his bed. There was no time for him to clear away the shirts and newspapers scattered around.

'I've just come back from a walk.' Kudo was stuffing his shirt into his trousers as he attempted to account for the mess. 'The room's in complete chaos.'

18

Anne gazed intently at the two packets of cigarettes, the books and notebooks left on his desk. She was short in stature, and her hair, though brown, revealed the occasional trace of white. It was hard to tell whether she had been attractive or not when young, but there was something stubborn about her face. For some reason, she had always looked kindly on Kudo, but occasionally this had the opposite effect of weighing heavily upon him. With such women, one never knew when their feelings would change.

Studying her face intently, Kudo asked, 'Do you want anything?'

'I have some good news, Paul.'

'Good news?'

'Yes. You're to give a talk to the little group we belong to.'

'Me?'

'Of course, Paul.'

Paul ... Paul.... In this household Kudo was called Paul by Monsieur and Madame Vealeaux as well as by Anne. That was the name he had been given at his baptism long ago. It also happened to have been the name of the Vealeauxes' dead son. When Madame Vealeaux had heard that Kudo's baptismal name was the same as her son's, she had literally shouted for joy. 'From now on, I'm going to call you Paul. That way, we can feel much closer. I suppose you feel the same way?'

Every time he was addressed as 'Paul', Kudo felt an unbearable sense of shame. But by now he had already resigned himself to this and responded with a smile, 'It's impossible. My French isn't good enough to speak in front of a large gathering.'

But Anne shook her head. 'That's not true. First, make a rough draft. I'll correct it for you. Then all you have to do is read that.'

'But I have nothing to talk about.'

'Of course you have.' Anne had a tendency to inflict her opinions on others rather forcibly. 'We are all interested in how Christianity has spread in Japan. Or, failing that, you could talk about what you mentioned to us at the dinner-table the other day.'

'What I mentioned at the dinner-table?'

Kudo recalled that occasion. It had been one lunchtime a few days after his arrival. Thinking it rude to remain silent during a meal, Kudo always made an effort to think up some topic of conversation. At that time he had been describing with some passion the famous incident of the French priests arriving in

19

Nagasaki shortly after the reopening of Japan to foreigners in 1868. The priests believed that all traces of Christianity had long since perished, only to discover that some Japanese Christians had remained underground, generation after generation, for over two hundred and fifty years. This story had moved Madame Vealeaux to tears. However, Kudo recalled that, the more they were moved, the more had he become aware that he was trying to ingratiate himself with them, and had then lapsed into an embarrassed silence.

Anne changed the subject, as though a decision had already been reached. 'This used to be my nephew's room. He had his desk up against that window to study.'

Everywhere one looked in this house, there were memories of the boy. Kudo recalled the picture of the boy that adorned the downstairs living-room. The same picture was also to be seen in both the dining-room and the hall. Like his mother, there was something classical about both his slender build and the expression of his face. And yet there was also a certain suggestion of a nervous disposition, the way his right hand was inserted inside his jacket and his narrow eyes stared at one from behind his rimless spectacles.

'If he had lived...' – Kudo was trying to humour Anne – '...he would doubtless have become a magnificent priest by now.'

'That's true. But now we have you, Paul, to return to Japan and do all that he was hoping to do.'

After Anne had left the room, Kudo sat down on the bed biting his nails. The house was all quiet again. So, you're Paul Kudo, are you? he thought. He pursed his lips, but his smile became distorted and then disappeared.

Kudo had still not forgotten the empty feeling he had experienced on that day when, having taken his leave of the old priest at St Lazare station, he had boarded the train for Rouen alone. Equally vivid was his memory of Madame Vealeaux who, despite her physical limitations, had been brought to the station exit at Rouen to meet him off the train. When he thought of the reasons why she had come to meet him, he realized that he had no choice but to accept the fact that she called him Paul.

When the train reached Rouen, Kudo had timidly ascended the stairs behind the five or six French people who had alighted with him. Putting down his heavy suitcase in front of the barrier, he had searched for his ticket. At that moment a man sporting a moustache had called out his name from the other side of some iron railings.

'Monsieur! Monsieur!'

Behind him, a lady with brown eyes who was dressed in black and wearing a hat with a veil stood staring in Kudo's direction. She looked very pale – possibly the result of sickness. The man held her arm with one hand as though preventing her from falling.

'This is Madame Vealeaux.'

Hastily Kudo tried to take the slender hand she had extended. However, noticing that his palm was still sweaty from carrying the heavy suitcase, he hurriedly wiped it on his jacket. She made some remark, but he was unable to catch what she said in her girlish voice.

'She's asking whether you had a good trip.' The man laughed as he spoke to Kudo. 'Let me take your case. I'll put it in the car.'

When the man had left, Madame Vealeaux spoke again – this time more slowly so that he could understand. Every time she spoke, she gasped painfully.

'I've been so looking forward to your coming. This is the first time I've met someone from Japan, but since we share the same faith, I'm sure we'll be able to understand each other soon.'

As they crossed the station precincts, three or four people spotted Madame Vealeaux and raised their hats respectfully. Then they looked back with curiosity at Kudo who was walking beside her. He gathered from these reactions that Madame Vealeaux was treated with respect in this town.

As the car moved off, the man he had just met, who now occupied the driver's seat, introduced himself. His name was Claire, Monsieur Claire, and it transpired that he was responsible for running the Vealeaux household.

'This may be a small town, but it's a nice place to live.' As he drove, Claire turned round to Kudo, who was seated in respectful manner, both hands in his lap. 'This road leads into the busiest street of Rouen. There's a medieval clock tower that you should see tomorrow or sometime.'

The town was bathed in afternoon sunshine. The houses, with roofs of red or yellow, had been built in an orderly fashion, and the roads were kept clean. And yet whatever he was told, it was all

Kudo could do in his tense state to keep smiling. The fragrance of eau-de-Cologne emanated from Madame Vealeaux's handkerchief, causing him to feel even more disconcerted.

'We'll soon be there. I expect everyone's there by now.' Claire spoke to try to help Kudo relax.

The car raced up the paved slope and passed through an iron gate surrounded by poplars, their leaves fluttering in the breeze. Behind the trees stood an old, white, three-storey house, with four or five women standing at the door. 'Voilà,' Claire shouted out.

Under the full gaze of the women in this reception party, Kudo blinked as he left the car. He did his best to smile and cut a fine figure, but there was no stopping the sweat that poured from his brow. Standing behind the women who swarmed around the entrance like ants stood the sturdy figure of a middle-aged priest clad in black, his hands outstretched. 'Well,' he said, taking Madame Vealeaux by the hand, and looking Kudo up and down as though appraising him. 'Please come in. There's no need to stand on ceremony. Everyone's here to welcome you. Madame Vealeaux, you must be tired.'

The smell given off by the plaster, combined with that of body odour and cosmetic perfume from the women, pervaded the hall. At the end of the hall with its well-worn carpet was an open door leading into a bright living-room. There, Kudo could see women in a variety of hats milling around. He was led inside by the priest, and immediately the voices of the women, who had divided themselves into small groups and been involved in animated conversation, became hushed.

With one hand on Kudo's shoulder, the priest introduced the new guest. 'It's all thanks to you, the faithful of Rouen, that he has been able to come here – or perhaps I should say, thanks to Christians from all over France. Baptized in Japan, he believes in the same God as you and I. Unfortunately, we Frenchmen know hardly anything about Japan, but, according to St Francis Xavier who once travelled to the Far East, the Japanese are the most spiritual race in the whole of the Orient.'

Lowering his gaze, Kudo stared fixedly at the floor and worried about his clothes. This was a kind of ceremony. Since there is a ceremonial side to everything, there was nothing for it but to grin and bear it.

'We all hope that his studies here will bear some fruit in the work of the missions in Japan. I once read how, at the end of the sixteenth century, four Japanese youths were dispatched as envoys all the way to Rome ... and how these four continued, even after their return to Japan, to work as ministers of the word of God throughout Japan.'

Kudo sensed an increasing heaviness in the hand placed on his shoulder.... No, not just on his shoulder: the priest's hand weighed heavily on his whole being. It was like a heavy stone on his heart. Taking a handkerchief from his pocket, he wiped the sweat from his brow.

'I should like him to be added to your daily prayer list – pray that he might take advantage of this opportunity to study abroad to strengthen his faith and increase his learning.'

The priest gave Kudo a look of encouragement. He seemed to be requesting a few words by way of greeting.

'Um . . . thank you very much.' Kudo's voice was very quiet as he addressed the women. He probably should have said more, but, just at that moment, his head was swimming and he had no idea what else to say.

Everyone seemed disappointed by his contribution. They were probably expecting something much grander. Two or three of the women began distributing teacups, as though they had sensed the chilled atmosphere. They began circulating a silver tray laden with cakes.

'I've been wanting to know for some time. . . .' There was a look of childish innocence in the eye of the middle-aged woman who had approached him. 'How do the Japanese and Chinese manage to use chopsticks like that?'

With a dextrous movement of two fingers, Kudo gave the woman an introductory lesson in the use of chopsticks. Then, with a sombre expression, she continued, 'When you return to Japan, you must take a fork with you. There's nothing as useful as a fork.'

Once more the priest placed a hand on Kudo's shoulder.

'So, do you like what you've seen of Rouen?'

'Yes, thank you. It's the kind of place I'd like to settle down in.'

'You've got a lot to thank Madame Vealeaux for, you know. If you have any problems during your stay here, don't hesitate to contact me.'

The priest literally dragged him to the corner of the room. On the wall in that corner hung 'the picture'. It portrayed the nervous face of a young man, with narrow eyes gazing out from behind his glasses.

'This is Madame Vealeaux's son ... the one who died. I knew him when he was just a lad. Even as a young boy, he was always respectful of his parents. He was a good student too. When we heard that he was going to go to the seminary, we were both surprised and happy. He wanted to go to Japan as a missionary.'

The priest glanced over at Madame Vealeaux, who appeared to be exhausted and had sat down in the corner of the room listening to her friends' conversation.

'I expect you've already been told, but it was as a result of her son's death that her heart grew weak. She's now living entirely on that memory. You'd do well to remember that.'

Dinner at the Vealeauxes' started at eight. In summer, the days in France are much longer than those in Japan. Even at eight there was still plenty of sunlight in the garden outside the dining-room window: indeed, it was only on those parts overgrown with trees that a faint haze was to be detected. The wind rustling in those trees sounded cool.

Anne would sit beside Monsieur Vealeaux, and Kudo was placed beside Madame Vealeaux. The family had realized the importance of teaching table manners to their Japanese visitor as quickly as possible, and it was for this reason that Kudo's seat was fixed like this.

'In France, unlike England, we always place our cup in front of our plate,' Anne explained. 'Before drinking wine you should always wipe your mouth with your napkin first. If you don't, you leave dirty lip marks on the glass. What's more, it's not the men but the women who are the main focus of the meal. You should never start eating before your hostess. And it's rude to put your knife and fork down before she's finished.'

Kudo sat up straight as he tried to hammer these lessons home. But when he tried putting all this into practice, it proved extremely difficult. In Japan, he had been used to finishing his meal as quickly as possible, and so, by the time he had emptied his plate, his hostess had not finished half of the food set before her. And despite all he had been told, when he finished drinking wine he would notice dirty lip marks on his glass and suddenly realize he had forgotten to use his napkin.

'You must never eat in silence. You should always find something to talk about. That's another important lesson.'

'I see,' Kudo replied obediently.

'And you must learn not to talk with your mouth full like that!'

Throughout the meal Kudo remained in a state of confusion, his head feeling like a waste-paper basket. He always ended up exhausted. Monsieur and Madame Vealeaux felt obliged to ask him about Japan. But he felt quite unable to answer any of their questions.

'I've heard the Japanese sleep on the floor. Is that true?' Monsieur Vealeaux was a portly man who sported a goatee, and there was a tenderness about his features that reminded one of Bergson, the philosopher. But he knew virtually nothing about Japan. Kudo went to great pains to explain how the Japanese sleep, not on the floor but on tatami mats, though he was unsure how to describe these rush mats.

'It's a kind of straw matting you find everywhere in Japanese houses.'

'So you mean you sleep on straw?'

'It's just like the barns you find on farms,' Anne ventured to conclude. 'In France, too, they spread out dried grass in such barns. It's like that. Isn't that right, Paul?'

Kudo tried to say something, but the conversation had already digressed. Thanks to his maladroit explanation, the Vealeaux household was now convinced that the Japanese were a weird and unenlightened race.

'This means that, if my nephew Paul had gone to Japan, he would have slept on straw too. Right?'

'Yes, but that boy loved camping,' Madame Vealeaux remarked as she rolled up her napkin and flung it on to the table. 'He would have enjoyed that too.'

After dinner, Monsieur and Madame Vealeaux would retire to the living-room – the 'salon' as they called it – and spend the time reading the paper and knitting, all the while gossiping about the tenant farmers and the priest. At such times Kudo would gaze at 'the picture' on the wall, trying desperately to stifle a yawn. He had little choice, for it would soon be time for family prayers. After a while Monsieur Vealeaux would put down his paper and say, 'Very well. Shall we start?'

Kudo would kneel and listen intently to Monsieur Vealeaux as he read from the prayer-book.

'Let's pray for Paul and for Japan,' Anne added.

When this was over, Kudo finally found release from the tension of the day. He was freed both from the need to keep smiling in front of everyone and to speak French, which he found so hard.

When the rest of the house was fast asleep, Kudo was in the habit of standing in front of the mirror and adopting various poses. The mirror had presumably hung there for many years, so when the son had used this room, he too must have stood in front of it in the same way. Kudo could not help thinking how the motif, *Use this mirror to change your appearance*, seemed like an ideal aphorism for the seminarian.

There was no escaping the fact that the figure reflected in the mirror looked dirty. This was not merely because his appearance was plain, but also because his 'true appearance' was nowhere to be seen. Was the miserable-looking figure with hands clasped in front of his body really himself? That was the figure of the Japanese youth he presented to Monsieur and Madame Vealeaux and to Anne. On the day of his arrival Kudo must have looked like this as, surrounded by all those women from the church, he had listened to the priest's speech in the living-room downstairs. And, from that day on, whenever he appeared in public, he had taken to adopting exactly the same pose. Once, as he walked the streets in the early afternoon, someone had stopped him and said, 'You must be the Japanese boy staying with the Vealeauxes. Do you like Rouen?'

At that time a smile had come to his lips as he replied, 'Yes, it's the kind of place I'd like to settle down in.'

As he made this reply, Kudo had adopted the same pose. He thought of himself placing part of the money which had been collected for him by the French Christians in an envelope and attaching it to his jacket pocket with a safety-pin. All of these believers were convinced that Kudo would be able to contribute to the evangelist movement in Japan. He also thought of the way in which such expectations made him more gloomy by the day. All of these weighed heavily upon him, just as had the priest's hand on his shoulder.

'I didn't come here for this,' Kudo reflected as he faced the mirror. He pursed his lips as he muttered, 'I could do without such misplaced favours.'

On such occasions Kudo would smile faintly as he stared at this aspect of himself in the mirror. And, in a low voice, his *alter ego* would accuse him of being a little hypocrite, a liar.

At such times Kudo would turn to his *alter ego* and explain in self-defence, 'But I don't want to destroy everyone's confidence in me. Just think of poor Madame Vealeaux were I to shatter all her dreams about her dead son.'

'Yes, but for all their confidence in you, there is a certain degree of egotism and unconscious calculation. Madame Vealeaux for her part is trying to force her dreams about her son on to you, and the Christians gain a sense of self-satisfaction through their act of charity. You must realize that.'

Kudo shook his head, a clear expression of abhorrence at his *alter ego* which was unable to believe in the goodwill of the people of this country. He despised himself for attempting so readily to detect another dimension in the feelings expressed by the Vealeauxes behind their devout faces.

On such occasions Kudo could not help but sense the presence of the dead son, Paul, in the centre of the mirror staring at him through his glasses with that nervous look. Turning to the face, he would say, 'Why did you decide to go and spread the Gospel in Japan?'

'Paul. Paul.'

Kudo was sitting reading a book on the bench in the corner of the garden when Anne summoned him from the house. Her shrill voice hit him like a well-struck tennis-ball.

'You have a visitor, Paul.'

Kudo gave his usual smile, and, book in hand, he crossed the lawn under the already scorching sun. In the living-room overlooking the garden he could make out the profiles of Madame Vealeaux and the priest. They were seated with their backs to him. Anne was bent over the table pouring some coffee.

'He studies in the garden until it gets too hot.' Madame Vealeaux toyed with a handkerchief imbued with the scent of eau-de-Cologne as she addressed the priest in that childlike voice of hers.

'That's good.' The sturdy priest dressed in black was much too powerful for a typical cleric. Kudo felt that he would have done well in the army.

'Paul studies really well.' Coffee-pot in hand, Anne spoke as though flaunting her own achievement. 'At night, his light seems to be on till all hours. We keep telling him he mustn't get ill.'

Anne was unaware that it was to the mirror that Kudo turned in the middle of the night.

'Yes, you mustn't get ill.' The priest drew his pipe from his trouser pocket and scraped it with his large hands. 'All the believers around here are hoping that you'll be able to complete your studies without any problem.' Then, glancing at the book Kudo held in his hand, he continued, 'What are you reading?' Raising his head abruptly, he looked at Kudo inquisitively and said, 'I never thought you'd be reading this kind of book. This is not the sort of book you should be reading. I don't recommend Gide. He was anti-Church.' He almost spat out the words.

Bemused, Kudo tried to make some sort of response. But before he could do so, Anne interposed. She was like a mother hen protecting her chicks.

'He bought that book without knowing anything about it. How can you expect a foreigner to know that Gide's books have been banned? Isn't that right, Paul?'

Kudo could not bring himself to upset Anne's goodwill. With eyes downcast, he mumbled as he sat down quietly in the chair in the corner that he would be more careful in future. He put both hands to his cheeks and recalled the words he had just read on the garden bench: 'Don't choose! Don't take a stance! And don't choose one set of ideas! If you do, you will only be able to view life from that one angle.' That fits the priest perfectly, Kudo thought. And the Vealeauxes. Their opinions have been hardened by the creed they have inherited, and they see everything simply from that perspective.

In his own abstruse way Kudo tried to feel disdain for the three who sat before him drinking coffee. But he ended up feeling this sense of contempt rebounding upon himself like a sharpened sword. If these people are as you suggest, then what about yourself? At least these people have some firm religious convictions. You're just a coward who changes colour as the occasion demands.

He raised his head and peered up at the photograph of the dead son which hung in this living-room too. From the centre of the photograph Paul was staring fixedly in Kudo's direction. Did you, who were born and bred in this house, never experience the kind of feelings that I've experienced? Did you manage to cope with everything without any problem? Such were Kudo's thoughts as he gazed at the picture.

'I've come to tempt you out for a walk.' With saucer in one hand and the other hand gripping his coffee-cup, the priest seemed to have completely forgotten about Gide. 'Are you coming?'

The summer sun blazed down on to the stone pavement as they set off. After a while a dog went by, bearing a sand-covered beef bone in its mouth.

'Well, how is everything? Have you got used to French life?' The priest forced some tobacco into his pipe with his fat finger and continued, 'I'm really pleased. You seem to have gone down really well with the Vealeauxes. But please do nothing to mar their opinion of you.'

'Yes, I see,' Kudo replied.

'Nothing's troubling you? If there is, be sure to tell me at once.'

Kudo continued to glance at the priest out of the corner of his eye. He remained silent, like a peevish child. The thing which troubled him most at the moment was that the Vealeauxes and everyone else were pleased with him. It was because of this that he felt stifled. But the priest would never understand it.

'About their son . . .'

'Their son?'

'Yes, the Vealeauxes' son. Why did he want to go to Japan as a missionary?' Kudo was inquisitive.

'As I've already told you, Paul had a great respect for St Francis Xavier, and, from the moment he entered the *lycée*, loved to read the letters written by the great missionary as he preached the Gospel to the Japanese. You must have read the letters he wrote about the Japanese?'

Of course Kudo had read Xavier's views on the Japanese. They were recorded in the first letter Xavier sent from Japan to his colleagues in Goa in 1549. It had been one of the first letters to leave Japan.

'They are the best race yet discovered, and I think that, among non-Christians, their match will not easily be found.' It was in such glowing terms that St Francis Xavier had described the Japanese. 'They are exceedingly affable, full of courtesy in their dealings with one another, uphold the highest level of moral conduct and possess a voracious appetite for knowledge.'

'Is that why you have such great expectations of us Japanese?' A furtive smile lit Kudo's face. 'And the reason the son. . . ?'

'Yes.' The priest failed to detect the sarcasm in Kudo's voice.

In just the same way that Madame Vealeaux and Anne were guilty of overestimating Kudo, so St Francis Xavier had held out excessive hopes for the Japanese. But had not the Japanese of Francis Xavier's dream averted their gaze and smiled when in his presence, in just the same manner as Kudo was now doing?

'There just happens to be a book in the Rouen library about the envoys and Catholic students who came from your country in the sixteenth century. It seems that Paul – Madame Vealeaux's son – loved reading that book during the summer holidays.'

'Is that what inspired his dreams? Didn't he read anything else about Japan?' Kudo asked.

'Hmm. I wonder. Unfortunately there are not many books about your country here in France.' The priest drew a match near to his pipe. The sun had grown gradually fiercer. Before long the number of people in the streets would begin to dwindle. Kudo felt both sweat and a dull pain at his back and removed his jacket. But the priest, who seemed to be sweltering in his black robes, continued with long strides.

'I have a lunch appointment with some Moroccan students now – that's another of the projects we've been involved with in this parish. They're all studying in Paris. Have you ever seen any in Japan . . . blacks, I mean?'

'No.'

'The students in Paris are all on their own. They have no one to talk to, and, instead of the warmth of a family, they have to live in dormitories. As such, they are prone to temptation, and so we invite them up here whenever they are free. In that respect, you were lucky right from the start.'

The July sun reflected off the tower of Rouen castle. For the past two weeks there had been no real rain and so the roads and surrounding ground were totally parched. When they got to the place de Corneille, the priest entered a narrow alley which was bathed in distinct shadows, and said, 'I'm sure it was this restaurant.'

As they entered, Kudo's nostrils were greeted by the smell of onions and of meat being cooked. There was a long, thin table covered with a white table-cloth, and seven or eight of the women who had been part of his welcoming party that day were there too, busily engaged in passing round glasses and trays of sandwiches. In their midst stood a solitary black youth, a white handkerchief hanging from his chest. His teeth appeared incredibly white as he spoke, and he gesticulated like a puppet. His manner of speech was more akin to shouting than talking, but every time he spoke, the women all burst out laughing. There was another black youth seated in the corner who had placed both hands on his lap and was staring in Kudo's direction with a penetrating look.

'That's fine. Just fine.' Apparently satisfied with the proceedings, the priest nodded and introduced Kudo to them. 'Here's one more friend for you all.'

The surface of the hand which one of the black youths held out to him was black, and yet the palm was white and sticky, as though the raw flesh had been peeled away. Kudo felt uncomfortable and involuntarily withdrew his hand.

The black youth, for his part, appeared to have felt some kind of jealousy, and looked on with scorn as the women approached to talk to him.

'We were just about to have a song. Paulin was going to sing something from his homeland.'

One of the women, who had spotted nothing, came up and addressed Kudo. The priest nodded, explaining how this was indeed a rare opportunity. The black youth called Paulin had forcibly parted his wiry hair in the French manner and matted it to his brow. This aroused in Kudo a wretched feeling of sadness.

'All right. Let's hear what you have to say, Paulin.'

Spreading his legs wide, Paulin began beating time with his hands. He moved his whole body as he sang. His voice was shrill, and his movements were so exaggerated it was embarrassing to watch. The priest chewed on his pipe and stifled a laugh. But the women were helpless and had to look away. It was clear, even to Kudo, that they did not consider this song or dance the least bit appealing. And yet Paulin continued to sing. For his part, he knew exactly what was going on in the minds of the women and had worked things out accordingly.

Kudo found himself turning his eyes away from the youth as much as possible, for Paulin's feelings as he sang reverberated painfully inside him. Here's a boy with black skin attempting to endear himself with this party of white women by singing a funny song, Kudo thought. He knows that's the way to win their affection.

At the end of the song, the priest placed his hand on Paulin's shoulder, his pipe still clenched between his teeth. Several beads of sweat ran down the forehead and cheeks of the black student. It was the sweat of a slave following a period of hard labour.

'Do the Japanese like to sing and dance in that way?'

Kudo glared at the priest and, in spite of himself, almost spat out his reply. 'Definitely not. We. . . .'

The priest did not grasp what was going on in Kudo's mind. He looked a bit surprised, but then said quietly, 'No, that's right. We've all heard how tasteful Japanese songs are.'

One of the women began passing round the glasses of wine and the sandwiches. Then suddenly a heated discussion erupted between Paulin and the other black student. Since they were both speaking in their native language, Kudo had no idea what they were saying. But they seemed to be involved in an argument. All the women and the priest looked on in silence.

'That's it!' The black student spoke in French, loosening his tie as he did so. 'I've had enough! I'm going back to Paris!'

'What's happened, Maguillot?' It was the priest who was attempting to intervene. 'Don't get too worked up.'

But the black student called Maguillot grabbed his cap in silence and pushed his way through the crowd of women. Thrusting the door open with the full weight of his body, he went outside. One of the women started to go after him, but she must have given up, for she was back in no time.

'Maguillot wasn't like that before, was he?' The priest was mumbling to himself. 'I heard that he's recently started hanging around with some communist students in Paris. He must have been influenced by them.'

With the crestfallen look of a naughty puppy, Paulin stood holding his head in his hands. The women around him tried to console him, as though showing compassion to a sick man.

Leaning against the wall, Kudo gazed at the chair which Maguillot had just vacated. Of course he had no idea of the cause of his anger. Maybe he had been thinking along similar lines to Kudo himself during the course of Paulin's song. Rather than finding himself enveloped in a surge of goodwill and becoming transfixed, he had opted to court hatred. He certainly has guts, Kudo thought. Kudo felt a sense of jealousy towards Maguillot and the way he had barged through the crowd of women on his way to the door. He wished he could muster such courage.

The heat had removed his appetite for reading. The sky visible from his window was so blue as to be painful on the eyes. It had not rained once since Kudo came to Rouen. It was not as humid as Japan, and yet his body sweltered under the midday sun.

He could hear Monsieur Vealeaux ringing a tenant farmer. He was afraid that the grapes on the land he cultivated would wither. 'We haven't seen anything like this for fifteen years.'

He continued to grumble even at the dinner-table. Madame Vealeaux ventured into the dining-room only at night. With her weak heart, she was apparently particularly sensitive to the heat. On occasion, the doctor would come with his black bag to examine her.

I could hardly imitate him, Kudo thought.

Every day Kudo would reflect on the figure of the student Maguillot pushing his way through the crowd of women and going outside. Compared with Maguillot who had brushed aside the goodwill which everyone had heaped on him like sugar candy and reacted against it, there was no doubt that it was Paulin who should be disliked. There was something repulsive about the way he had buried his head in his hands as the women had attempted to placate him. And yet for some reason Kudo lacked the confidence to act as Maguillot had. To be sure, this was partly due to an innate moral cowardice, but also to a reluctance to betray the goodwill of everyone. After all, their intentions are not evil, he thought.

Every time he looked in that mirror, he would hear a voice from somewhere telling him that, behind all this charity, lay a certain egotism. There was an element of truth to this – and yet goodwill is goodwill. Kudo now felt sorry for Madame Vealeaux, with all those visits from the doctor. He was loath to do anything that would shatter her desire to fulfil the dreams of her son. He did not want to hurt the feelings of Anne who always stood up for him. And yet he still felt an unbearable abhorrence towards himself when he was doing all in his power to live up to everyone's expectations. It all seemed like the film he had seen recently.

The other day, overcome by the heat during one of his walks, he had gone to the cinema. The place had been half empty and he had sat near the back absently watching an old film. All the time he had worried about when he was expected home. The film had been the story of a man who, unable to endure the sight of his wife bedridden and in pain over a long period, had given her a lethal injection. On the day he had killed her, there had been a festival with fireworks in the town. For a while Kudo had been unable to forget the expression of the man who had brought destruction upon himself through his own timidity.

The following day Madame Vealeaux did not come down to lunch. Anne sat in Madame Vealeaux's chair and ladled out the soup.

'Did you hear about the fire this morning?' Monsieur Vealeaux had tucked his napkin into his shirt like a child. 'It was by the town hall. About half the house was gutted.' Since this was such a small town, word of even the most trivial of incidents spread rapidly. 'It's because of the drought. Out in the suburbs they're afraid of a forest fire. It only takes a couple of dried-out twigs to rub together and the whole place could go up in flames.'

Kudo looked up and stared at the sky which was almost unbearably clear. The sun shone like a white dot. The air was so dry, there was a real danger of fire.

Kudo was deep in thought as he drank his soup. I don't know. If I had lived here for a long time, I might do something horrible.

'Is your preparation coming along all right?' Anne passed him a new plate as she spoke. 'We can't wait to hear your talk.'

'Yes, thank you. It's coming on fine.' Kudo forced the customary smile to his lips.

'Even the wife of one of the city councillors has come.' Anne surveyed the living-room on the far side of the garden from a second-floor window as she spoke with a certain pride. For about half an hour now the priest and the women had been crowding into the living-room.

'All right. I want something I can be really proud of today. I want everyone to know how much your French has improved. So just relax . . . and speak slowly.'

Kudo gave a wry smile as he thought how like a child attending school open day she was. But, oblivious to his thoughts, Anne examined his clothes once more and removed a piece of thread from his shoulders.

'Right. Let's go.'

It was painful to have to wear a tie on such a boiling hot day. His collar was already drenched with sweat. It angered him to be subjected to such an ordeal. And yet there was nothing for it. This, too, stemmed from the goodwill of the local Christians. They were doing him the favour of listening to his lecture in French.

Kudo swallowed hard and followed Anne down the stairs. A silence fell over the room, and the women welcomed him with beaming smiles. There, on the large leather chair in the centre of the room, sat the priest, his legs firmly crossed, and a middle-aged woman with the face of an eagle. She must be the wife of the city councillor whom Anne had mentioned earlier. Beside her sat the pale-faced Madame Vealeaux clasping a handkerchief. The smell of sweat and perfume pervaded the air.

When a silence had fallen on the whole room, the priest stood up, as was his custom, and said a few words by way of greeting. 'Unfortunately we know all too little about Japan. But today I am sure that Kudo will satisfy our curiosity. Right, then. Please begin.'

As he sat down again and crossed his long legs, there was a touch of sarcasm to be detected in his smile. His well-polished shoes glistened in the sunlight.

'How many Christians are there in Japan?'

'There were about thirty thousand until the end of the war. But since then the number has risen to eighty thousand, I believe.'

'Did you hear that? What a magnificent increase. Doesn't that

35

just go to show how our faith has appealed to the suffering and uncertainty of the Japanese?'

An increase in numbers does not necessarily imply progress. Kudo raised his head to explain how it was not merely Christianity which had appealed to the uncertainty of the Japanese – but, noting the look of elation on the priest's face, he stopped himself. Following the war, Japanese women and girls had been attracted by the atmosphere of churches, and consequently were baptized. That accounted for the increased membership.

'What percentage of the total population is that?' One of the middle-aged women raised her left hand tentatively and put her question to Kudo.

'The population of Japan is about one hundred million – all squeezed into a tiny island.' Kudo had failed to answer her question properly. 'The population crisis has long been a problem for Japan. In a way, it can be seen as one of the causes of the war.'

No one seemed interested in his answer.

Then, one of the women said suspiciously, 'Eighty thousand out of one hundred million! That's still not nearly enough. Is the rest of the population Buddhist?'

'Only by force of habit.' Kudo lowered his eyes and mumbled his reply. 'Buddhism in Japan is not as dynamic as Catholicism in this country.'

'That means there is hope that it will be Christianity which captures the hearts of the Japanese.' There was a note of conviction in the priest's voice.

The sunlight streaming through the window struck Kudo full in the face. Feeling the sweat beginning to trickle down his neck, he looked for his handkerchief.

'But the percentage of Christians amongst the intelligentsia is small.'

'Doesn't that depend on the education system? If the Japanese attain an intellectual level whereby they are able to comprehend Catholicism, all such worries should disappear.'

'I don't believe that our universities are in any way inferior to those of this country.'

A vague smile came across the priest's face. 'That's not what I meant. But how many universities do you have in your country?'

'Even the smallest of towns has one. I've never actually counted them, but there must be at least fifty or sixty.'

'But those are not real universities, are they? In France we don't go round recklessly building masses of universities.' The priest was persistent.

Kudo wiped his face and neck with his handkerchief, but there was no stopping the sweat that poured down his cheeks.

'I have a different question.' It was the woman who had come to him the first day asking him how to use chopsticks who now stood up. 'I've been dying to ask this for a long time.... We always read of how Japanese houses are made of paper and wood. Is it true?'

'We use paper instead of glass,' Kudo replied.

'Instead of glass!' The woman looked surprised. 'That's hard to believe! What happens when there's a strong wind?'

Just as he had when describing tatami mats to Madame Vealeaux, Kudo sat firmly in his chair and began to explain. But the more he explained, the more the women built up this weird image in their minds.

Exhausted, Kudo wiped his brow with his handkerchief. He grew more and more angry with his inadequate French. But he was mad not merely at his French but at having to answer this question which revealed such a lack of understanding.

From somewhere nearby came the wailing of a fire-engine. There had been another forest fire in the suburbs. He sensed feelings of anger welling up inside. Why did he have to go on living in this town? Why did he have to spend his summer dealing with people who were unable to distinguish between tatami mats and straw and who imagined that *shoji* sliding doors were no more than pieces of paper?

'Let us pray that the spirit of Christianity may find greater acceptance in Japan,' the priest interposed.

'I'm sorry?'

'We are going to do our best to see that the spirit of Christianity strikes a more receptive chord in your country than at present.'

Japan is totally different from Chad or the Congo. You know nothing about Japan. Do you think anything will come of your simplistic comments? The prevailing climate in my country causes the very roots of Christianity to wither and die. It's not the simple-minded country you all take it for. Wiping his neck with his handkerchief, Kudo groped for suitable French words to convey such sentiments. But his head hurt and it was too much of an effort to answer.

At that moment he looked at Anne, who was discussing something with the woman sitting next to her in the back row. When she caught sight of him, she nodded vigorously, presumably by way of encouragement. Right in the middle of the room he could see the emaciated face of Madame Vealeaux, both hands in her lap despite the heat. There was no way he could hurt the feelings of such good people.

'Thank you very much.'

Kudo forced a smile to his sweat-covered face. At dusk the women retired. They all shook his hand and congratulated him on an excellent talk. After Madame Vealeaux and Anne had gone out to see them off, Kudo felt physically and mentally drained. He stood around aimlessly in the centre of the room.

The setting sun fell on to the teacups and the plates which had been used for cakes. The glass in the frame on the wall sparkled. As he approached it, he could see the son staring down at him with that nervous expression of his. Kudo wondered whether he would feel the same for the rest of his stay. For a while he remained, looking at the picture.

Part Two

Araki Thomas

The only extant information about Araki Thomas, the Japanese man who studied in Rome in the seventeenth century, consists of a few short articles to be found in some of the records about Japanese Christians during the period of isolation. Even the date and place of his birth are uncertain. Although his baptismal name of Thomas is known, his real Japanese name remains a mystery to this day. A considerable amount of study has been devoted to those Christian priests and students of theology who were martyred for their faith, but those who apostatized have been largely ignored. This is presumably because the missionaries and Roman authorities of the day attempted as far as possible to gloss over and conceal information about those who had sullied the name of the Church.

According to one theory, Thomas was a descendant of Araki Murashige who was killed on suspicion of insurrection against Oda Nobunaga. Despite the counsel of Hashiba Hideyoshi, Murashige was determined to perish along with Itami castle, but his survivors fled to Kumamoto in Kyushu.

Another theory holds that Araki Thomas was related to Araki Shutaro, the Nagasaki merchant who had been so involved with the ships granted licences by the shogunate. Shutaro was born in Kumamoto in Higo, and, although he started out as a samurai, he travelled to Nagasaki and became a townsman. Subsequently he was involved in trade with Siam and Annam.

At any rate it is clear that Thomas was raised in Kyushu, baptized as a child – hence the baptismal name, Thomas – and received a

Catholic education at the hands of European priests.

There is no record of where he studied theology, although it is not too difficult to conjecture. At that time the priest Valignano had come to Japan from Macao in order to oversee the propagation of the Gospel in Japan. Realizing the urgent need to nurture some native clergy, he had established a couple of theological colleges, or *seminarios*. Both of these colleges, one in Arima in Kyushu, the other in Azuchi on the shores of Lake Biwa, survived until the great persecution of Christianity began in 1614 – though not without their share of difficulties and misfortune. Presumably it was in the *seminario* in Arima that Araki Thomas pursued his studies.

There is currently considerable information available about the *seminario* in Arima. The initial intake of students was twenty-two; and these scholars studied in an old Buddhist temple which had been donated by the Lord of Arima. There they studied not only Portuguese and Latin – that would be necessary for them to proceed to ordination – but a foundation course in religious studies, ethics, Japanese literature and calligraphy. For the physical well-being of the students, a training ground and bathing area were also established. Amongst the graduates of this college were those, like Kimura Sebastian, who would subsequently be sentenced to burn at the stake in similar manner to the twenty-six Christians who were martyred on the hill of Nishizaka in Nagasaki. Alternatively, there were those, such as the priest Kibe Kasui who, like Araki Thomas, was sent to study in Rome, but was arrested on his return and subjected to a cruel death following days of hanging upside-down in a pit.

Today, all that remains on top of the hill where Arima castle used to stand is a solitary Shinto shrine. The castle apparently stood right on top of the hill and it is rumoured that the *seminario* stood about a hundred metres lower down – the site is now reduced to paddy-fields. If one stands on top of the hill on an autumn day, one can clearly see the fields stretching all the way to the Ariake Sea and, beyond that, the plateau of Hara castle, the focal point of the Shimabara rebellion of 1637.

In those days, the graduates of the *seminario* would help those foreign missionaries who still had problems with the language, whilst performing their own ministry under the title of *irmaos* or *doshuku*. Those who had pledged their whole life to the service of

God were called *irmaos*, a kind of monk, and, of these, only the very best were advanced to the rank of fully fledged priest. Those of the *doshuku* category made no such promise, but were engaged in the propagation of the Gospel in the secular world. Nevertheless, they too shaved their heads, wore black robes and lived within the confines of the church. There is no way of determining whether Araki Thomas became an *irmaos* or a *doshuku*.

Until the year 1587 the Gospel continued to spread throughout Japan at a steady pace, despite the occasional setback. Oda Nobunaga, who had manifested a tolerant attitude towards the Christian faith, died at Honnoji, to be succeeded by Toyotomi Hideyoshi. The latter, too, established friendly relations with the missionaries, and several of the warriors in his immediate entourage were converted to the faith. As a result, Christianity developed into a kind of vogue. Araki Thomas was one of those new-style intellectuals to emerge in Japan during that period, having studied Latin and Portuguese and acquired a nodding acquaintance with ethics and the basics of religious study. It is unclear whether he worked with the foreign missionaries in Kyushu or in the Kansai area, but, at that time, wherever he went, he must have been able to experience a sense of pride as an intellectual.

During the same period there was a man called Sanemon living in the province of Settsu. It is unknown whether he belonged to the samurai or townsman class. He professed a belief in Buddhism, but, profoundly affected by a chance observation of the life-style of some members of the Franciscan community, developed an interest in Christianity, the dominant influence on their lives, and determined to study the tenets of Christianity in Nagasaki.

In Nagasaki it was none other than Araki Thomas who supervised Sanemon's studies. But, in contrast to Thomas, who would ultimately renounce the faith and become one of the apostates, his disciple Sanemon changed his name to Sanemon John and was martyred with three blows of the sword at the execution ground in Omura. Nevertheless, as can be seen from the example of Sanemon, there was a time when Araki Thomas was happy to devote his life to the propagation of the Gospel.

But in July of 1587 an unexpected halt was called to the previously uninterrupted diffusion of the Christian faith. Hideyoshi, who until that point had evidenced a tolerant attitude towards the faith, suddenly promulgated an anti-Christian edict. To this day, the reasons for this volte-face remain clouded. In the previous year, on the occasion of his audience with the famous priest, Father Frois, and the deputy Bishop Coelho in Osaka, Hideyoshi had been in high spirits and even declared his intention to donate Nagasaki to the Jesuits, following the subjugation of Kyushu. The missionaries struggled in vain to comprehend the reasons for this abrupt change of heart. If one studies the edict of proscription carefully, all that one finds is a series of ambiguous statements about the evil way in which Japan, the land of the gods, had adopted aspects of witchcraft from Christian countries and how these had been used to destroy the shrines and temples.

Counter-measures had to be hastily implemented. Included in the edict was a clause to the effect that no priests should remain in Japan, that they should all be out of the country within twenty days. In short, all foreign missionaries were to be banished. There was little doubt that the colleges at Azuchi and Arima, designed to nurture native priests, were destined to be closed. As a desperate measure, Father Valignano, the overseer of Christianity in Japan, determined to build a new theological college in Macao and send the Japanese there.

It must have been about this time that Araki Thomas left Japan and travelled to Macao. And yet, although the names of virtually all of the Japanese students who studied at the Macao college are known, the name of Araki Thomas is nowhere to be found. Since he was already versed in Latin and Portuguese, the priests presumably saw no need to continue to detain him in the college. They had determined to confer on him a more important role. In anticipation of the day when the proscription edict would be lifted, they decided to broaden his horizons by having him pursue his studies at the hands of some learned priests. He was to study the same theology and philosophy as was studied in the West.

In this way Araki became the first Japanese student to travel to Europe. To be sure, there were at least five Japanese who preceded him to Europe. The first of these was a man called Bernard 'Something or other' from Kagoshima, who was escorted by Francis Xavier first to Goa and subsequently to Lisbon. The other four were the so-called 'Tensho envoys' – four young men who travelled to Rome bearing a letter from their Christian daimyo, or feudal lord, in Kyushu. But Bernard fell ill and died in Lisbon, and the four young envoys were sent with a clearly defined goal. They did not travel to Europe to pursue their studies. Thus, strictly speaking, it was Araki Thomas who was the first Japanese scholar to study in Europe.

Araki left Macao on a ship bound for Goa in India. This town was both the Portuguese base in the Orient and the place where St Francis Xavier stayed whilst making plans for his forthcoming mission work in Japan. The houses in the town revealed considerable European influence, and missionaries to both India and the Far East were gathered there.

It was here that Araki received the first news of his homeland. Suppression of Christianity in Japan was becoming ever more intense, and in Nagasaki twenty-six priests and other believers had been sentenced to death. At Nishigaoka in Nagasaki six missionaries, including Father Baptista of the Franciscan order, had been burnt at the stake along with twenty Japanese believers. Araki was acquainted with Father Baptista. And there were others among the martyrs whom he had had occasion to meet in the past. On the one hand, he was secretly grateful that he had been able to escape from such a country, but, at the same time he must have contemplated his own future, since he was destined one day to return. And yet his return to Japan was in the distant future. By that time the situation would doubtless have changed.

From Goa there were two ways of travelling to Europe. One option was to cross over to Ormuz on the Persian Gulf – the route chosen by Kibe Kasui who would subsequently be martyred – and there join up with one of the caravans crossing from Palestine to Italy. Alternatively one could opt for the sea route, arriving in Portugal and then cross over to Rome. It would appear that Araki chose this latter route.

There is no record of Araki's actions before his arrival in Rome, but he is known to have reached Italy in 1600 or 1601. This was both an auspicious and inauspicious time for the first Japanese student to reach Rome. For, at that time, there was a kind of 'Japan boom' in Christian circles in Europe. It was only about ten years since the 'Tensho envoys' had come all the way from Japan and received such an enthusiastic welcome all over Italy before their departure from Lisbon. The warmth which the envoys had aroused in the Europeans had yet to subside. The people of Rome still retained a mental image of the four young envoys marching to the sound of drums behind the cavalry and papal officials, flanked by bishops and archbishops. At that time people had thronged the roads and squares like ants, and a hail of cheers had rained down upon the envoys from the windows and balconies. When they had arrived in St Peter's Square, an artillery salute had echoed forth in welcome both from the Vatican palace and from Castel Sant' Angelo. As they knelt, Pope Gregory XIII had bent down and planted a kiss on each of their foreheads. From Rome they had travelled to Venice and thence to Milan – and everywhere they went they were welcomed in a triumphal celebration. There were even those who, in a rush of excitement, kissed their clothes. In Venice the envoys' boat had been escorted by a throng of gondolas adorned in ceremonial fashion, and the scene had been painted by the famous artist Tintoretto.

Even after the envoys had returned home, a wave of curiosity and a determination to spread the Gospel in Japan persisted in Europe, like molten lava which continues to flow even after a volcano has ceased erupting. The Society of Jesus claimed that it had never known such a hectic period, as applications from those wishing to travel to Japan came flooding in. It was at this time, too, that such famous works as Degelman's *A History of Missions to the East* and Archbishop Theotonio's *Correspondence from the Society of Jesus in Japan* were written.

As he finally arrived in Rome exhausted from his long and arduous journey, Araki could hardly have imagined such a state of affairs in the Church. At first it was a source of great joy to him, but he had not realized that it would shortly become the seed of a great burden of unhappiness. Just because he was Japanese, he was surrounded by people trying to force their dreams of spreading the Gospel to Japan upon him.

In the case of Kibe Kasui, who also came to Rome to study about ten years later, a conscious effort has been made to honour the name of the man who later became a martyr and, as such, considerable records remain. His report cards from the Collegio Romano (the modern Gregorian University), which he attended, have been preserved, and there are clear records of where he received his training and when he became a priest. And yet in the case of Araki Thomas, the apostate, such records are sparse. Nevertheless, it is known that he was appointed to the rank of priest whilst in Rome, and it is believed that he, too, attended the Collegio Romano and took his examinations there.

It is also easy to imagine what kind of life he led in Rome from one particular report which has been handed down. In this report, it is recorded: 'Cardinal Robert Belamino loved Araki above all else – so much so that, every day, they would recite the daily prayer together.'

This is a valuable record; for, at that time, Belamino was eminent in Christian circles both for his faith and for his scholarship. He was a priest as well as a scholar, and he was subsequently canonized by Pope Pius XI. For such a cardinal, famed even within the Vatican, to recite the daily prayer with a mere student of theology and priest was an unprecedented honour.

So, why was Araki Thomas able to enjoy such a distinction? The reason for this is clear. It was because he was Japanese ... because he was the only Japanese to be studying in Europe at the time. Everyone was deeply impressed by the fact that this youth from the island country in the Far East should be studying the same religion as themselves. Inspired by the example set by St Francis Xavier, several young missionaries who were driven by a passionate desire to help spread the Gospel in Japan formed a constant stream of visitors, each one curious to know more of the current state of affairs in the Far East. And the other believers, seeing in this Japanese student the fulfilment of their own personal dreams, frequently invited him to their homes for dinner.

Yet the more he enjoyed their friendship and expectations, the more melancholy Araki Thomas became. Although he hated himself for the pious attitude he adopted before Cardinal Belamino, he was aware of his own inability to repudiate the warmth of friendship with which he was surrounded.

The affection and kindness which the people of Rome showered upon him gradually developed into a heavy burden. He tired of having to assume an attitude that accorded with their expectations whenever he was in their company – and of having to force a smile to his lips from morning to night.

Araki fell to thinking about the Japan to which he would shortly have to return. He could not forget the news of the twenty-six martyrs which had reached him in Goa. What had amazed him more than anything else about them was that, included in their number, were Father Baptista and other Christians he knew personally. Of the twenty-six, he had had occasion to talk with Miki Paul, a graduate of the Azuchi college, and Father Baptista, who had occasionally come to the Arima *seminario*. Araki realized that a similar fate probably awaited him on his return to Japan. He, too, would doubtless be executed in similar fashion. Would he be able to accept death as they had?

Yet there was no one in Rome to fathom the secrets of Araki's mind. When word of the twenty-six Japanese martyrs finally reached Rome, the Christians there praised Araki – as though he were one of them! They believed that, when he returned to Japan, he too would act in the same way. Araki must have been praying secretly that the situation in Japan would change, that the day would soon come when preaching the Christian Gospel would once again be permitted. For that was his only hope of saving himself.

A description by one of Araki's classmates has been preserved: 'Early one evening, I visited Thomas in his room. He did not hear my knock at the door. Bathed in the sunlight which streamed through the window, he held his head in his hands. He seemed to be crying, so sad and lonely did he look.'

There is no way of knowing which route Araki took on his return to Japan following his stay in the holy city. The next mention of him occurs in 1615 when he was in Macao *en route* for Japan. By that time the priest Valignano had already died, but the number of new Japanese students who had come to the theological college there had increased.

On learning of conditions at home from these Japanese students, Araki felt his last vestige of hope disappear. Following the death of the twenty-six martyrs, far from there being any relaxation in the persecution of the Christians, this had been intensified. During his stay in Rome, the Toyotomi clan had perished, giving way to the Tokugawa era. And yet the first Tokugawa shogun, Ieyasu, had continued the proscription of Christianity, issued edicts of banishment on such Christian lords as Takayama Ukon and Naito Tadatoshi, and dissolved all extant churches. In Kyoto Christians were systematically arrested, and there were reports of increased persecution of Christians even in Yamaguchi and Tanba.

Valignano's dying wish has been recorded. He requested that Araki return to Japan and, from his place of hiding, ensure that the light of the Gospel continue to burn. In 1614 Ieyasu had declared all missionaries and priests in Japan be banished from the country, and yet thirty-seven priests, unable to abandon the Japanese Christians, had defied this edict and secretly remained. These priests were now crying out for even one more source of support. For there was no way that a mere thirty-seven priests could tend to the spiritual needs of all the hidden Christians, scattered as they were throughout the country.

'What's needed more than anything else is a Japanese padre.' This was the unanimous opinion of the missionaries in Macao at that time, since it was impossible for any of the foreign missionaries to enter the country in disguise. The foreign missionaries during this age of persecution may have continued to proselytize with shaven heads in imitation of a Buddhist priest or as Portuguese merchants, but they were still all too identifiable. And the lay Christians, too, preferred a Japanese to a foreign priest, in view of the diminished danger to which he would expose them.

Not surprisingly, everyone believed it to be Araki's duty to return to Japan. Having spent time studying in Rome, he was a great source of hope to both the missionaries and Japanese studying in Macao. He could never repudiate this fact. He must have considered staying in the safety of Macao until the flame of persecution had perished in Japan, but it was evident how such cowardice would be treated were it to come to light. There was an unspoken understanding that this student, of whom so much was expected, should act in accordance with his status.

In the winter of 1617, with a heavy heart, Araki boarded a Portuguese ship bound for Japan. It was two and a half months before he saw the islands of Japan. He was now over forty-five years old.

On landing secretly in Nagasaki, Araki immediately realized that the Christians there were being hounded and persecuted even more than he had expected. This was the work of the head of the fief, the grandson of the Christian lord, Otomo Sumitomo, who had, until recently, defied the shogunate by acting with magnanimity towards the local Christians. But of late, Otomo had shown a complete change of heart – the result of a rebuke from the shogunal household. In the town of Kikitsu near Nagasaki the Franciscan, L'Assomption, had been arrested and thrown into Omura jail. And in a farmhouse near Hirado the Jesuit Father Tavora had been surprised by a police raid during the course of a mass. Both were executed in a district about five miles outside Nagasaki. Likewise the Dominicans, Father Navarette and Father Joseph, were escorted to one of the several islands scattered around Omura Bay and put to death.

Araki and his fellow priests changed their location every day in an attempt to elude the officials. But it is said that, on learning that Sanemon, whom he had converted to the faith, had been put to death at the Omura execution ground in response to Buddhist pleas, Araki held his head in his hands and wept bitterly.

As one by one the foreign missionaries were put to death, the Christians who were in hiding came by night to Araki's secret abode requesting the sacraments and penance. He was their last strand of hope. It was encumbent on Araki as a Japanese priest to hold secret masses, to hear their confessions in an underground cellar and to offer them words of encouragement. Yet the words he offered them by way of support always stuck in his throat. He must have realized that he was unqualified to pronounce such words.

By 1619 the number of Christians being arrested began to increase steadily. On 31st January a blind Christian called Yasujiro was put to death and, on 14th March a Dominican, Father Mena, was escorted from the farmhouse where he had been in hiding to the jail at Omura – again in response to Buddhist demands. The houses where Christians were discovered were put to the torch and members of these families burnt at the stake.

It was from about this time that a gradual change was to be detected in Araki Thomas's demeanour. He was known on occasion to voice anti-Church sentiments to those around him. There are no records to substantiate this claim, yet Araki's thoughts during the process of change must have developed in roughly the following manner.

Whilst fully aware of the ban on Christianity, foreign missionaries continued to steal into Japan. Fired by an intense vision to convert Japan to Christianity, their heroic spirit spurned even death. But what was to be done about the poor Christian peasants who were implicated along with them? The missionaries urged dreams of martyrdom upon the Japanese Christians. They expected them to die as martyrs. Martyrdom was now the only path which led to God, and they believed that, if they were to ignore it, they would be guilty of ignoring God. But did their faith offer nothing but this cruel path?

At about this time Araki came to compare the Japanese Christians who had been ensnared by the ideals of the missionaries to the image he retained of himself when he had been in Rome. Recalling his life as a student studying abroad – a life in which he had found himself totally cramped by the need to stand up straight and conform to the dreams of others – he must have wished to call out, 'That's enough! Leave me alone! Don't try and force your ideas on the Japanese!'

On 10th August 1619, when the officials from the Nagasaki magistrate's office arrived, Araki shook as he was arrested. When ordered to renounce his faith at the magistrate's office, he refused once – but soon apostatized under torture.

Araki was held for a while in Hirado jail, in order that the sincerity of his apostasy could be verified. But news of his apostasy spread amongst the Christians in Nagasaki. He may have been Japanese, but the fact that a priest had apostatized was a severe blow to morale in the Christian community. He was immediately dubbed 'Peter, the fallen padre'. In other words, he was the 'Father of all apostates'.

It is clear from the following story that this nickname spread not only through Nagasaki but as far as Arima and Omura.

In 1620 a Japanese Christian from Arima was dragged to the magistrate's office and subsequently compelled to lie down on some girders formed in the shape of a cross. Water was then poured in through his nose and mouth. The officials told him that he had only to reveal the whereabouts of the hidden priests and his life would be spared. Following hours of interrogation, he finally muttered, 'I know where a priest lives. He lives in Hirado.'

'Who is in Hirado?' shouted the official, whereupon the victim replied weakly, 'Peter, the fallen padre, is there.'

This man was immediately subjected to a succession of cruel tortures and died around dawn.

Having been held for two years in Hirado, Araki Thomas was moved to Omura jail. By now the officials were convinced that this coward would not recant, and it was decided to set him to work. His job was to persuade the Christians held in Omura jail to apostatize.

It was 1622, and there were eight foreign missionaries as well as numerous Japanese Christians held in Omura jail at the time. Today we have a fairly good idea of the conditions under which they were held. It is said that thirty prisoners were squeezed into a twelve-mat room (each mat was approximately two square yards in size). Unable to move, they were forced to sit all day long with their legs crossed. By way of food, they received one bowl of unwashed rice with a small salted sprat and the occasional bowl of turnip-leaf soup. Nevertheless, in the middle of the night, the prisoners would recite their prayers in chorus and then conduct silent prayer for two and a half hours.

It is uncertain whether Araki Thomas was placed in the same room. But it is known that he was dragged out as a witness whenever they were being questioned. At that time there were numerous instances in which the Christians would protect each other by maintaining before the officials that they were uncertain whether the others were Christian or not. On such occasions a witness like Araki was needed at the magistrate's office.

Virtually no mention has been made of Araki's subsequent actions in the Christian records. It is not even known when he died. The only subsequent record is of the conversation he held with the Dominican Father Michael Ozaraza at the Nagasaki magistrate's office in 1637, fifteen years after his transfer to Omura jail.

In 1634 a Spanish ship was driven by the wind on to the shore of the Ryūkyū Islands. There were four missionaries in lay-man's dress aboard. They were immediately seized, bound and sent off to Satsuma. Three of them were subsequently brought to Nagasaki. Under interrogation all three confessed to being Dominican priests from Manila who had come to spread the Gospel in Japan. They also declared that there were some Japanese studying at the theological college in Manila, even though they were few in number.

At that time Araki Thomas was in the magistrate's office, and he spoke with one of the missionaries, Father Ozaraza, in fluent Latin. Araki informed him how, in Japan, enough Christian blood had already been shed, and how, every time more missionaries slipped into Japan, more Japanese blood would necessarily be spilled. He begged the Church in Rome to forsake the people of Japan, to stop forcing its dreams and ideals upon the Japanese.

Father Ozaraza heard Araki out in silence. He then exclaimed simply, 'Your Latin is good. But your faith is rotten. Your period of study abroad was in vain.'

The three missionaries were subjected to cruel water torture – terrifying amounts of water being poured in through the nose and throat. In addition, they were covered with planks and trampled upon. Such torture persisted for several days, before all three eventually succumbed to death.

There is one theory which holds that Araki Thomas, the first Japanese to study in Europe, was subsequently tormented by his conscience to the point that he, too, suffered the death of a martyr. But of course that is wishful thinking. Catholic sources describe him in the following terms: 'Japanese apostate. Studied in Europe. Received a rapturous welcome wherever he went – but ultimately succumbed to pride.'

Part Three

And You, Too

1

The plane landed in Hamburg at 8 p.m. The airport was shrouded in a light drizzle, though this was not enough to penetrate right through to the skin. As they stepped out through the doors of the plane, the passengers, tired of the stifling atmosphere they had endured for so long, were suddenly greeted by the damp smell of the outside world. There was a freshness to the air which they had come to forget during the long flight. Airline employees dressed in navy-blue uniforms standing at the foot of the landing-steps greeted the passengers with a smile and offered each an umbrella. The passengers' legs were still shaky as they reached the tarmac and the sound of the engines continued to reverberate in their ears. Puddles of water at their feet were illuminated by the lights of a refuelling truck as it drove past. In the distance the terminal building could be seen bathed in light.

'Brrr. It's so cold here.'

'Anchorage was colder.... Hardly surprising, since it's up by the North Pole.'

From the shadows of the black stream of passengers which crossed the rainy tarmac behind a stewardess, it was easy to spot the Japanese. Probably in their excitement at having crossed from Tokyo's Haneda airport to Anchorage and, from there, finally reaching Europe by way of the polar route, they were chatting noisily, totally oblivious of those around them. True to the stereotype of the Japanese traveller abroad with camera forever round his neck, these were typical Japanese tourists.

On their arrival at the terminal building, a thin German official with a moustache quietly began collecting all the passports.

'*Bitte* is the same as "please" in English, right?'

'You don't have much of a flair for languages, do you, Tada-san! That's the very first word we learnt as students.'

There were two groups of passengers: those who were to stay in Hamburg and those bound for Orly airport in Paris. The two groups parted and the passengers in the latter group were led into one of the airport restaurants. They were to wait there while the plane was being checked and refuelled. Passengers seemed to split up into smaller groups by nationality as they sat down at their respective tables, but on every face were the telltale black, sootlike marks of travel fatigue.

'They say Hamburg's a really interesting place. Apparently it's the best place there is for picking up white women.'

The Japanese group had established itself in the very middle of the restaurant, and one of them glanced back at the window, by now quite wet from the rain, as he spoke in a subdued tone.

'There you go again! Is that all you can think about, after coming all this way?'

'But, Tada-san, above and beyond our work, we should never stop observing how the masses live. You know Takahata-kun of Nippon Textiles? He's the one who told me that Hamburg is the most interesting place he knows. He said there are even women there who know how to sell their services in Japanese.'

A waiter dressed in white began serving bottles of German beer to each table. At one of the tables where foreigners were sitting one of the women was frantically gesturing that she didn't drink beer.

'Hey. That person sitting over there is Japanese, isn't he?' The man who had just been holding forth about the Hamburg women was using his chin to point out for everyone's benefit an Oriental sitting all alone in the corner of the room. 'He was sitting in the very front of the plane. If he's Japanese, why doesn't he come over here and sit with us? I wonder what's up. Shall I call him over here?'

'No. Leave him alone. He was all alone at Anchorage as well, wasn't he? I passed him by in the plane, too, when I was on the way to the toilet. But he just looked the other way and ignored me. I thought he was pretty conceited then.'

'He must be on a business trip for some trading company.'

'I bet he's not. I saw him sitting there smugly reading a foreign book, so I bet he's some kind of intellectual. He'll have nothing to do with the likes of us ...'

'But if he's so good at languages, perhaps he'll be able to help us when we get to Customs in Paris.'

The solitary Japanese man must have known he was being watched, for the face behind those heavy-rimmed glasses tensed visibly. And, sure enough, whenever his eyes met those of the other Japanese, he immediately looked away towards the framed picture which hung on the wall of the restaurant. Everything about him seemed to be saying, 'We may all be Japanese, but I'm of a different race from you.' Having finished about half his beer, he put on the beret which had been lying on the chair beside him and, book in hand, left the restaurant alone.

'What's he up to?'

Just as such spontaneous tongue-wagging and light invective began to develop in the Japanese group, a blonde stewardess arrived to announce to them that the aircraft was ready for boarding.

Once more the passengers formed a single line and crossed the wet tarmac in silence. Apparently refuelling had just been completed, for the little truck which had been parked alongside the aircraft had just started its engine and was pulling away.

'Bienvenu ... mesdames et messieurs.' Until now the welcome at the cabin door had been in German, but now it was in French. From Hamburg, it was only a short flight over Belgium to Paris.

No sooner had the *No smoking* and *Fasten your seat belt* signs appeared than the aircraft began to shake a little.

When they had been in the restaurant, it had not been quite so obvious, but now they were all seated in the plane it was clear that the number of passengers had decreased considerably. Even those areas of the plane which had been full until Hamburg were now half empty, the empty seats being covered with newspapers and glossy magazines which had been left scattered around. There was something stagnant about the air, filled as it was with the sound of passengers yawning. The stewardesses continued to go round distributing toffees, even though by now there were very few takers.

The plane droned on across the leaden sky. Wiping the steamed-up window with his hand and placing his face to it, the lone Japanese man could make out a faint light on the dirty wing, which, every now and then, emitted bright-red sparks, like flames. The roads and villages were enveloped in the mist and cloud and neither the stars nor lights below were visible. It was as though the tiny plane were surrounded on all sides by a vast and infinite void. Presumably the group of Japanese, who had been in such high spirits in the restaurant earlier, were tired of talking, for almost all of them were now lying back in their seats, deep in sleep. But the man who had been sitting all alone in the corner continued to gaze intently from behind his heavy glasses at the world outside.

It was raining in Paris too. After the plane touched down, passports were stamped and, in Customs, suitcases were marked in a most perfunctory manner with a chalk circle. From there the travel agent had laid on a bus to Les Invalides.

The Japanese group was led away by a young Frenchman in a navy-blue suit who appeared to have been sent specially by the host company to meet them. They were still shouting happily as they left Orly by car.

Passport in hand, the man wearing the beret and the thick glasses remained standing in the suddenly deserted building. There was an announcement over the loudspeaker about the free bus for Les Invalides, urging passengers to board quickly, as the bus was about to leave. But apparently he was as yet unable to pick up such rapid French.

'Monsieur.' The blonde stewardess, her bag hanging from her shoulder, passed by and pointed out the bus to the guileless Japanese man who was still hovering around.

'Vous feriez mieux de . . . profiter.'

'L'autobus. . . ?'

'Yes.' The stewardess quickly changed to English. 'To Les Invalides.'

When the stewardess realized that the man had finally grasped that the bus would take them to Les Invalides, a sympathetic smile played across her face. Her legs were shapely and elegant.

The Japanese man's face stiffened out of a sense of humiliation. Not only had the stewardess's smile pricked his pride like a thorn, but added to this was the disapproving look in the eyes of the other foreign travellers as he hurriedly boarded the bus. They were clearly annoyed at having been kept waiting almost ten minutes. But wasn't he a lecturer in the literature department of a Japanese university? There was no reason why he should be ridiculed in this way.

The bus passed down a long, narrow street. The paved surface appeared leaden, glistening in the rain as far as the eye could see. And, on both sides of the street, the street lamps stretched out like extended bows, creating a bluish blurred effect. Scribbled on to the long wall, black and dirty like that of a prison, the words *la paix* could be made out under the light of the street lamps. Two or three people were huddled together under the dim lights of a café. There was a young man on a bicycle wearing no coat in spite of the rain. Apart from one pharmacist with an advertisement for *Vitapointe*, all the other shops were closed.

'Paris.... So this is Paris. I've finally arrived.... But what a drab place it is!' Then he realized that this was the Paris equivalent of the district filled with drains and dirty buildings which one passes on the way from Tokyo's Haneda airport to Omori. The real Paris was still to come.

The sense of shame he had experienced earlier had gradually dissipated. The other passengers seemed to have forgotten completely about the Oriental man sitting at the back of the bus.

Just as he had expected, the dirty streets gradually turned into broad boulevards. They passed by a cinema where the smiling face of Michele Morgan could be seen surrounded by neon lights which looked like enormous beans. Even the cafés on the street-corners were now larger, brighter and altogether more magnificent. And as they passed by one of the squares, there was an illuminated merry-go-round which was being enjoyed by several children. Despite the rain, a small crowd had gathered to watch.

This was more like the Paris he had come to know through books, pictures and films whilst he was still in Japan. Time and again he raised his heavy glasses with his finger as he drank in every single scene of Paris by night. There was a silver streak of light to their left. It was the Seine. The bus was passing along the quai

Anatole France on the bank of the river on its way to Les Invalides. And in the flood of light from the taxis along the river-bank they could even make out the dark shadows of the barges on the river.

On arrival at Les Invalides, the passengers picked up their luggage. Emerging from a small exit on to the conveyor belt, there were all kinds of cases: cream-coloured suitcases and even exotic hatboxes. Spotting a dirty blue bundle tied up in a Japanese cloth, one of the officials with a cigarette-end in his mouth exclaimed in surprise, 'Tien! C'est à qui?'

Although he was asking for the owner of the bag, once more the Japanese man appeared flustered. Eventually he stepped forward.

'Voilà.'

Both the bundle and his suitcase were dumped down before his eyes. But, completely forgetting his 'merci', the Japanese man grabbed his bags and rushed out of the building.

The drizzle had finally stopped. But there were still enormous black puddles as far as the eye could see in the esplanade des Invalides. There were hundreds of taxis about, causing water to spray in all directions; but, unable to hail one of these, he just stood around in a daze. Look at me. I'm acting like a fool, he thought. Shivering in the rain, he began to recall all those members of the literature department who had come to this country before him to study. Had they, too, experienced a similar sense of self-pity as they passed through Customs at the airport and in that building at Les Invalides? Had they, too, had their luggage thrown at them by some official with a cigarette-end in his mouth as though it were no more than a piece of dirt?

'Whilst I was there, I met the poet Dupuis.'

'This girl studying philosophy was constantly pestering me to go to the theatre with her.'

On their return, they made no mention of feelings of shame and self-pity when they had spoken of their experiences abroad. They spoke as though they had been treated as intellectuals, just as they were in Japan. It was as though, from the moment they had arrived in Paris, they had as a matter of course been respected as members of the intelligentsia.

He now knew that those stories and reports of life abroad were nonsense. He was also aware that the man who now stood at his wit's end in the pouring rain on a Paris street-corner with heavy

58

luggage in both hands, totally incapable of hailing a taxi, was not the university lecturer who had left Japan. The awareness of himself as an intellectual, which had helped him sustain his self-respect, that gratifying feeling of being able to issue orders to students in the lecture-room and the self-confidence he had felt as he strutted around the campus with French originals under his arm ... all these he now felt being peeled away and crashing to the ground. What was left of him was like a statue from which the plaster had been ripped off, leaving only an ugly skeleton. But at least, with a statue, the skeleton remains even after the plaster has been torn off!

At last a taxi came to a halt in front of him and the driver, wearing a beret, put his head out of the window to ask him something. No sooner had he climbed in with his bundle and his suitcase than the driver placed his foot on the accelerator, seemingly by mistake. The young Japanese man bumped his head hard on the window and cried out in pain. Not surprisingly this involuntary cry was not in French but in beautiful Japanese.

'Oh, pardon....' The driver was smiling. 'Where do you want to go?'

Rubbing his painful cheek with his left hand, he groped in his inside pocket with his right. Eventually he pulled out his passport. Somewhere inside his passport was the name of a hotel he could use for the time being which had been given him by one of the senior members of his department. At the same time a couple of envelopes fell out of his passport on to the floor. He gave the driver the piece of paper on which the name of the hotel was written and picked up the muddied envelopes from between his shoes. One of them was from his wife, Kikue, the other was a letter from Nozaka Kazuko.

His wife had slipped him her envelope as he had waved to the crowd which had come to see him off at the boarding gate at Haneda airport. He had opened it just after the first meal had been brought to him on the flight from Haneda to Anchorage. The envelope contained no letter, merely a photograph of his wife and their child, now almost two years old. He had taken it one Sunday or on a national holiday in his back garden. Standing in front of the garden hedge, which was striped with sunlight, his wife was holding the baby in both arms. On one side, the baby's nappies and some shirts could be seen hanging out to dry.

When he opened the letter from Nozaka Kazuko, there had been a distinct smell of perfume. He felt a definite sense of nostalgia from that fragrance. He had read and reread that letter several times during the course of his meal. When he had grown tired of reading it and looked up, he had seen clouds like snowballs floating past beneath the plane. He had left Japan – and his wife and Kazuko – far, far behind.

The taxi set off and raced up the narrow slope of the rue Hamelin. A corner greengrocer's was still open, and from the taxi he could see a thin young man carrying a box full of green vegetables.

The car came to a halt and the young Japanese man offered the fare as indicated on the meter; but the driver angrily demanded a tip. Even in Japan, he had known only too well that, in France, one should always offer at least ten per cent as a tip not only to taxi-drivers but even in cafés and cinemas. This latest mistake of his must be the result of the nervous tension he had felt ever since landing at Orly.

The reception desk at the hotel was quiet. A young man with a blond moustache was reading a book with a picture of a nude woman and a cat on its black cover. The blond moustache seemed somehow vulgar, and the way in which he raised his head and smiled in such a professional manner served only to add to this impression. To the right of the desk, there was a staircase with a cheap-looking red carpet.

'Do you have a room? A single would be fine.'

As he spoke, he was only too well aware that he was using an expression straight out of a French phrase-book.

'For how many nights, sir?' The clerk was obviously used to foreign guests, for his answer, spoken in slow and clear French, was also such as could be found on page one of any guide-book.

'About a couple of weeks. Maybe longer.'

'Are you from Indo-China?'

'No, from Japan.'

The man with the blond moustache allowed himself another smile as he stretched out to take one of the room cards from the shelf behind him.

'You're lucky. There's another Japanese guest staying in the hotel.'

A middle-aged man sporting a felt hat and a white woman

60

wearing a black fur overcoat came slowly down the stairs. The woman was wearing incredibly high-heeled shoes but, hanging on to the man's arm, she passed outside without so much as a single glance in the direction of the reception desk. Perhaps she was a prostitute. For some reason or another the Japanese man felt that he was acting out a scene from a novel by Maurice Kessel.

On the check-in card he had to fill in not only his name but his date of arrival in France, his passport number and his profession. Smiling all the while, the young Frenchman continued to watch the Japanese man's pen as it moved across the page. Sensing this, the latter suddenly found himself reliving all those miserable moments he had experienced in the past two hours – at the airport, at the baggage reclaim area at Les Invalides and in the taxi. He adjusted his glasses with one hand and, in an attempt to eradicate such memories, in the section marked 'Profession' he wrote: 'University lecturer, chargé de cours'.

He was handed his key and told that, since his room was on the fifth floor, his baggage would be brought up later. When he was still in Japan, he had been taught by some of his superiors that, in France, 'I will bring your baggage up later' was another way of asking for a tip. Realizing that this was how French hotels are run, he nodded in agreement.

There was a strange smell of butter on the staircase. Perhaps some of the rooms were equipped with a kitchen and some of the guests were busy preparing a meal. As he climbed the stairs he felt for the first time a deep tiredness welling up in his whole body. All he wanted to do was to lie down on his bed and sleep.

He heard footsteps descending. The man who came down was tall and thin and sported a red Scotch wool tie. Just like a dog trying to sniff out one of its kind, he was sniffing out a mate with the same physical features and appearance.

'Ah, you're Japanese, aren't you?' The visitor was the first to speak. 'I've just heard from downstairs.'

Although he had been loath to speak with his fellow countrymen in the plane, he now felt a sense of relief. In the plane he had not even wanted the stewardesses and other passengers to think of him as coming from the same Oriental stock as the other Japanese passengers. He had somehow wanted to show that they were mere businessmen who had no idea how to behave on a journey, whereas he was a well-educated university lecturer. But now he was exhausted both physically and mentally.

How useful it is to be able to speak one's native language. I am now able to speak freely without thinking about it. Such were the thoughts that rushed to his head at that moment.

'Hello. My name is Sakisaka.'

'I'm Tanaka.' He hurriedly bowed and, using his finger, pushed up the glasses that had slipped down over his nose.

'Where's your luggage?'

'They told me that they'd bring it up later.'

'Oh, you mean the man at the reception desk? Did you spot it? . . . He's queer. You must have guessed, didn't you?'

Sakisaka was showing just how much he knew about the hotel. 'What's your room number?'

'Um . . . 416.'

'Oh, so you're on the fifth floor. It's the top floor in the hotel. I'm on the floor below. Would you like to come in for a second?'

He was absolutely exhausted, but did not want to offend Sakisaka, the first Japanese he had met since landing in Paris. Moreover, he had been sensing for a while now his lack of contact with fellow Japanese for such a long period of time. Perhaps this was the reason why everyone starts talking about 'Japan this' and 'Japan that' as soon as they return home. As he followed Sakisaka up the staircase in which the smell of butter still lingered, he was suddenly assailed by such incoherent thoughts.

Whilst in Japan Tanaka had occasionally thought it strange that each of his fellow students who returned from a period of study abroad become so ardently nationalistic. Each had attempted to justify such feelings of nationalism with his own respective reasoning, all of which sounded perfectly plausible. One such person had argued that the Western spirit was more firmly rooted than its Japanese counterpart and had concluded that the Japanese way of thinking, unconcerned with cultural roots, was totally meaningless. Confronted with such logic, Tanaka had found himself half in agreement, half unconvinced.

Such ideas must follow from feelings like those I'm experiencing right now, he thought.

As he watched Sakisaka strutting up the staircase to the third floor as if he owned the place, Tanaka could not help sensing how typically Japanese was his skinny physique. At the same time he was aware of his own present timidity, and wondered whether, given a month or two, he too would have grown used to life abroad as Sakisaka so clearly had. He felt a distinct sense of jealousy.

'This is it. Please excuse the mess.' On opening the door, Sakisaka took off his red Scotch wool tie and threw it down on the bed to his left. Everything about his pose at that moment suggested that he was completely at home in this foreign land. Nevertheless, wherever one travels in the world, there is a peculiarly Japanese smell to a Japanese room. It was not only the wooden Japanese doll that stood on the desk which came with the room and the tin of Yamamoto-yama seaweed; the fragrance of the whole room was permeated with the distinct smell the Japanese seem to effuse.

'Please sit down. I'll make some tea.'

Opening the desk drawer, Sakisaka took out a black can of Japanese rice crackers.

'I'm afraid they're a bit old, but please help yourself. And what about tea . . . ?' Let me see, where did I put the tea . . .'

'I've got some Japanese tea in my luggage if that would help.' Raising his glasses, Tanaka spoke with an air of deep respect. 'I've also got some pickles in soy sauce. I'll bring them down later.'

'Oh, I love pickles. I haven't had those for over two years.'

'Have you been here long?' Tanaka felt a slight inferiority complex as he spoke.

'It's been two and a half years. I'm studying architecture.'

In the little bookcase to the right of the desk there were about twenty or thirty magazines and books with the word 'Architecture' on the cover mixed in with various Japanese books on the subject. 'How about you?'

By way of an answer Tanaka hurriedly took out his name-card holder from his jacket pocket. Nozaka Kazuko had given him the holder just before he had left. Apparently she had bought it at the Daiwa store on the Ginza in Tokyo.

He gave one of his cards to Sakisaka. His name was written in Japanese on the front, and on the back he had had printed the words *Lecturer, Department of Literature, S University*.

'Oh. I see you teach French literature at S University.'

'Actually I've only just started. I don't know my left hand from my right over here, so I would really appreciate your help.'

He bowed slightly, and for the first time there was the vague hint of a smile in Tanaka's eyes. At last he had been able to convince himself once more in the presence of a fellow countryman that the pitiful figure he had presented ever since his arrival in Paris was not his real self.

Sakisaka placed the name-card in his drawer and asked, 'Did you know that Ono-san is in Paris too?'

Ono was Professor of French literature at a different university. When in Japan Tanaka had despised him as a mere linguist, a self-styled seventeenth-century literary specialist. A short, rotund man, he was a frequent contributor to magazines for beginners in the French language, the sort of man whose double chin and somewhat common features frequently adorned the advertisements for language tapes.

'And then there's Honma-san staying in a hotel on the boulevard Saint Michel.'

Having poured the boiling water from the coffee-pot through the tea-strainer, Sakisaka took a sip himself as, one by one, he reeled off the names of those scholars working in the field of French literature currently resident in Paris. Included in this list were several for whom Tanaka had received letters of introduction from some of his superiors. There were also some professors whom he had been told to contact immediately on arrival in Paris.

The strict hierarchical network that existed in Japanese academic circles had already spread to Paris. To ignore that fact was to invite charges of presumption and egotism upon one's return to Japan.

'Are you the only Japanese here?' Tanaka surveyed every corner of the room as he spoke, a hint of caution in his voice.

'Yes. At first I stayed in a hotel in Montparnasse – a hotel swarming with budding Japanese artists and designers. I couldn't stand the way they lived and so I escaped here. You'll see what I mean soon enough.' Sakisaka allowed a sarcastic smile to play across his pale face. Picking up the blue carton of cigarettes lying on the desk, Sakisaka offered it to his guest. 'They're Gauloises. Do you smoke?'

Tanaka was not a regular smoker but was eager to try a real French cigarette. He lit one clumsily and began to inhale. It was painful.

'They taste really fresh, don't they?'

'I suppose you still can't buy them in Japan. They keep on importing American tobacco. But once you start smoking these, you won't be able to stop. It's the same with Paris itself. You end up settling down here. Of course it has its bad moments. And yet, whenever you go anywhere, you find yourself confronted by irresistible feelings of nostalgia for the place.'

Tanaka had frequently heard much the same opinion expressed by those returning from abroad. He recalled the drops of rain shining like thousands of needles under the street lights and the ugly, leaden grey streets which he had just seen from the bus on his way from Orly to Les Invalides.

'By the way, Tanaka-san. What's your specialist interest in French literature? . . . Not that it will mean anything to an architect like me.' Presumably in an attempt to clear the smoke-filled air, Sakisaka took hold of the handle of the french windows. 'Phew. It's so stiff. That's the problem with old hotels like this.'

'Well, I can hardly call it my specialist field yet, but I'm hoping to do some work on the Marquis de Sade.'

'Hey. . . . The Marquis de Sade?' For the first time there was a distinct note of interest in Sakisaka's voice. 'You've certainly picked a weird topic, haven't you?! Of course I don't know anything at all about him.' The smile that now played across Sakisaka's lips could not be described as either sympathetic or sarcastic. 'People have so much ambition when they first arrive.' It was almost as though he were talking to himself.

Once more Tanaka's self-confidence was severely wounded. He felt an urge to explain why he had chosen that topic, but refrained from doing so. When he realized that Sakisaka knew nothing about it, his face tensed.

Sensitive enough to realize that Tanaka was upset, Sakisaka tried to humour him. 'I'm really jealous. We get this constant stream of excellent young students coming here, while people like me end up wasting our time ... and before we know it, two and a half years have gone by.'

'Really?'

A moist breeze came in through the window Sakisaka had just opened. The light from the window could be seen projected on to the wall across the small courtyard.

'This is a really old hotel. Did you notice the copperplate sign over the entrance?'

'No, I didn't.'

'It says that Proust died here. Not that I've ever read anything of his.'

'He's the author of the book called *A la recherche du temps perdu*.'

'Oh?' Sakisaka put his hand to his mouth disinterestedly.

Leaving Sakisaka's room, Tanaka made his way back to the fifth floor. There were no signs of life in the corridor, and from the rooms arranged like cabins on a small liner not a sound was to be heard. The light bulbs, like small beans, cast faint patches of light on to the ceiling.

He finally managed to unlock his door, but could not locate the light switch and ended up groping around the wall with both hands like a lizard. Banging his knee against something, he staggered and cried out in pain. In the darkness he crouched down and held both knees in his hands. He had apparently bumped into the corner of the bed.

When he finally managed to switch on the light, he saw his bundle wrapped in the Japanese cloth and his suitcase lying there. It was both sad and pitiful.

He sat down on the edge of the bed, his eyes downcast. This was his first night in Paris. He had not imagined such a night at the time his selection to study abroad had been confirmed, nor when he had arrived with the crowd of well-wishers at Haneda airport. He recalled how, as he had started to leave everyone and pass through the steel barrier, his wife Kikue had suddenly held up their baby in front of him.

Once more Tanaka took the photograph out of his passport and stared at it. He could not help blinking. He then reread the letter from Nozaka Kazuko. In addition to his jet-lag, he was assailed by a profound awareness of being entirely alone in a strange country. He wondered what time it was in Tokyo. It would be just after midday. Kikue would probably be in the kitchen warming some milk for the baby. Perhaps Nozaka Kazuko was in the noodle shop just off the campus with the students Izaka and Fujimura. And in the deserted office the midday sun would be shining in on the two or three teacups left lying around.

Standing up from his bed, Tanaka pressed his face to the window. Adjusting his glasses with his finger, he stared down at the narrow courtyard enveloped in darkness. Most of the windows on the three sides of the courtyard were dark. There were just one or two rooms in which the light from some kind of table lamp could still be seen through the thin curtains. Tanaka wondered which was the room where Proust had died. Although at the time he had paid little attention to it, he recalled what he had just heard from Sakisaka and felt a sudden searing pain in his chest. A long time ago he had read Mauriac's account of his visit to the dying Proust. If Tanaka was not much mistaken, Proust had moved into a furnished apartment three years before his death. Tanaka had also learnt from his reading that Proust had spent the next three years fighting severe bouts of asthma, but that, despite being virtually confined to bed, he had continued to write little by little. 'All the lights were out, and there was an overcoat instead of blankets on his bed. His face seemed like a wax effigy and only his hair seemed to be alive as he watched me eat.' Tanaka could still remember the extract from Mauriac's account of his visit.

Tanaka was overcome by an awareness that he might be in the very same room. Suddenly everything about the room, with its marks on the ceiling where the rain had seeped through and the yellowish paper on the walls, seemed unbearably oppressive.

2

Tanaka had no idea why he suddenly felt so stifled. It seemed that this feeling was inspired by more than his painfully agitated state at finding himself in the very same building where, some forty years previously, Proust had finally succumbed to his asthma and died. He remembered another article he had read about the room Proust had occupied: 'Nothing could have been more arid, more poverty-stricken, than this room, the only ornament in which was the pile of notebooks, which formed the manuscript of his novel, stacked on the mantelpiece.'

In this room which Edmond Jaloux described as an 'artistic

penitentiary', Proust was denied the use not only of a hearth and gas, but even of matches in case his asthma developed into some bronchial disorder. Tanaka pictured the room with the bottle of ink to the side of the bed and Proust sitting there writing every day, and he wondered whether the ceiling with its damp patches and the faded walls he now saw were just as they had been in Proust's day. But, given that that was all he saw, Tanaka had no idea why he felt this indescribable pressure closing in on him from all sides. Once more, in an attempt to escape that suffocating feeling, he put his head out of the window into the fine drizzle outside, but the lights that had been on when he had last looked out were now extinguished and the courtyard had been enveloped in a darkness like coal tar.

There had been times in Tokyo, too, when, tired of studying in his small rented accommodation in the Kyodo district of Setagaya, he would open the window and take a deep breath of the fresh air outside. But on such occasions, even in winter, the moist air would be filled with the smell of dust, so typical of the Musashino district. In sharp contrast, however, this courtyard exuded the smell neither of dust nor of trees. The only smells that assailed his nostrils now were those of man-made stone buildings and of cement. Even the colour of the darkness seemed somehow colder and thicker than in Japan.

Removing his clothes, badly creased after the long flight, Tanaka took from his suitcase the yukata he wore instead of pyjamas. Putting this on over his briefs, he felt at last that he had recaptured his Japanese identity. Removing the shoes and sweaty socks he had worn ever since leaving Haneda the day before, he rubbed the soles of his feet on the floor. It felt good! Really good! Suddenly he found himself yearning for the tatami-mat floors he was used to in Japan and realized just how Japanese he really was.

When he awoke the following morning, the sun filtering through the chinks in the Venetian blinds formed several long, faint streaks on the floor. He sloppily opened the front of his yukata and stifled a yawn as he opened the window. The leaden sky hung heavily in between the black roofs of the buildings. Immediately opposite him stood the bare wall of the house next door. Two or three grey pigeons had gathered at the corner of the eaves on the roof. But not a single tree was growing in the cement courtyard down below.

Right in the middle of the courtyard stood a buxom French girl wearing a dark-blue apron and carrying a bucket filled with rubbish, and when she threw out some breadcrumbs for the birds, the pigeons came flocking down. Immediately the young girl looked up and saw Tanaka casually dressed in his yukata. She stared up at him in surprise. He hurriedly stepped back from the blinds.

He washed, put on his shirt and trousers and went down to Sakisaka's room in a pair of slippers. He wanted to take him the tin of tea he had promised him the previous evening. A bleary-eyed Sakisaka opened the door only a fraction.

'Hey. You're up already? I'm sorry. I always sleep until just before noon. If you don't get enough sleep, you won't be able to take the hectic pace of Paris life.'

He thanked him for the tea, but, unlike the previous evening, did not invite him in. The change in attitude made Tanaka feel strangely deserted. Perhaps this was some Western concept of individualism which Sakisaka had picked up in Paris.

'All right.'

'Hey.' With the door still only partly open, Sakisaka pointed at Tanaka's feet. 'In this country you mustn't walk around outside your room in bare feet and slippers. It's like going around naked. They don't like it. In the hotel at Montparnasse all the Japanese used to walk around like that. It was a real problem for the manager. I'm free this evening, so I should be able to show you around.'

Even after returning to his room, Tanaka continued to feel strangely embarrassed – a feeling aggravated by the painful memories of various incidents the previous evening at Orly and Les Invalides.

The guest in the neighbouring room must have been getting up, for Tanaka could hear him ordering coffee on the phone. His French was clearly audible through the wall. Lying down on his bed, Tanaka tried to picture himself in his Japanese university as he had been until the week before. He thought of himself happily talking away with a group of students in the coffee shop facing the university gate. On that occasion he had been able to recite a verse from a poem by Rimbaud or lines from a classical play without any self-consciousness, as though it were a piece of everday conversation. At the same time he had been profoundly conscious of the female students who were sitting there staring intently at him as he spoke. He had been particularly aware of Nozaka Kazuko, sitting in the corner. By that time Tanaka had become a lecturer in the department of French literature at one of the private universities, a position he had held for only about a year. Such happy memories served, in part at least, to heal the wound to his self-respect that had just been inflicted by Sakisaka.

I'm in Paris at last. The flight was most enjoyable. And now that I'm here, I feel as though I've returned to our intellectual and spiritual home. Please give my regards to all those who came to see me off: Suganuma, Nakagawa and Inoue. I'll be writing properly to Professor Ueda and Assistant Professor Imai in the near future. . . .

Seated with a cup of coffee in the corner of a café on the avenue Kléber, Tanaka wrote this card to his wife and another quick one addressed to his department. Strangely enough, he did not feel he was writing a series of untruths. Between the lines of the letters he had received from all those above him in the department who had come to study in Paris before him, he had detected similar feelings of satisfaction, even superiority, at having arrived in France. It was a kind of accepted norm for all students who travelled abroad, and Tanaka found himself using just such logic to justify his actions. In all probability he would adopt a similar tone even during his report on this study trip following his return home, and he would certainly never ask the others just how miserable some of their experiences had been. It was the same with doctors, who not only keep quiet about their own faulty diagnoses but feel duty bound not to talk about those of a fellow doctor.

On finishing these cards, he summoned the waiter with a loud 'Merci' and went outside with the same cowardly smile he planned to show to Professor Ueda and Assistant Professor Imai. There were few signs of life in the street that morning. A four-storeyed, soot-coloured building towered above the dark-red boulevard. On the other side he could vaguely make out the Eiffel Tower. Some workmen in blue overalls were clearing rubbish from the gutter, using water from a long hose. An old woman dressed in black emerged from a bakery carrying some bread in the shape of a long

70

stick, and a couple of Frenchmen bought the morning paper at a kiosk at the entrance to the Métro before disappearing down the stairs.

This was more like the Paris Tanaka had come to know from films and photographs during all his years in Japan. These were the scenes he had dreamt about so often since he had taken those first preparatory courses at university. Since then, how often had he mulled over such visions, determined to see them for himself. His passion for anything French had grown steadily ever since those days when he had gone to see the old films of René Claire and Duvivier over and over again at the Shinjuku cinema. He could recall equally well the subsequent daily trip to the dark, damp classroom of Aténé Français in Ochanomizu. Of course there were various factors involved in his decision to enter the French literature department at university, one of the more significant of which was a somewhat childish fascination with the dark Parisian landscape.

Nevertheless, as he looked at the Eiffel Tower reaching up into the cloudy sky, he could see something inordinately 'popular' about its appeal. It was like a pagoda, explicitly aimed at the tourist. And yet as he stopped to consider himself standing in the centre of Paris, even that 'popular' spectacle was enough to make him smile. He kept repeating to himself, 'I've actually managed to come here to study! I'm actually here!'

Compared with those immediate post-war years of hardship, it was no longer quite so difficult for young Japanese students of foreign literature to travel abroad to study. From his own department, he knew of about four who had gone off to study in London and Berlin. And he had heard that, including artists and designers, there were over four hundred Japanese studying in Paris alone. Nevertheless, for the young Japanese student of foreign literature, the opportunity to study abroad still constituted an important mark of esteem.

'I heard Ponty speak at the College de France.' Tanaka had been able on occasion to see for himself just how much weight such words, spoken by a proud returning student, carried amongst those who had remained behind in Japan.

'What can you achieve in just one year studying abroad? He doesn't seem to have made any progress. And he's certainly none the wiser!'

'He walks around as though the whole world of French literature hangs on his shoulders, doesn't he?'

Yet even such malicious gossip, exchanged in the privacy of the coffee shop out of earshot of the student in question by those not chosen to study abroad, bore adequate testimony to the fact that they felt a distinct sense of inferiority.

By doing this, I've got two steps ahead of the assistant, Suganuma, he thought.

Tanaka adjusted his glasses, which had slipped down his greasy nose, and walked towards the Eiffel Tower, which seemed to hang in the leaden sky in front of him. His head was full of unresolved questions. When deep in thought, he had this habit of pushing his glasses up off his nose with his finger. It had been the female student Nozaka who had pointed out this idiosyncrasy to him. He could still remember her mischievous grin as she had done so. Tanaka was comforted by the thought that, for the time being at least, Suganuma could not possibly overtake him.

Just as Tanaka was considered Professor Ueda's senior student, so Suganuma, Tanaka's junior by two years, was being trained to succeed Assistant Professor Imai. Then, just a year after Tanaka had become a lecturer, Suganuma had risen to the rank of assistant. He seemed to be following closely on Tanaka's heels. Given that Tanaka had chosen to study the rather drab eighteenth century, whereas Suganuma was engaged on research into post-war literature, it was only to be expected that it was Suganuma who was the more popular with the students. His translation of *Tour du Pin* had been well received by the critics and his discussions of novels were occasionally to be seen in the various literary magazines. As a result, his name was much more widely known in journalistic circles than that of people like Tanaka.

'There's no douting his ability. But what about his contributions in academic circles? He'll never make it if he keeps pandering to the media.' There had been occasions when, out drinking with some of the graduate students in Shinjuku or Shibuya, he had carelessly let slip such thoughts. Afterwards, aware that such comments smacked off jealousy on his part, he would keep quiet. But it was in just such moments that his own sense of inadequacy *vis-à-vis* Suganuma had been revealed.

Professor Ueda was due to retire in another year and a half. He would be succeeded by Assistant Professor Imai, whose eye was clearly on Suganuma. There was the distinct possibility that, at that stage, Tanaka would be transferred to another private university or to a post in a different department.

Between the roofs of the buildings there was a break in the ashen sky and a penetrating ray of light was cast on to the leaden road. The bells rang out coldly from the clock on the grey church. There was more traffic on the roads now.

Tanaka came to a square, in the middle of which a lawn had been created. According to the map, this was the place du Trocadéro. From this square, the Eiffel Tower, which had been no more than a vague blur against the smoggy sky, now appeared vivid and imposing before his eyes. In the café on the opposite side of the square a group of people, dressed in thick overcoats, sat gazing at the Tower. They looked cold. From one corner of the square he could look down on the Seine, which he had seen as a silver streak the previous evening. A thin veil of mist hung over the river and, although this was not the tourist season, there were a few sightseeing boats milling around. A solitary bird skimmed over the ice-cold water before flying off in the direction of the Eiffel Tower. Looking out on this scene, Tanaka felt really glad he had come to Paris. He felt alive. He suddenly recalled the famous depiction of the ambition of Julien Sorel by Stendhal. Julien was standing on top of a great rock: 'From time to time a hawk, risen from the great cliffs above his head, caught his eye as it wheeled silently in vast circles. Julien's eye followed mechanically the bird of prey. Its calm, powerful motion impressed him, he envied such strength, he envied such isolation.'

At about four o'clock that afternoon Tanaka was in his room writing postcards to the people who had come to see him off at the airport and to whom he had not been able to write that morning. Suddenly there was a knock at the door and Sakisaka walked in.

'I'm sorry about this morning. I felt bad about leaving you all alone like that just after your arrival, but there was nothing I could do about it. I'm awful in the mornings. Recently I haven't been feeling too well.'

Tanaka had not noticed the previous evening, but now that he mentioned it, he could see that Sakisaka looked pale. He looked strangely yellow.

'What did you do after you left me?'

'I went to the Trocadéro. I walked down the Champs-Elysées from the Arc de Triomphe. But I haven't begun to find my way around yet.'

Sakisaka passed a hand through his long hair and smiled wryly. 'It's the same for everyone at the beginning. The sooner we teach you how to use the Métro, the better. What do you particularly want to see in Paris?'

As a student of the literature of the Marquis de Sade, Tanaka wanted to see hundreds of places connected with him. First and foremost he had to meet the scholar Ruby, who was involved in research on Sade. Tanaka planned to use introductions from the latter to meet Sade's ancestors and to examine the literary records on Sade that were kept at the Bibliothèque Nationale. In Paris alone there were numerous places essential to a study of Sade. For example, there was the house that still stood in the town of Arcueil in which, one Easter Sunday, Sade had outrageously assaulted a beggar woman. In addition, he wanted to see the prison of Vincennes in which Sade was confined as well as the remains of the Bastille destroyed at the time of the Revolution. Then there was the psychiatric hospital at Charenton in which the writer was confined during his final years, and his gravestone – both of which Tanaka wished to visit at the earliest possible opportunity.

'You don't give yourself a breather, do you?' Sakisaka seemed to be scorning Tanaka's enthusiasm as somewhat simplistic. 'You can go round all these places of specialist interest on your own later. Tonight I'll take you to the Café le Dôme where all the Japanese get together.'

Tanaka had heard of both the Café le Dôme and La Coupole. They were the places in Montparnasse where all the young literary scholars and artists congregated – and the favourite haunts of the Japanese artists and other visiting scholars.

'You really should meet people like Ono-san and Honma-san.'

Both Ono and Honma had cropped up in the conversation the night before. The former was Professor of French literature at H University, the latter Assistant Professor at M University.

'If you go to Le Dôme, you can be sure to get hold of Ono-san.

He goes there every night for a drink. Shall we have a bite to eat in my room before we go?'

'Oh, do you cook for yourself? Really?' Tanaka had just eaten at a restaurant near the Trocadéro and been amazed at the cost! A bill like that would be inconceivable in Japan. He could not conceal his surprise from Sakisaka.

'I was thinking of starting to fix my own food from now on, too. If not, I don't think my grant will last long here.'

'But if you do, you'll find yourself growing weak – like me. There's a place called Chez Julianne near the Sorbonne. Or else there's the student cafeteria. You're all right if you stick to either of those. They're cheap and the food's not too bad.'

Dinner was a simple affair of bread with rabbit pâté and Camembert in Sakisaka's room. The two of them then went down the rue Hamelin, upon which a thin film of mist was beginning to descend. Through the mist they could just make out the blurred lights of a greengrocer's and a pharmacist's. The streets of Paris seemed not so much melancholy as gloomy and desolate. Once more Tanaka was overcome by the sensation that the buildings and dirty walls on either side were rejecting him.

Sakisaka seemed to read his mind and, coughing gently, asked him what he thought of the place. 'What are your first impressions?'

'Well, somehow it doesn't seem like the Paris I had imagined.... The whole place seems so cold.'

The architect in Sakisaka was evident in his reply. 'That's probably because the houses, streets and churches are all just accumulations of stone. And each of those stones bears the whole weight of history. It's a long, long history. Living in Paris is a constant process of coming to terms with that history. For someone like me who has been here for a couple of years, the pressure and burden that that history imposes causes both physical and mental anguish.'

Tanaka recalled the suffocating feeling he had experienced the previous evening in his room with the damp marks on the walls. He also recalled the great void he had sensed from his window as well as the pungent smell he had experienced when inhaling the night air through that window – the smell emanating from the ground which had been artificially hardened with cement. Proust had spent three years with that smell, almost completely cut off from the outside world. And during that time he had succeeded in creating a whole new world through his writing.

'There seem to be three types of Japanese who come to Paris,' said Sakisaka. 'Those who completely ignore the weight of that history, those who try to be smart by imitating that weight and ... there are plenty of this kind swarming around in the Café le Dôme we are going to now.'

Putting his hand to his mouth and coughing drily, Sakisaka did not mention the third group of Japanese visitors. When one heard that weak cough, one realized that this man was exhausted by life in Paris.

The staircase of the Métro was dank and muddy, but the air coming from the exit was lukewarm. On the wall was a poster of a semi-naked woman with a bright smile, clutching a bottle of Cinzano. A swarm of Frenchmen, exhausted from a hard day's work, rushed past them. They looked more hostile than their Tokyo counterparts.

'Paris is no longer in its *belle epoque* either. Life is hard for these people too,' Sakisaka hurried to explain to Tanaka as he watched those faces. 'At any rate, if there's no resolution of the protracted war with Algeria, then the economy has had it. Everyone knows that the recent spate of new political parties has not helped the situation. But, by the same token, the ingrained character of the French wouldn't allow a dictator to come to power.'

A train, shabbier and seemingly in a worse state of repair than those in Tokyo, pulled into the platform. The train was filled with a variety of smells, and Tanaka realized that this was the smell of people, the smell of life. It was strange that when he was in Tokyo he had not noticed this smell of people and of life in the subway. It must have been the fact that he was a visitor to this city which caused him to be overcome by such a wave of sentimentality. A black student was leaning against the doors of the train with a blonde girl, discussing dancing. Opposite him was an elderly man of ruddy complexion wearing a beret and buried in the third-rate newspaper *France Soir*. The headline on the front page read: MOTHER THROWS CHILD INTO SEINE. There was an accompanying photograph of a hollow-faced woman.

On emerging on to the streets of Montparnasse, Tanaka had to admit he was disappointed. He had read so many novels about

Montparnasse whilst still in Japan and had subsequently formed his own mental image of the place and its unique flavour. This was the town which had inspired the artists of the Parisian school like Matisse, Derain, Utrillo and Picasso. It was the nightly haunt of such novelists as Apollinaire, Jacob and Carco. It was in one of the little cafés here that the Symbolist poets had first congregated. But the Montparnasse which now appeared before his eyes was darker and more deserted than the area in front of Ogikubo or Nakano stations in Tokyo. The few neon signs that were lit were far more shabby than those of the bars in Shinjuku and Shibuya he had frequented with other students. A dark man in a shabby coat approached them and rubbed Tanaka's palm with a sweaty hand. He was mumbling something in an inaudible voice.

'Take no notice.' Sakisaka shook his head. 'They try and fob you off with some ridiculous so-called pornographic photos.'

'Are there prostitutes too?'

'I suppose you want to get hold of a white woman, do you?' There was a distinct note of sarcasm in Sakisaka's voice as he spat at a horse-chestnut tree by the side of the road. 'If you do, I'll give you the name of a bar I know. Of course you don't have to go to such places to.... Look! That woman in the fur over there on the corner by the cinema. She's one too.'

Feeling he had betrayed his own despicable longing, Tanaka remained silent. Even in Tokyo he had never resorted to paying for a prostitute. He was well aware that this had little to do with his own moral stance; he had refrained rather out of a fear of venereal disease and a sense of social dignity. But he could not deny that somewhere in the recesses of his mind lurked the desire of the yellow Oriental to sleep with a white woman sometime during the course of his stay in Paris. But Tanaka, the university lecturer, was as yet unable to confess as much to Sakisaka.

The Café le Dôme was divided into a glass-roofed terrace and the interior of the shop. The glass partition had steamed up as a result of the heat from the stove, but it was clear that the terrace was crammed full of young people. From their long hair down to the nape of their necks, their goatee beards and the loud colours of their sweaters, it was immediately apparent that most of these were students, budding artists and youthful literati from all corners of the globe.

Tanaka felt strangely out of place in his suit and tie; but, at the same time, he remembered that there was a scene, near the beginning of Hemingway's *The Sun Also Rises,* in which a café similar to this one in Montparnasse was portrayed. In the novel, these youths had lived out an empty existence in this place, day after day.

'Hey.' In the corner of the shop, which was enveloped in cigarette-smoke, they could make out four or five Japanese men, and it was one of these who was now addressing them, his arm raised in greeting. Just like the other clients in the shop, these, too, sported goatee beards and turtleneck sweaters. Even to Tanaka, this all seemed incredibly superficial and somewhat pathetic. Such sweaters looked somewhat incongruous on Japanese of such unimposing physique, and goatees did not suit their plain faces.

'Well, if it's not Tanaka!' A portly man had spotted him and shouted out in surprise. It was Ono, the Professor of H University whom Sakisaka had mentioned earlier.

'When did you arrive?'

'Um . . . I got here yesterday.'

'Really. I got a letter from Japan saying that you were coming. You must be tired after the long trip.' As if to show off his superiority to those around him, Ono sat in his chair and nodded magnanimously just as though he were in the department office.

'This is Tanaka-kun. He's also studying French literature.'

'Another specialist in foreign literature! We can't keep up with them all!' This time it was a middle-aged man who spoke, his wineglass pressed firmly to his lips. To judge from the colour of his face, he was clearly drunk and there was something provocative about his manner as he stared at Tanaka. But he was the only person, apart from Tanaka, to be wearing a suit and tie, even though the suit was badly worn.

'Shut up, Nabe-san! You don't start picking a fight with someone straight off the plane!' A youth in a corduroy jacket who was sitting to one side attempted to intervene on Tanaka's behalf. He continued, as though baiting a dog. 'He's the author Manabe-san. He's just stopped off in Paris on his way home from the PEN club meeting in Stockholm. He was just having a heated discussion with Ono-san.'

'What can I say?' A mean smile played across Ono's rotund face.

'Nabe-san always starts arguing when he's drunk!'

'What are you talking about?'

'It's all right. Never mind. Just be quiet!'

'It's not all right! Who do you foreign literature experts think you are? What sort of relationship is there between you lot and the literature you read? Are you trying to tell me you have the same sort of unseverable ties that we writers have? You lot are just getting a free ride at someone else's expense. Or perhaps we should call you irresponsible commentators!'

The author's words and facial expression smacked more of a Shinjuku or Shibuya bar than of Paris. The whole place reeked of the salted fish guts and dried fish to be found in the bars of Shinjuku and Shibuya where the Japanese literati were always arguing with the scholars of foreign literature. For some reason or other Tanaka recalled the impression he had formed the previous evening in Sakisaka's room. There had been something about that room which had, over the course of time, transformed the room itself into Japanese body odour. And now, here in the Café le Dôme in Montparnasse, was a Japanese writer exuding the odour of a Japanese writer. Ono, too, for his part was manifesting in his pose the power relationships rife in the realm of higher education in Japan.

'Well, how goes it? How are things with you, Tanaka-kun?' Ono had skilfully diverted the barb of the attack towards Tanaka. 'Well, say something, won't you? Remember you've been sent to Paris as one of the outstanding scholars of foreign literature in Japan.'

'What do you mean, "outstanding scholar"? Don't be so conceited! What do you mean by that? Since when have you given of your own flesh and blood for literature?'

This notion of 'giving of one's own flesh and blood' was currently much in vogue amongst the Japanese literati. But again the word smacked of the salted fish guts and dried fish of the drinking world.

'What do you mean, we've never given of our own flesh and blood for literature?' Sensing that the eyes of the young artists were focused on him, Tanaka continued in a quiet voice. 'Are you saying that we are incapable of creating a work of literature?'

'I mean that those who don't write can't possibly understand the pain and suffering of the writer.' At the sound of Manabe's booming voice, the foreigners in the shop all looked round. The waiter, bearing a silver tray laden with aperitifs and cognac, was clearly perplexed and raised his index finger. The smiles which had formed on the lips of the young Japanese artists comprised a mixture of guile and sarcasm. Their cynical expressions betrayed a sense of superiority that they, like Manabe, were creative artists, whereas all that the students of foreign literature like Tanaka did was merely denounce such efforts.

'But rather than judging whether someone actually creates something or not, isn't it more important to judge him by what he has created?'

'What the hell do you mean by that?'

'What's the point in creating a tedious novel and then feeling a sense of pride and superiority just because one has created something? The world is full of writers, but the only time they justify their existence is when they create a masterpiece. Right? As far as I'm concerned, that's the only justification for their existence.' Tanaka sensed his voice growing louder as a result of his agitation. With his finger he repositioned the glasses that had slipped down his sweaty nose and, painfully aware of the look of consternation in Ono's gaze as well as the animosity in the eyes of the young artists, Tanaka rose to the challenge.

'I suppose you're trying to say that Japanese writers and critics are no match for their French counterparts in whom you seem so interested?'

'That's right. No match at all.' Tanaka had finally said what he had no right to say. 'Even someone like me is able to say that with absolute confidence. I know I shouldn't say this, but even your most representative works are third rate in comparison with the best French works. Over here, you have possibly yet to pass muster as any kind of writer.'

'Listen to him! I'll take your criticism at face value.' Manabe put on a bold front, but his nervous facial expression belied his true feelings. 'But I never asked you to pass judgement on my works. Stop changing the subject. Instead of criticizing others, just take a look at yourself. If you're not creating works of art as I am, then what do you stand to lose in your study of literature?'

'For a start, I'm planning to translate some of the great works.'

'Oh yes! You mimic the words of another human being like a mina bird and call it translation! In which case you students of foreign literature are mina birds. No, there's nothing wrong with that. But if that really is so, then I wish you'd reveal the pain and suffering of living like mina birds in your lives! There's absolutely none of that with you Japanese students of foreign literature.'

'How do you know that?' Tanaka's glasses rested on the tip of his nose and there was anger in his voice. 'How can you be so sure that we don't know the pain and suffering of living like mina birds?'

The whole party fell quiet and a tense silence reigned. The young artists who, until that point, had been listening to the argument with wicked grins, now began idly to blow cigarette-smoke up to the ceiling and to discuss quietly amongst themselves the latest news of their deals with the picture dealers and the current market prices.

'Anyway, let's leave it at that.' Manabe had noticed the tense atmosphere and smiled in an unaffected manner. 'Ono-san, there's much more of the samurai about this one than you. I like him. I really like the way he told me my works are boring.' Then, extending his hand to Tanaka, he continued, 'Here. Let's shake on it.'

Tanaka took the writer's clammy hand and felt a sense of humiliation and sadness welling up inside him. I failed. I didn't know when to stop ... and so soon after my arrival in Paris! This was obvious from the look on Ono's face as he glanced uncomfortably at Tanaka out of the corner of his eye.

'Let's try another place, Nabe-san.' Coat in hand, Ono was trying to humour Manabe. 'Let's go and have another drink at La Coupole.' Then casting a cold stare in the direction of Tanaka, he continued, 'Well. We'll be seeing you.'

He slowly raised his portly body from the chair. The other artists followed him with not a word to Tanaka. As they left the bar, it was clear that they considered him a conceited newcomer. Sakisaka sat silently smoking in his squeaky chair.

'I'm sorry. I didn't mean to cause you any trouble.' Tanaka stiffened and hung his head in shame.

'What are you talking about? Don't worry about it. Ono-san was just defending you.'

But Tanaka could picture the scene all too clearly. He could see Ono turning his portly frame to the others as soon as they had left Le Dôme and saying, 'We've got a real problem with that one! Even among the students of French literature, he's known as the country bumpkin.' Tanaka knew that, at the very least, Ono would be offering such an explanation.

'It's not only you. While you're in Paris you have both the physical exhaustion and the intricate relationships to contend with, and so . . .' – Sakisaka seemed to be saying this for his own benefit – 'you find yourself becoming strangely edgy. There is also this strange tendency amongst Japanese when they are abroad to feel a real professional rivalry and jealousy. It's like the ladies-in-waiting at the Palace. That's what I hate most about the Japanese in Paris. That's why I decided to live on my own.'

Behind his glasses Tanaka blinked sorrowfully and nodded.

'Shall we go back? Or do you want to go to another café?'

'No. Please take me back to the hotel.' Tanaka was almost in tears as he replied.

Sakisaka nodded and called for the bill.

They returned to the hotel in silence. When they came to the third-floor staircase, Sakisaka turned to Tanaka and said 'Bonne nuit'. He then disappeared down the corridor.

Left all alone, Tanaka returned to his room and groped for the light. In the dim light he could see the letters he had finished just before leaving strewn around on the desk. The bundle of clothes tied up in the Japanese cloth and his suitcase were also scattered about untidily. His whole being was pained by the memory of his failure in the café. But what pained him more than anything else was the way Ono, his senior at college, had fixed him with that icy stare. Having only just arrived in Paris, he had completely overstepped the mark in front of a group of Japanese who had been here for some time. He could just picture how they would look on him in future.

It was nevertheless true that he secretly despised most modern Japanese novelists. Furthermore, this trait was not unique to himself: he had detected similar sentiments amongst the majority of the people in his department at the university and other foreign literature specialists he knew. There was no way in which Tanaka could divorce himself from his opinion that the works of the modern Japanese novelists were, if not inferior, at least no better than those of their French counterparts. Yet the fact remained that, as was the accepted practice of all the students of foreign literature in Japan, if he were to be introduced to a novelist in a bar in Japan, he would never have ventured to express such sentiments quite so readily. The fact that he had openly confessed to such opinions within two days of his arrival in Paris must, as Sakisaka had surmised, be the result of frayed nerves caused by travel fatigue.

'How can someone who has never created anything possibly understand the struggles of the true artist?' Manabe's attack was that traditionally employed by Japanese literati when taking critics and specialists in foreign literature to task. Tanaka was fully aware how simplistic and foolish such criticism was; and yet, ultimately, he had to confess that he had yet to develop the confidence simply to laugh such attacks off. Tanaka, who at one stage during his university career had contemplated a career as a novelist, had never quite managed to throw off his sense of inferiority at his lack of creativity, even as he proceeded with his studies of foreign literature.

'Well, well! What is it? What's so difficult about finding your works in the pages of the literary magazines every month?' Lying flat out on his back on his bed, Tanaka shouted out to himself, just as though Manabe and his friends were present in the room. And yet his voice echoed off the ceiling with its damp stain and disappeared into the void within the room. But then he found himself recalling Proust who, on a similar winter afternoon some forty years ago, had lain dying in one of the rooms of this hotel, nursed by one solitary maid. It is said that the ailing writer had continued to work on his fifteen-hundred-page manuscript until the very morning of his death and that he had experienced respiratory problems at about three o'clock that morning. On regaining his breath shortly afterwards, however, in an attempt to work the pain and presage of impending death he had just experienced into the death scene he was in the process of creating, he had apparently continued to dictate to his maid, breathing heavily all the while.

That's what it takes to create a work of art! Tanaka had this feeling that the batlike shadow of Proust lived on to the present in the walls of his room. He felt as though the tenacity of the artist adhered to these walls. Maybe it was the existence of this image of Proust that lingered on in his memory which had been the cause of his feelings of suffocation since the previous evening.

The fact nevertheless remained that he was pained by Manabe's assertion that he and the other students of foreign literature were merely translating the works of these men and introducing them like mina birds. For Tanaka was only too well aware that, in the case of Japanese students of foreign literature, there was some truth in the claim. Opening the window, he was confronted by the same sea of darkness he had witnessed the previous evening. It lay before him like a thick castle wall. Tanaka was suddenly overcome by a sense of the extraordinary devotion to literature evidenced by a writer like Proust. He was gradually overcome by doubts as to the function of the specialist in foreign literature in response to such passionate dedication.

3

On his tenth day in Paris he received the reply he had been waiting for from Gilbert Ruby. There was no letter of introduction, merely an invitation for Tanaka, the scholar involved in the study of Sade, to come to his house at three o'clock the following Thursday afternoon.

Tanaka knew nothing about Ruby apart from his enormous two-volume *Life of the Marquis de Sade*. He knew nothing about his background or about his other publications. And yet he had been able to infer from a casual perusal of the *Life* that Ruby was unique in France in having devoted half his life to studying the hidden aspects of Sade and to collecting his various letters and manuscripts which were scattered about. Tanaka imagined him as a man somehow lacking both social standing and a formal teaching position. And even whilst still in Japan, Tanaka had pictured a man interested in nothing but Sade, obsessed by his desire to resurrect the image of this man long since confined to oblivion.

'That's what they call over-indulgence.' Professor Ueda had once made this remark with a grin on hearing about Ruby from Tanaka. This elderly professor, formerly a distinguished scholar of seventeenth-century classical French drama, but now aware that retirement was impending, had recently diverged from his area of specialist interest and begun to discuss nothing but Chinese art and other Chinese writings.

'You see this trait a lot in the characters of Balzac. And there are some in Japan too. I know men who focused all their attention on the clay figurines discovered in classical Japanese burial-mounds and ended up losing everything they owned. Such people are completely blind to other things. It's the amateur who becomes too caught up with his own research. The true scholar is different.'

And yet for all Professor Ueda's advice, Tanaka's curiosity about Ruby had not waned. Furthermore, he knew of nobody else in France except Ruby who was involved in any serious study of Sade. Since he was used to typed letters, Tanaka had to read and reread the one he had received from Ruby, which was written in a distinctly idiosyncratic style and in light green ink. The letter concluded with the words 'Yours affectionately', intended as no more than a formal greeting, but Tanaka chose to interpret this literally and was delighted at such warmth. Ruby had probably never dreamt that his work was read in the Far East; and anyway, for some time now, Tanaka had been assuming that there was no reason for Ruby to be inhospitable to a Japanese student who wrote him a complimentary letter, however awkward his French might be.

With the letter in his hand, he raced down the staircase and knocked on Sakisaka's door. From inside the room he heard the sound of coughing and a faint 'Come in'. His hair totally dishevelled, the architect was flat out on his bed.

'What's the matter?'

'I've got a slight fever. I seem to have caught a cold somewhere. I was coughing so much I couldn't sleep last night.' His face was grey and his cheeks hollow.

'Don't you think you should see a doctor?'

'I hate doctors. Doctors over here are so expensive.' A streak of fear flashed across the architect's face. 'And anyway I'm afraid they'll tell me it's some nasty disease.'

Tanaka blinked in bewilderment. As Sakisaka lay there with his hair in such disarray, his face looked like a wax mask. Once more Tanaka recalled Mauriac's description of Proust towards the end of his life. His face had been 'like a wax effigy and only his hair seemed to be alive'.

'Yes. But if you really are sick, then you should get it seen to – whatever the cost.'

'No. It's all right. It's all right. I know my body better than anyone else. It'll be all right in the morning.' Sakisaka waved his hand, more to assuage his own increasing fear than for Tanaka's benefit.

'Well. Is there anything you want?'

'No. I've just received a letter from Ruby, the expert on Sade. He wants me to go to his home in the rue des Capucins. At last I'm going to make a real start. This is it.' As Tanaka opened Ruby's letter on his knee, there was a note of triumph in his voice. In his excitement he completely forgot Sakisaka's sickness.

'It's all right for some, isn't it?' The architect sighed heavily and spoke with obvious envy as he explained how to reach the rue des Capucins.

'Two and a half years ago ... I was just as keen. But now.... It's not just a physical problem.' Sakisaka was staring vacantly at the ceiling and repeated this almost in tears. 'It's not just a physical problem.'

Returning to his room, Tanaka stripped and set about the pile of dirty underwear he had accumulated. As he scrubbed his long underwear, he found himself thinking about Nozaka Kazuko again. Had those who had come to Paris to study before him also gone to a cheap hotel and done their washing in this way? He wondered what his wife would say if she could see him right at that moment – not to mention Nozaka Kazuko! He could see his thin but compact figure in the mirror.

'At least I have no worries about my health,' he muttered to himself. 'I'm not going to get sick in Paris like Sakisaka.'

Since there was nobody to go out with, he left his room alone. He had planned to go to the Louvre, but the letter from Ruby had made him change his mind. He decided to visit Arcueil, the scene of one of Sade's famous acts of violence.

He spread out his map of Paris on the pavement and passers-by kept turning round to take a closer look at him. There was even one little old woman dressed in black who was kind enough to stop and ask him where he was going. But, on hearing the name Arcueil, she shrugged her shoulders and informed him that there was no such place in Paris. At the sound of her voice, a youth with a characteristically Jewish hook nose approached them.

'Arcueil? It's out in the suburbs, close to the university. You can

86

go there by the Métro. You're a foreign student, so you must know where the university is.'

Tanaka had heard, whilst still in Japan, that there was an area in the suburbs of Paris where students from all over the world lived. Indeed, many of those who had preceded him from his own university had lived in the Japanese house there. Tanaka nodded and the young man with the hook nose placed a large finger on the map and said, 'Voilà'. He pointed to the spot and smiled. The finger bore the telltale traces of paint of a labourer, but there was a tenderness about his smile, like the rays of the sun in winter, that appealed to Tanaka.

After Denfert Rochereau the Métro emerged above ground and the carriage, which had hitherto been completely dark, was suddenly immersed in light. The train was crowded with students returning to the university and Tanaka detected one who appeared to be Japanese. However, on spotting Tanaka, this student immediately looked the other way. Holding on to the leather strap and pretending to be looking out of the window, he seemed to be afraid of being rudely approached in Japanese by this fellow countryman in the midst of a whole group of foreigners.

The rays from the winter sun beamed down from the overcast sky on the woods and fields of the Paris suburb like a volley of arrows. The scenery was very similar to that which he knew so well between Kyodo and Tamagawa on the Odakyu line in Tokyo. The natural scenery had been buried beneath factories and apartment buildings still under construction which were covered with advertisements for Vitapointe and Cinzano. Tanaka considered how, one April some hundred and ninety years ago, the Marquis de Sade must have ridden through these same unremarkable woods and fields with the beggar woman on his way to Arcueil. Immediately the various details of the incident as he had read about them in Ruby's *Life* and Maurice Heine's *Study of the Incident of Arcueil* appeared vividly before him.

This was one of the most famous incidents in the whole of Sade's life. On Easter Sunday in 1768 he had tricked the beggar woman, Rose Keller, into accompanying him to his second home at Arcueil. This was the house in the avenue Fontaine which Sade was renting at the time with the express purpose of spending the occasional night there with his various women. There, on the second floor of the house, Rose was threatened by the Marquis, bound to the red and black Indian-style bed with a hemp rope and mercilessly beaten with a whip. After every lash of the whip Sade stopped to record the number of strokes by carving a notch in the wainscot with a small knife. Taking advantage of Sade's temporary absence from the room, the woman had escaped through the window and reported the incident to an official of the town of Arcueil.

Tanaka had learnt from his reading that this incident offered a couple of leads for the student of Sade. First there was Ruby's claim that the fact that Sade chose Easter Sunday to perform this act was evidence of Sade's anti-Christian outlook. On the other hand, there was the view of Simone de Beauvoir that the way in which he stopped to record the number of lashes by marking notches with a small knife on the wall suggested that Sade sought to observe his own lust with a dispassionate eye.

When he was in Japan Tanaka had written an article for the literary magazine *A View of Man,* in which he had discussed both the Arcueil incident and Sade at the time of the incident. At the time, whilst Tanaka cited the interpretations of the various foreign critics, there was part of him that had felt he was resorting to a somewhat strained interpretation. He saw no inevitability about Sade's choice of Easter Sunday: one could equally well argue that the choice of date was pure coincidence. Similarly, there was always the possibility that the way in which he had stopped to mark each lash with a notch carved in the wall had been a mere caprice, a desire for absolute conquest over his victim. To the Japanese Tanaka, the conclusion that these were expressions of Sade's anti-Christian ideals and of his desire for objective observation of his own passions had seemed absurd and ridiculous.

In his article for *A View of Man,* however, Tanaka had not given expression to his own personal opinions. Rather, he had been able to convince himself whilst writing the article that the views of these other critics coincided exactly with his own interpretation. To Tanaka, as a Japanese scholar, words such as 'Christian' and 'anti-Christian' did not carry the same heavy or oppressive connotation. In fact, the concept of objective observation failed to evoke any real sense of poignancy for him. As a Japanese critic, Tanaka had merely employed such words as convenient tools when introducing and discussing Western writers.

Tanaka alighted at the little station of Arcueil with half a dozen other passengers. The wheels screeched as the train pulled out of the station and a copy of *Le Figaro,* which had been lying around on the platform, was caught up in the swirl of wind and blown down on to the tracks.

At dusk this town was strangely quiet and gloomy. Tanaka spotted a solitary cat slowly crossing the stone square. Tanaka asked a station official to help him find the avenue Fontaine, the location of Sade's second house, and began walking in the direction the official had indicated. As he passed by the neighbourhood factory, he could hear the sound of a machine planing raw materials. Three or four children in aprons stopped their game of hoop-rolling as Tanaka approached and stared at him suspiciously. He could hear one of the elder girls whisper to her friends, 'He's Chinese.'

According to research performed by Ruby, Arcueil retained hardly a vestige of its former appearance and Sade's second house had completely disappeared. Only one section of the road remained as it had been in Sade's day. Nevertheless, when he arrived at the gloomy and deserted street-corner on that wintry afternoon, Tanaka involuntarily came to a standstill and stared up at the dimly lit houses and the overcast sky above them. Everything was still. The sky appeared even darker as a result of the smoke spewing out of the tall factory chimney. A labourer on a bicycle descended the hill and disappeared out of sight. So this was the old avenue Fontaine. To his left, there was a small building which looked like a kindergarten with a swing in the garden. Beside that stood a two-storey house from which the plaster had peeled away in great strips. There were Venetian blinds over all the windows and two or three shirts and handkerchiefs hanging out to dry on the washing-line.

At that moment, beside the house with the peeling plaster, Tanaka noticed a well-worn, narrow lane which merged with this road. If he was not mistaken, it was somewhere in this lane that the house in which the Arcueil incident had occurred had stood. And, according to Ruby's work, this was the road along which the blood-spattered Rose Keller had escaped. Rubbing the road with his finger, Tanaka realized that the dark-red stones had been completely eroded by almost two hundred years of wear and tear.

In the winter evening light he could also make out a couple of grooves, like railway lines, which had apparently been created by the wheels of passing traffic. He had never seen such a road in Tokyo. He was convinced that no such road existed in Japan. He had never before experienced such a road, tinged as it was with the smell of human habitation and the sweaty odour of human feet. If it had been possible, Tanaka would have liked to dig up this road – the road along which Sade had walked and Rose Keller had run – and take it home with him. And had he not felt so inhibited, he would even have liked to run his tongue over it. Sensing the arousal of certain animal passions, Tanaka repositioned his glasses with his finger time and again. He didn't feel as though Sade was anti-Christian or that he had resorted on frequent occasions to dispassionate observation. He could claim, with but little exaggeration, that he had written that article only in order to see his name in print and so that he would be able to show the magazine to Nozaka Kazuko in the coffee shop. He could not help feeling, however, that the giddy sensation he was experiencing as he stood pushing up his glasses on that road was genuine and, as such, an integral part of himself. Professor Ueda would presumably call this 'over-indulgence'. But there was no denying his pressing desire to bend down and lick that stone road. Tanaka felt that, even if this were to be labelled as 'over-indulgence', it was nevertheless that part of himself which was the most real.

The following Thursday at three o'clock he arrived at the rue des Capucins, as arranged. He had with him a box containing a copy of Ruby's *Life of the Marquis de Sade* and a crêpe wrapping-cloth. Just as Sakisaka had told him, as he came out behind the church of St Sulpice, blackened as a result of years of buffeting by the elements, he found himself in a pungent-smelling cul-de-sac. The dirty walls of the houses on both sides of the street were covered in children's graffiti and all the grey doors were closed. Somewhat surprised that Ruby should live in such an impoverished neighbourhood, Tanaka looked at his map. There could be no question that this was the rue des Capucins.

He rang the bell and a middle-aged maid chewing a slice of bread opened the door. When he gave Ruby's name, the portly woman smiled somewhat contemptuously. She pointed silently to the second floor. There was no elevator, so Tanaka had no choice but to use the stairs. The whole place seemed dilapidated and the wallpaper was peeling off in patches, as though afflicted with some skin disease.

He rang the bell, and this time an elderly lady opened the door just a fraction. She motioned him inside. All he could see was a room which appeared to be the kitchen straight ahead of him and a single room on either side of the corridor. So this was where Ruby, the great Sade expert, lived. He could hear a man clearing his throat in the room to his right. But, on opening the door, he was greeted by a large, discontented face.

Tanaka stepped into the room tentatively, but the French greeting he had been planning on the way eluded him temporarily. For some reason or other, even before receiving his letter, Tanaka had pictured Ruby as a man whose angular face was of a pale, sickly complexion. But the man standing in front of him was a large, portly man somewhat thin on top. There was a vaguely wily glint in his small eyes. Noticing the sheets in complete disorder on the bed beside the desk, Tanaka assumed that Ruby had just woken from a nap. Tanaka had imagined receiving a rapturous welcome and a hearty handshake from this scholar. But Ruby did not even offer him his hand. His arms folded, he just stood there looking Tanaka up and down with his small eyes.

In an attempt to ingratiate himself with his host, Tanaka offered him the box containing the little present he had brought with him. Ruby's small eyes did light up somewhat, but it was clear that this was more an expression of satiated greed than of any genuine pleasure. This was obvious from the way in which, on opening the box and discovering that it contained a Japanese-style wrapping-cloth, Ruby muttered a perfunctory 'Thank you' but then immediately reverted to his previous morose demeanour.

'I'm only free until four.' Ruby was staring at the clock on the desk as he broke the silence. Even when Tanaka took out his copy of *The Life of the Marquis de Sade* and asked him to sign it, Ruby just stared at him suspiciously over his spectacles and made no attempt to take up a pen. Finally he muttered, 'I have no idea why an Oriental like you should be studying Sade.'

Tanaka shook his head and asked Ruby to repeat himself. Ruby's

French was easy to understand, but he was certainly not expecting such a question straight away.

'Even in France, there are hundreds of people who know nothing about Sade and yet continue to discuss him. Take Simone de Beauvoir for a start.'

On hearing that, Tanaka recalled the excitement he had experienced years ago in Japan on reading de Beauvoir's 'Study of Sade'. Her article had been published in four instalments of the magazine *Les Temps Modernes*, a publication with which both she and Sartre were affiliated. He recalled with what pride he had deliberated upon that article in the coffee shop in front of the university before Nozaka Kazuko and several other students. The article had offered a completely fresh approach to the study of Sade.

'That woman knows nothing about Sade. But she's nevertheless used him to amass a fortune.'

Tanaka had no idea how to respond to such a comment. Of course he did not feel confident enough to attempt to defend the work of Simone de Beauvoir. Besides, he failed to see why Ruby had to start by confronting him with such unsolicited criticism.

'But sir, your book is widely read even by Japanese scholars like myself.' Tanaka emphasized the words 'your book' in an obvious attempt at appeasement.

'I don't believe it! That book only sold about two hundred copies in France.' Ruby proceeded to stride across the room and raised the filthy curtain with one hand. The great pile of yellowing paper which lay behind reminded one of a junk dealer's shed. 'How many years do you think I spent on this? It's the manuscript for the third volume of the *Life*. Eight years! It took me eight years to write this lot! But the company which brought out Simone's "Study of Sade" has refused to publish this manuscript! Why? Because the second volume sold only two hundred copies. Simone writes about Sade knowing nothing about him … and I have to publish this manuscript at my own expense! What am I supposed to do?'

Ruby's face appeared horribly contorted. Tanaka could recall seeing similarly ugly expressions in Japan too. It was the expression of one writer jealous of the achievements of another. For example, it reminded him of the expression of Kenmochi, lecturer at Y University, as, in a fit of drunken pique, he had wreaked his anger on some of the students under him on the night that his fellow

92

lecturer Imai had been made assistant professor. He also recalled his own contorted face reflected in the bathroom mirror on the day he had learnt that Suganuma, in hot pursuit of Tanaka, had been appointed an associate. But, unlike the Japanese, Ruby was here venting the anger and jealousy he nourished towards Simone de Beauvoir in front of a foreigner he had never met before. The thick veins on his large, balding brow stood out prominently. It was like the face of a lecherous and greedy old man. Alternatively, it was like the pictures of the anatomy of the head found in medical manuals portraying large cranial blood vessels.

'Sir, the reason I'm interested in Sade . . .'

'I've no idea why you're interested in Sade.'

Frantically Tanaka tried to recall the various essays he had written on Sade whilst in Japan. He stammered and fidgeted with his glasses.

'I believe Sade is relevant to contemporary Japan. I see the circumstances in which the aristocracy to which Sade belonged found itself before the French Revolution as similar to those confronting the intelligentsia in Japan today. For that reason, I. . . .'

Ruby was paying little attention to his inept French. As soon as Tanaka had finished, he shrugged his shoulders in an attitude of silent contempt.

'Sir. For me, the eighteenth century . . .'

'As a Japanese, you know nothing about Greece. I've been fascinated by Greece since my childhood. That's why I understand Sade. But you know nothing about that.'

'But sir . . . I . . .'

'I just don't understand why you are studying Sade.'

'But sir.' In an attempt to steady himself, Tanaka was about to put his hand on the eighteenth-century style chair covered in silk which stood nearby.

'Don't touch it!' Ruby's voice trembled. 'That's my chair which Sade . . . the chair that Sade used. I don't let anyone sit on it.'

It was not until he noticed the surprised look in Tanaka's eyes that Ruby became aware of his own agitation. Motioning Tanaka to sit down on a wooden chair, he opened out the Japanese crêpe wrapping-cloth he had just been given and commented on its beauty. He began to ask Tanaka whether the Japanese use such cloths as scarfs. With the conversation now focused on the harmless topic of the Japanese, Tanaka could not help looking towards the bundle of yellowish papers piled up in the corner of the room. That manuscript! That was what he really wanted to look at. He had not come here to become involved in a boring conversation about Japan. If he were merely to be allowed to read that manuscript, he would have succeeded in satisfying one of the objectives of his period of study abroad.

Noticing Tanaka's wandering eyes, Ruby quickly closed the dirty curtains. He seemed to be afraid that someone would steal his great secret. Then, by way of consolation, he remarked, 'You should go down to La Coste. The sooner the better.'

The village of La Coste had been part of Sade's domain and his château had been located there. Needless to say, Tanaka was aware that that château, too, had been destroyed during the course of the French Revolution.

'Some crazy man from Marseille bought the castle site. Apparently he's a middle-school teacher who knows nothing about Sade. Of all the stupid things to do, he's cutting up stones from the ruins and selling them off to some architect. In a couple of years, there'll be nothing left of the castle.'

Once more Tanaka noticed the beads of sweat and the veins swelling up on Ruby's forehead. But unlike the moment shortly before when he had been cursing Simone de Beauvoir, the wry expression on his face suggested he was close to tears.

'That's terrible.' Tanaka made another attempt at ingratiation. 'Won't anyone make a formal protest about it?'

Ruby appeared to have seen through Tanaka's sycophancy, shrugged his shoulders and smiled.

'It's four o'clock. I'm very sorry but I....' The implication was clear. Ruby stood up in front of Tanaka and opened the door. 'I'm pleased to have met you. I hope we can meet again.'

But it was patently obvious to Tanaka that these words lacked sincerity.

Tanaka treated himself to a glass of wine in a small café in front of St Sulpice in an attempt to alleviate the humiliation to which he had just been subjected. He formed a mental reconstruction of Ruby's large face as though producing a rough sketch on a piece of drawing paper, and added to this the thinning hair, the thick bull neck and those small, cruel-looking eyes. Even the blue lines of those protruding veins remained firmly in his mind. It was as though he had been invited with the express purpose of being shouted at. What had Ruby done but voice his complaints and rancour towards society at large at the way in which his study had been so totally rejected? But Tanaka was aware that he had done little better. All he had wanted to do was to look over that manuscript piled up in the corner – just a look at the table of contents would have sufficed. So Ruby hadn't understood Tanaka's motivation as a Japanese student of Sade. Did he think that he had the sole right and qualifications to pursue such research?

Tanaka found himself involuntarily giving vent to such mutterings, which were like numerous air bubbles floating up to the surface of a pond with a hissing sound.

Inside the dark café a woman with chestnut-coloured hair was seated on one of the bar-stools talking to the waiter. The latter was busy polishing the cups and glasses with a white cloth.

Why had he picked on Sade as the focus of his studies? As he sat sipping his wine, Tanaka meditated painfully on the reasons for his decision, dating back to his days as assistant in the department, to pursue his research on Sade, the imprisoned writer. There were several reasons. For a start, there was certainly nothing untrue in what he had just told Ruby. As a student interested in eighteenth-century literature Tanaka had long been intrigued by the similarities he detected in the circumstances surrounding the aristocracy in France as they watched their privileged status being gradually eroded in the years immediately preceding the French Revolution and those of the intelligentsia in contemporary Japan. Thereafter, learning that the author of *Vice Amply Rewarded,* which had attracted the attention first of Baudelaire and then the surrealists, was being re-examined by post-war literary critics, Tanaka had slowly begun to collect Sade's works. The fact that he had been unable, even in broken French, to explain this to Ruby was a source of the deepest regret to Tanaka. And yet, at that moment, the image of Ruby's ugly, contorted face crossed his mind. He pictured those sparkling little eyes scowling at him and asking derisively, 'Is that right? So you, too, like de Beauvoir, are just using Sade for your own purposes, aren't you?'

95

Tanaka tried to blot the image of that contorted face out of his mind. But he knew that most of the major French writers were being cultivated by students above him in the hierarchy. The only one left untouched was Sade. Tanaka himself was the first to confess that his decision to set his sights on Sade had been prompted, in part at least, by the ulterior motive of thereby ensuring for himself recognition as a scholar of French literature. Moreover, he could not in all honesty deny that his decision to study Sade had been, to a certain extent, a calculated attempt to check Suganuma whose presence at his heels was a constant goad.

When the waiter left, the woman with the chestnut hair who was seated on the stool turned towards the mirror hanging on the wall and began to touch up her face. As she applied her lipstick, she cast the occasional glance in Tanaka's direction. Just like the woman he had seen in the street when Sakisaka had taken him to the Montparnasse bar, this woman, too, wore a cheap-looking brownish fur.

Shortly afterwards she smiled and raised her glass in his direction. But this was the cue for Tanaka to look away. Hurriedly he placed some money on the table and went outside. The piercing sound of her laughter reverberated at his back.

A thin veil of mist had descended on the city. The blue light from the gas lamps around the place St Sulpice seemed blurred. Tanaka sensed the arousal of carnal desires he had forgotten ever since his arrival in Paris, stimulated both by the dank mist and the lipstick of the lady in the café. He regretted his failure to initiate a conversation with her. There was no telling what might have happened, had he done so.

Tanaka was, however, well aware that he lacked the courage to strike up a conversation in such a situation. It had always been the same, back in Japan. As a consequence both of his fear of disease and awareness of his position as a university lecturer, Tanaka had not been intimate with any woman apart from his wife. There had been the isolated instance when he had taken hold of Nozaka Kazuko's hand – on the night the two of them had opened the French literature society. But even that had required the additional stimulus of alcohol.

For a long time after that incident Tanaka had been ashamed of his inability to take things any further than that. But the fact remained that, at that moment, he had been overwhelmed by an awareness of the shame and ignominy he would incur as a teacher were Kazuko to reject his advances.

That's the kind of man I am. I can't even go and buy a woman, he thought.

But it was such a man who had chosen Sade, the inquirer into carnal desires, as subject of his dissertation. Were Japanese writers like Manabe, whom he had met in the Montparnasse café, to discover this facet of his personality, they too, like Ruby, would probably shower scorn on him – though for somewhat different reasons. That was why Manabe had suggested he couldn't trust students of foreign literature.

Confronted with the ridicule of Manabe, Tanaka felt that he knew how to respond. But when it came to Ruby's contemptuous smile, he felt totally helpless.

Tanaka recalled the giddy sensation he had experienced the other afternoon in the streets of Arcueil. He had no idea of the root causes of that feeling. He could not be sure whether he qualified as a dedicated scholar of literature, but there was nothing more genuine than that feeling.

4

Greetings from us all. We have heard nothing since your letter of 19th December, so I assume you must be feeling the effects of travel fatigue. As instructed, I sent postcards to everyone who came to the airport to see you off. In addition, I sent formal letters of thanks to Professors Ueda and Imai. Somehow I, too, have been feeling a bit despondent recently and seem to spend most of my time rather aimlessly. I imagine it's because all that tension has finally been relieved. Don't worry about Keiichi. He's fine. Last Sunday, Sota-san came and took him to Shinjuku park. Keiichi was so excited. Sota-san took this picture for us.

A strong wind was sweeping down the boulevard and the letter looked as though it would be blown out of his hands at any moment. Kikue had covered every available space of the airmail paper with her intricate Chinese characters. She had obviously calculated that, the heavier the letter, the more it would cost to post. She was the sort of woman who even hesitated before buying items on special offer in the department stores! Strangely enough, though there had been several occasions since Tanaka came to Paris that he had recalled his son's face with almost painful clarity, he had scarcely stopped to consider his wife. It was as though hers had developed into some uninteresting and distant existence.

Along the left-hand side of the road, the high wall of the prison of Vincennes seemed to stretch on for ever. Every now and then the wall was capped with a small tower. The feeble afternoon sun smudged the drab, grey wall. Beneath him lay the dried-up moat into which had been thrown empty cans and the remains of old cardboard boxes. A hundred years ago, when Sade had been incarcerated there, the moat must have been filled with water to foil any attempts made by the prisoners to escape.

There were still about ten minutes to go before the three o'clock guided tour.

A cheque for royalties came from the Bunrin publishing company. It was a cheque for twenty-nine thousand yen for the reprinting of that translation you did. It was an unexpected windfall and I took two thousand yen out to buy Keiichi some winter clothes. I put the rest into the bank as you told me. I discussed it with Grandfather in Omori and he suggested I use it to buy some shares. So I'm thinking of doing that.

Adjusting his glasses with his finger, Tanaka felt he should reply as soon as possible. She had this terrible tendency to hang on his father's every word. Every time she opened her mouth it was 'Grandfather said so'. But this was not so much a stock phrase on her part as a continuous attempt to be seen in everything to accord with her parents-in-law's wishes – in a desperate attempt to be accepted as a wife worthy of the Tanaka family. Nevertheless, when an amateur dabbles in the stock market, he is bound to lose out. Tanaka had been most adamant before leaving that, if, while he was away, there should be some unexpected income like royalties, she was to deposit it into a bank account where it would be safe. But already she appeared to have forgotten her promise. He had constantly told her that nothing could make one happier than the mundane. And how many times had he stressed that shares were dangerous, whereas one could not go wrong with a bank account, even if the interest rate was low? Tanaka grew steadily more and more angry.

Their marriage had been arranged and Tanaka had not been close to other women before their marriage. Despite a tendency since his university days to feel affection for every young woman he met, the possibility of being rejected had always caused him to recoil at the last moment. This fear of having his pride wounded always made him shy in front of women. In his graduating class there had been those like Yasui and Fujita, who became journalists, who dated girls steadily during their university days. But Tanaka had merely looked on enviously from afar.

As soon as their arranged meeting had been successfully concluded and the engagement had been announced, Tanaka sent her a letter in which he had copied out Verlaine's poem 'La première oui' as well as some of his own poems which he had as yet shown to no one. The first six months of married life were like a dream. To a man with no sisters, objects like a mirror-stand and dolls were strangely refreshing. Looking back on it now, he could not understand why he had developed such romantic feelings for that ordinary and not particularly attractive girl. She was the kind of woman who treasured the household menus which appeared in the supplements to the women's magazines and the publications about the knitting of spring sweaters.

By the time of the opening of the Vincennes jail to the public, four or five visitors had gathered in front of the iron railing. There was one courting couple who appeared to have nowhere else to go, a woman in a black raincoat who looked for all the world like a schoolteacher and a black youth who whistled continuously. The guide was chewing on some tobacco as she approached with an enormous key and slowly opened the gate.

Tanaka started to put his letter away. But, as he was folding the envelope, he caught sight of a scribbled postscript on the back: 'Yesterday I happened to bump into Suganuma on the Odakyu line and thanked him for coming to the airport. He said that there was a chance that he too would be going to Paris to study in the near future. He said he would be relying on you to show him round if he really did end up going.'

The visitors were already in the inner courtyard. The uniformed guide was shouting at Tanaka, who was still standing in front of the railing staring at the letter, asking him whether he was going to come in or not. But as he walked across the large, bleak courtyard, Tanaka kept on running his eye across that postscript, convinced that he must have somehow misread it. There was no reason why Suganuma should follow so closely on his heels in coming to France like that. For a start, since he himself had come to Paris, Suganuma had been left behind as assistant. If Suganuma were to leave as well, who would there be to deal with all the odd jobs around the department office? There was the Associate Izaka, but there was no way that he could be entrusted with such responsibility as yet. Moreover, in view of the limited university budget, there was no precedent for sending two members of staff from the French department to study abroad in the same year. Tanaka's head was besieged with such negative reasoning. Kikue must have misheard something somewhere along the line.

The five visitors had turned left out of the courtyard and were standing in front of the prison building adorned with its four tall towers. In addition to that, the prison was surrounded by thick, square walls, and, at each corner of this wall stood an observation tower in the form of an iron grille. The small windows in the wall were fitted with thick iron frames, again in an attempt to foil attempts by prisoners to escape.

The sky above was light grey and there were patches of black cloud to be seen approaching from the direction of the forest of Voici.

'It's cold.'

'Yes, it really is.' The young lovers clung to each other like two birds. The boy had his arm around her shoulder, trying to keep her warm. The woman who looked like a teacher was frantically jotting down the guide's explanation in a small notebook.

For over five years from 7th September 1778 to February 1784 Sade was confined in Vincennes prison, the converted castle. This was as punishment not only for the Arcueil incident but also for that in Marseille where he had attacked five women in a most perverted manner. Tanaka had learnt from Ruby's work that the house in which this Marseille incident had taken place was still standing and he planned to visit it when time permitted.

Since his arrival in Paris, Tanaka had come to realize more and more the considerable impetus which the five years in Vincennes prison had exerted upon the literature of Sade. Since his cool reception by Ruby, there had been no alternative for him but to continue his own research of Sade by trial and error. Fortunately the Bibliothèque Nationale in Paris had preserved several of the reports and much of the correspondence about these various incidents and he had consequently started to pay daily visits there, spending his time taking notes from these documents. In addition, in order to learn more about the eighteenth century, which comprised the background for these events, he had been a regular attender at the lectures of Professor Bady at the Sorbonne. In this way he was gradually able to form a much clearer picture of Sade the man and, in so doing, Tanaka had come to the conclusion that the greatest turning-point in Sade's life had been the years he had spent in Vincennes prison from 1778 to 1784. In 1778 Sade had been thirty-eight years old, and his life to that point had been that of the man of pleasure – one long round of extravagant sexual encounters with various actresses and prostitutes. The first time he had taken the plunge and tried his hand at 'writing' had been during the years he spent in Vincennes prison. The walls of the prison assumed a religious significance as they stood between him and his sexual freedom as well as his gradually awakening philosophy of life. They came to represent for him the walls of sovereign authority. The only weapon left in the hands of the individual whereby he could break down these walls imposed by society was to create a realm of the imagination. For the first time, on reaching this conclusion, Sade asked his jailer for pen and paper and began to write a novel. He staked his life on his vision of an ideal world in which neither religion nor sovereign power could deprive the individual of his freedom.

It was because he wanted to see for himself the walls of the prison that had been responsible for forging Sade into a man of letters that Tanaka had come here that afternoon. Nevertheless, as the guide noisily brandished the key and the five of them followed her up the spiral staircase that wound its way up the tower like a snail, Tanaka was more interested in those two lines of postscript to his wife's letter than in Sade and Vincennes prison. The possibility of

Suganuma's coming to France was enough to shatter the pride he had felt in his heart until the previous day. He had seen the very fact that he had been sent to study abroad before Suganuma as a subtle manipulation of personnel within the department which guaranteed his position in the university hierarchy even after Professor Ueda's retirement. But now, less than two months after his arrival in Paris, if there were any truth in his wife's announcement, there was the possibility that Suganuma too would be sent abroad to study. Who could be behind such a decision? Might it not conceivably mean that Professor Imai was planning to have Tanaka farmed out to the College of Liberal Arts or demoted to the French department in another university upon his return?

For nine days after his arrival in Vincennes, Sade was allowed the luxury of neither a shave nor a change of underwear. There had been no light in his room. At night he would hear the mice scampering about, and for a long time even sleep proved elusive. The twice-weekly walk, too, was of a mere one hour's duration and performed in complete silence under the scrutiny of the guards. There were only two meals a day, one at eleven in the morning, the other at five in the afternoon. For breakfast prisoners were served a thin soup and a single dish, and the evening meal comprised some meat and one other dish. On Thursdays and Sundays this diet was augmented with two apples. The guide appeared to know nothing about Sade. Coming to a halt in front of one of the cells which reeked of plaster, the guide explained how it had been in this room that Mirabeau, one of the main protagonists of the French Revolution, had been incarcerated. All of the visitors with the exception of Tanaka peered diffidently into the room. With its bare white walls and black, dust-covered floor, it looked just like an ancient storehouse. On the far wall there was one small window fitted with iron bars.

If he were not to come as an official university-sponsored student, the only other possibility was that Suganuma would be paying his own way. He had heard that Suganuma came from a quite wealthy family. But even if Suganuma were to decide to travel to France of his own accord, such a plan still required university authorization. To this end, Professor Imai must have gone to considerable lengths. Tanaka found himself troubled by a stream of groundless suspicions. Repositioning his glasses and distancing himself from the other visitors, he leant against the wall of the staircase and looked out through the small rectangular window. In the distance he could see bleak rain clouds borne on the rain-filled wind, and the forests of the Paris suburbs which stretched out beneath them. He was suddenly overcome by the realization that, some two hundred years ago, Sade too must have used this window, the only one to have been cut into the wall, to stare out on the same clouds and woods. He would have had a deep sense of anger. Compared with such anger, how miserable, how unliterary was his own instinct for self-protection. Tanaka felt distinctly ashamed at this. But, try as he might, he could find no way to suppress his fear. Galloping down the stairs, Tanaka left the prison building and emerged into the courtyard all alone. Just as before, a grey wind was blowing through the deserted courtyard. Burying his head in his scarf, he crossed the courtyard and came to the exit.

On leaving the prison, he was stopped by someone calling out his name in Japanese. A car stopped and he could see two faces, both Japanese, looking at him. One of them was none other than Manabe, the writer with whom he had become embroiled in heated debate that evening in the Café le Dôme in Montparnasse.

'I'm sorry about what I said the other night. I was really rude. That's what happens when I get drunk.'

'No, it was my fault. I'm sorry for being so conceited.'

Manabe received Tanaka's apology with a nod and introduced the man sitting next to him. 'This is Kohara-san. He's been in Paris over thirty years. And this is Tanaka-kun, a student of French literature. Kohara-san knows every nook and cranny of Paris.... And he's better at the language than any of you French literature specialists.'

The middle-aged Kohara gave a pitiful smile and spoke in a quiet voice. 'When it comes to the French language, I have never studied the basics. I simply learnt from my wife, so it's nothing like what's spoken by serious students of the language.'

'Kohara-san married a French woman.'

'I'm just like Urashima Taro. I haven't been back to Japan once in thirty years.' Kohara waved at Tanaka. 'This means I'm up to simple interpreting jobs, but that's all. I've spent today showing Manabe-san around Chartres.'

'Tanaka-kun, have you been to Chartres yet? What, not yet? It's definitely worth a visit. The stained glass windows in the cathedral there are magnificent. There's no other church with stained glass which can compare with that. Looking at it, I thought the only place which could rival it was Notre-Dame. Have you ever read Yokomitsu's *Travel Sadness*?'

'Yes. But I don't remember it very well.'

Tanaka had glanced at Yokomitsu Riichi's story during his student days. Actually all he could remember of the experience was his growing weariness with the superficiality of the Western perspective of that Japanese writer.

'Oh, that's right. You feel contemptuous of all Japanese works, don't you?' There was a tinge of sarcasm in Manabe's voice as he spoke. 'But when I was in Chartres today, I suddenly remembered Yokomitsu's remark about the similarity between the medieval spirit which inspired Notre-Dame and Chartres and the Japanese haiku spirit.'

Tanaka fell silent and stared out at the place de la Nation, which they happened to be passing. Since this was the season of Christmas and the New Year, the shops on both sides of the road were covered with garish posters advertising their bargain sales. Once they were past the place de la Nation, the roadside was again lined with the pitch-black, strangely cold-looking Paris buildings and bald horse-chestnut trees.

Manabe continued his discourse on one section of *Travel Sadness* in which Yokomitsu had claimed that the lyricism of the haiku form was the same as that of Notre-Dame. Kohara sat, hands in lap, listening to Manabe and occasionally nodding. But Tanaka could not believe that Kohara, who had lived here in Paris for some thirty-odd years, was really interested in Yokomitsu Riichi's foolish opinion. Tanaka was on the point of inadvertently giving expression to his belief that Yokomitsu's novel constituted an extremely random, Western-style interpretation. But, recalling the earlier argument, he said nothing.

'Where have you just been?'

'I went to the prison at Vincennes.'

'I didn't know there was such a place.' Lighting up a Gitanes cigarette, the novelist continued, 'But why did you want to visit a place like that?'

As Tanaka spoke briefly about Sade, Manabe interjected with a triumphant air, 'You mean Sade's like the post-war Japanese novelists. I know nothing about Sade, but, judging from what you've just said, it seems to me to be very much like a phenomenon seen in post-war writing in Japan. It reminds me of writers in Japan who, after years of feudalism, went their own way, using their own flesh and blood as their chief weapon. How interesting. Has he been translated?'

Tanaka smiled wryly to himself and looked out of the car at the window of one of the shops adorned with an advert for *Savoie Cointreau*. That's right. Unlike Japanese liquor, Cointreau was always Cointreau. If asked in what way it was different, he would be unable to answer. He just knew it was different. It was not merely a difference in taste and ingredients. There was a quintessential difference. Who said Sade and the sensual literature of post-war Japan were the same thing? How ridiculous!

Crossing a bridge over the Seine, they came to the Porte d'Italie. Here Manabe asked the driver to stop the car.

'I'm getting off here. Thank you very much, Kohara-san. I hope we can meet again soon.' His voice lacked sincerity; but that was all he said before slamming the door shut. He did not look round once before disappearing into the crowd. One could tell even from his back that there was still little love lost between Manabe and Tanaka.

'What shall we do?' Kohara spoke in a diffident tone. 'Where are you heading?'

'Anywhere's all right. I just have to catch the Métro.'

'Would you like a quick drink?' Having spent thirty years in Paris, Kohara seemed to feel duty bound to look after Japanese visitors. Or maybe he feared he would be totally abandoned and ostracized by his fellow countrymen. At any rate there was an air of wretchedness about his face and the rest of his being, as though he had been deprived of his roots.

The two of them left the car on the quai des Grands Augustins by the Seine and climbed up the boulevard Saint Michel which was swarming with university students who frequented the bookstores and cafés there. A salesman was advertising *France Soir* in a loud voice, and, beside him, an old woman was selling roast chestnuts. Kohara stopped, took some cash from the pocket of his old overcoat and bought some chestnuts wrapped in newspaper.

'Here you are. Do you want some?'

He placed them in his pocket and pressed his fingers against them; the chestnuts felt warm, like the warmth evident in Kohara's manner. Given that Manabe and the other Japanese resident in Paris were not well disposed towards him, as was evidenced by the writer's sarcastic laugh and the coldness Tanaka had felt as Manabe had disappeared into the crowd, the way in which Kohara was treating him and attempting to humour him did not feel at all bad.

'Chestnuts go really well with white wine. In Japan we used to eat what they called "imperial chestnuts". Do they still sell them?'

'Hmm. I wonder.'

'Japan must have really changed since the war.' Kohara rested his arm on the large iron railing of the jardin du Luxembourg as he spoke. 'I came here thirty years ago on business for the Bank of Japan. I married a French woman and so I had to quit my job. It sounds ridiculous. I ended up settling down over here.'

'Which university did you go to?'

'I was in the Law department at Tokyo University. I was with people like the former minister, Shimada-san, at the Tokyo First High School.'

In those days, entering the Bank of Japan from Tokyo University must have been a sure path to success. Tanaka found it hard to believe that Kohara had been forced to quit merely because he had chosen to marry a French woman.

'That's how things were in those days. Nationalized companies like the Bank of Tokyo used to hate men who married foreign women. I was lectured about that by my boss before I left Japan. So it was tough for me too.'

Faint rays of sun still shone down on the jardin du Luxembourg. They seemed to match Kohara's desolate smile. Tanaka recalled how Sade's birthplace, the Condé Palace, was located on the opposite side of the park. To this day, the name Condé was preserved in that particular area of the city.

The park benches were covered with leaves and a couple of birds were pecking at some food scattered around one of them. They looked so cold. On another bench sat a solitary old woman reading the evening paper.

'You mustn't do what I did. There's more to this country than just women. Somehow the culture of the place seems to captivate many foreign visitors. There are quite a few men like me who never

106

return to Japan and end up settling here. But none of them ever makes it.'

'How do you mean, "makes it"?'

'I mean they're not happy.'

The street lamps had begun to shine faintly through the trees in the jardin du Luxembourg. An official scolded a group of children still playing around the pond and they were obliged to leave. It was closing-time.

'I know a place where you can eat oysters standing at the counter. Let's go there. In France they don't have those stalls where you can stop for a quick drink as they do in Japan. It's a great pity.'

Two young students were distributing leaflets in front of the Métro exit. They were calling for an end to the war with Algeria. But most of those who received them just threw them away on the pavement following a cursory, disinterested glance at their contents. Trodden underfoot and covered in mud, these leaflets could be seen strewn around the street. At the stall, the oysters had just been thrown into a large basket like small pebbles. A woman in an apron took their order for a glass of white wine each and then Kohara set about opening the shell of an oyster. He squeezed a drop of lemon inside and, with a clack of his tongue, downed the raw oyster with relish.

'The juice inside these shells tastes really good. You must make sure you don't leave it.'

Relying on Kohara's explanation, Tanaka put the shell to his lips and sipped the salty liquid.

'Tanaka-san, have you been to Spain?'

'No, not yet.'

'If you go to Madrid, they have drinking stalls lined up in the streets, just like Japan. They fry up shrimps dipped in olive oil on a steel plate till they are sizzling hot and then you just pour on salt before eating them. They taste so good. When I went there, I was reminded of the old Asakusa. What's Asakusa like these days. Are the shopping arcades the same as they used to be? When I was in Japan, I often went to the flower and fruit stalls.'

With his glass of white wine in one hand, Kohara shut his eyes. It seemed that he was able in this way to bring back memories of the old downtown Tokyo he had once known.

'I really miss tatami mats. I can't tell you how I long to take my shoes off and walk around on those new greenish mats. I love the sensation of wearing a well-starched yukata next to the skin and walking around on those new tatami. But I suppose you wouldn't understand so deep a sense of nostalgia yet.'

Tanaka explained how he had been seized by a similar impulse on his first night in Paris. But Kohara was not convinced.

'But you'll be able to go back to Japan sooner or later. You can walk barefoot on those tatami mats again. I'll never be able to do so. As I grow older, I come to feel more and more depressed with Paris. The Paris I loved so much when I was younger has become almost intolerable to my body chemistry. The whole place is constructed of stone – the buildings, the streets … everywhere. Even in the countryside, none of the scenery seems suited to the Japanese make-up. There's no disguising it, Tanaka-san. There's something uniquely Japanese about the Japanese. Even if the worst comes to the worst, you mustn't end up settling down here.'

Kohara had lost count of how many glasses of wine they had drunk, and his face was red even around his eyes. He blinked as he muttered, 'There's something uniquely Japanese about the Japanese. People like me are like those who have been deprived of citizenship of any country. Half of me is Japanese, the other half isn't. And yet I can never assume French nationality.'

Tanaka tried to imagine Kohara as he had been when he first arrived in this country on business for the Bank of Japan. He could not have been as wretched as Tanaka himself had been on his first night in Paris. He superimposed on to Kohara the image of those four or five other Japanese who had been so full of zeal on that same flight. Yet here was this man, standing in the cold wind, one hand in the pocket of his dirty overcoat, the other clutching a glass of wine.

'There's something quite pitiful about someone who is neither Japanese nor French. Quite pathetic. I feel just like a weed with no roots.'

'Shall we go back?' Tanaka put his glass down.

'I'll take you home.'

'No. My apartment is really close. Would you like to come in?'

'Maybe next time.'

Kohara's house was situated in the block between the place du Panthéon and the Sorbonne. The cinemas and cafés on the main streets were still swarming with students like stray dogs. But in the narrow street in which he lived, all was dark except for the light from a solitary neon sign outside the pharmacist's.

'Do you know this song?' Kohara suddenly spoke in a quiet voice. 'It's all right. I won't embarrass you. It's a song I learnt years ago, back in Japan . . .'

'Go ahead.'

Kohara began to sing quietly. The song, which Tanaka had heard before, had been popular during the reign of the Emperor Taisho.

> 'Why does the crow weep?
> Off to the mountains, the crow . . .'

At the end of the song Kohara left, disappearing into the building with its crumbling walls. As Tanaka stood there, the sound of a woman's angry voice and Kohara's weak one offering some kind of apology came to his ears. Kohara's wife appeared to be shouting something.

1 Laure de Lauris. A woman deceived by Sade before his marriage. A woman influential in the formulation of Sade's view of young girls.
2 Renée-Pélagie. Sade's wife.
3 Anne-Prospère de Launay Pélagie. Sade's sister-in-law. Younger sister of Renée. Had a protracted affair with Sade even after his marriage. Died of smallpox.
4 The actress Beauvoisin. Sade's mistress immediately after his marriage.
5 The actress Colet. Actress with an Italian theatre group. Sade's mistress at the same time.
6 The actress M. Full name unknown. Sade's mistress between 1764 and 1765.
7 Rose Keller. Widow of a baker's assistant. The victim in the incident at Arcueil.
8 Marianne Laverne and three other prostitutes. Victims in the incident at Marseille.
9 Rosette. Connected with him at Montpelier.
10 Catherine Trillet. Victim in the incident at Trillet.

Spreading out a large piece of paper on his desk, which was covered with books and notebooks, Tanaka was making a list of the various women in Sade's life. He had only the Venetian blinds open, but could hear a pedlar in the street below shouting out 'Chou, chou' as he passed. Someone was using the toilet in the adjoining room and he heard the sound of the flush. The list comprised only a small percentage of all the women with whom Sade was connected. In addition, there were several women who were to exert a considerable influence on Sade in ways other than physical. For example, there was Madame de Montreuil, Sade's mother-in-law, who was always secretly plotting to have him confined in jail for life. Hers was an extremely important existence. It was Tanaka's belief that she had been responsible for inculcating in Sade his hatred of motherhood. Another person not to be forgotten was Rousset, who loved Sade like an elder sister but ultimately died of tuberculosis. Sade always referred to her as 'the saint'.

Subsequently Tanaka had to copy that list into several notebooks, for he had decided, as far as possible, to investigate details of the lives of all these women. He planned to undertake a thorough examination of the influence these women had exerted upon the female protagonists of *Vice Amply Rewarded* and *The Misfortunes of Virtue,* his intention being to include this as one of the main chapters of the doctoral dissertation he was currently preparing. Having completed the list, he began to reread his notes from the lecture on 'Erotic Literature of the Eighteenth Century' which Professor Bady had given the other day at the Sorbonne. Several of Sade's contemporaries had been specialists in this field, including men like Laclos. A study of the literary relationship between Sade and Laclos was much needed, but remained as yet uncharted territory.

Tanaka sat there for a long time, absorbed in his reading and writing. Gradually he formed a clearer picture of these women and they came alive. To Tanaka, the most interesting of all these women were Sade's wife and her younger sister. In addition to devoting the whole of her life to acting as Sade's partner in his epicurean life-style, his sister-in-law, Anne-Prospère, had eloped to Italy with him. Tanaka wanted to know in what ways Sade had influenced this woman before she died of smallpox. On the one hand, there was the example of her elder sister Renée, who, even in the face of the most inhuman treatment from her husband, continued to live as a virtuous wife. Throughout his fickle life, Sade vacillated between these two large and contrasting women, not only in the world of his literature but in the real world.

Once again someone was using the toilet next door. On hearing it, Tanaka looked up from his books and opened the drawer of his desk in order to take out a cigarette. The picture of his wife and two-year-old baby had slipped in between the notebook and his medicine box. It was a picture he had taken a long time ago in the garden of his house in Setagaya. The sun's rays formed stripes on the fence behind them, and beside it he could see the baby's nappies and some shirts hanging out to dry.

Tanaka realized that he had forgotten to write to tell her not to go playing around with stocks and shares.

He clicked his tongue noisily, took out some airmail paper and began composing a letter to Kikue. As he wrote, he found himself growing more and more angry. Despite all his injunctions to put all royalties that might accrue during his absence into their savings account at the bank, she seemed to have forgotten her promise already. Her forgetfulness was most frustrating. Perhaps she had been mistaken about the possibility of Suganuma's coming to France to study too. Nevertheless, he did not forget to include at the end of his letter a sentence asking her tactfully to ask Professor Ueda whether the rumours about Suganuma were true or not. As usual, when he mechanically placed the letter in an envelope and looked at the notebooks scattered around on his desk, he realized the huge difference between the descriptions of the acts of Sade that these books contained and his own actions. His own existence was little more than a constant round of worrying about putting royalties in his savings account. His life was dominated by a policy of safety first. But it was just such a man who was currently meddling with the capricious Sade. He knew that all those who meddle with fire invariably end up burning themselves. So why wasn't he covered with burns?

Tanaka put on his jacket and, letter in hand, left his room. The post office in the avenue Kléber accepted overseas mail only until four o'clock. Just as he was about to go down the stairs, he decided to drop in on Sakisaka whom he had not seen these past couple of days. He had knocked at his door once the previous day, but there had been no answer.

Sakisaka's door was slightly ajar. Through the crack Tanaka could hear the sound of violent coughing.

'Hey. You're still not right, are you?'

Sakisaka turned to look at Tanaka, who had stopped by the door. His face was ashen.

'You look really bad. Have you been to the doctor's?'

Sakisaka nodded stiffly. 'I went yesterday. I got the results today.'

'Nothing bad, I hope?'

'Not really. He just said it was TB.' Sakisaka paused for a while before resignedly making this pronouncement. His hand was over his mouth as he tried to cover his hacking cough. 'The doctor advised me to go to hospital immediately. Failing that, he suggested I go straight home.'

'You're crazy.'

'I'm not. I'm serious. I've finally been caught. I knew my trip would end in failure!'

5

The two remained sitting in silence for quite some time. The early evening hush in the rue Hamelin was disturbed only by the occasional truck, which shook the windows of the hotel as it passed. TB was the disease which those living abroad like Tanaka and Sakisaka had to beware of more than anything else. For, more than any other disease or accident, it was the one which could affect the course of their period of study abroad. To catch TB was basically tantamount to an order to return home; for, to the foreign student, far removed from all close relatives and without the financial means to cover medical expenses, a protracted period of hospitalization in France was hardly a viable alternative.

Tanaka ventured to break the silence. 'What did the doctor say?'

'He told me I should go to hospital immediately.'

'For how long?'

'At least two years. He warned me that otherwise I'd die.' Sakisaka pouted his lips and forced a smile. But it was the deathly smile of a Noh theatre mask.

'Really. . . ?' Tanaka averted his gaze and stared at the floor. He felt as though he were directly experiencing the heartfelt anguish Sakisaka himself must be experiencing. 'Can nothing be done about it?'

'No. At this point, it's hopeless.' Once more, Sakisaka tried to laugh. 'For the time being, I'll enter the hospital on the boulevard Jourdan … until I can get my return visa fixed up. As soon as it's ready, I'll return to Japan.'

'Can you find no way of staying?'

'How can I? My money won't last. How can I stay here if all I can do is just lie on a bed doing nothing?' There was a trace of anger in his voice.

Tanaka pushed up his glasses with his finger and muttered, 'If there's anything I can do for you. . . .' But then, aware that, were he Sakisaka, such sentiments would sound like an empty display of commiseration, he stopped short. Was he really able to empathize with Sakisaka? It occurred to Tanaka that, at the deepest level of his consciousness, he was feeling rather a sense of relief that he himself had not succumbed to the disease during the course of his stay in France.

'Anyway, please stay in bed. I'll go to the office and ask them to make something for your dinner.'

'No. Please don't tell anyone here that I'm sick. They really hate being troubled down in the office. Anyway, I'm not going to get better just by staying in bed for one day like this. I'll go out somewhere for dinner. I'd like to make the most of my last few days of freedom in Paris before I go to hospital. Will you keep me company for dinner, Tanaka-san?'

Sakisaka made a great show of vitality as he stood up from the side of the bed on which he had been sitting. Opening the door of the wardrobe, he took out a jacket and eagerly started to put it on. But as he wrapped his camel-coloured scarf around his neck, his whole body was racked by more violent coughs.

Afterwards, as they left the hotel and began walking along the stone pavement of the road covered with dirty water, Sakisaka continued to cough fitfully. And when he looked at him more carefully, Tanaka noticed that the sick man was dragging his legs and panting heavily as he walked. He found himself recalling the word *rōgai*, the term which had formerly been used in Japanese to describe victims of pulmonary tuberculosis. The exhaustion of living and studying abroad seemed like a lead weight that did not merely hang over Sakisaka's whole body but had penetrated to the depths of his inner being.

'You're not too tired? You seem to be struggling for breath.'

'No, I'm fine. But studying abroad is really exhausting, isn't it? When I was in Japan, I had no idea it was so tiring!' As though despising himself, Sakisaka gave another wry smile as he continued, 'I suppose its not surprising that we get tired. Here we are trying to drink in the culture of this place which has been more than two thousand years in the making – all in the space of one or two years. Every day, though, fully aware of the impossibility of the task, we tense ourselves like a taut bowstring for fear of missing or overlooking even the smallest detail of that culture. Tanaka-san, my sickness represents a painful defeat in my struggle to come to grips with this country.'

'Yes. You shouldn't have tried to adjust so quickly to something with so much tradition behind it.'

'I know. But as I told you once before, there are three types of Japanese who come to this country. There are those who ignore the weight of history embodied in these stones, those who cleverly seek to imitate the weight of that history and those who, like me, lack that ability and end up going under.'

The two of them had emerged into the place du Trocadéro without realizing it. Tanaka recalled his solitary walk to the same place the day after his arrival in Paris. On that occasion, as now, the sky had been grey and the top of the Eiffel Tower had appeared to shiver in the biting wind.

'Have you been to this museum?' Sakisaka pointed to a drab building enveloped in a dank mist. Apart from a solitary uniformed official who stood between two columns, there were no signs of life, let alone any visitors. 'There was a time when I used to come here almost every day before dinner. There were virtually no visitors at such times, and often I was the only one in the place.'

'What kind of museum is it?'

'It's a collection of religious sculptures from the various cathedrals throughout the country. They've been re-created as exact replicas of the originals and are displayed in chronological order.

114

It's worth going there even once. Somehow, by going there, you can get a feel for the various trends in the world of art from the Middle Ages to the eighteenth century at a single glance.'

'But they are only replicas, aren't they?'

'Yes. But even so, they've been designed by means of some special technique that enables the creation of exact models.' As he spoke, Sakisaka placed his hand to his brow as though checking for a fever. But he continued to talk passionately about the museum. 'I'd really like to pay one last visit there today. Tanaka-kun, will you come with me?'

Tanaka could not generate much excitement about looking at a collection of replicas. Besides, his knowledge of the European formative arts was severely limited. He was aware from the outset that the uninitiated visitor was unlikely to grow excited about a series of replicas. But noticing that Sakisaka's feverish gaze was fixed on that drab building, he could hardly refuse.

As they paid for their tickets, the attendant appeared morose and muttered in a clearly audible voice that little time was left before they closed. But Sakisaka just ignored him, buried his head in his camel-coloured scarf and pushed open the large glass door. Inside, there was a series of deserted rooms. Neither custodians nor visitors were to be seen – merely a collection of sculptures which, in the early evening darkness, appeared to have been organized so that each had a sense of space and tranquillity surrounding it. The sound of Sakisaka's feet as he stepped inside seemed to shout out in the darkness. But those heavy footsteps served only to increase the feeling of stillness in the room.

'You have to start from here.'

'I know nothing about any of this. Please explain as we go along.'

'I know nothing about art either.' Sakisaka's voice echoed around the room. 'But Tanaka-san, the major challenge I have faced since coming to this country concerns the religious architecture. Christian architecture. I've found myself gradually losing interest in modern architecture. What we have here are the sculptures and formative art works of the great French cathedrals. Virtually everything in this room can be dated from the Roman era up to the middle of the medieval era.'

The two men stood in front of the first sculpture in the first room. It was a carved stone pillar preserved in the old cathedral on

115

the rue Minerval. Three beings – whether human or animal it was impossible to determine – were playing the flute with both hands. Their backs bent like drawn bows, they were supporting a scrolled pillar of stone. Tanaka remarked that he could not understand why such weird creatures, seeming to bear many of the hallmarks of some ancient folk religion, should be carved on to the pillars of a cathedral.

'But Christianity in Roman times seems to have felt no compunction about absorbing various local elements of pagan French art. It seems to have looked on such art as a sustaining force.'

'You mean Christianity did?'

'Right.' The architect covered his mouth with his scarf and suppressed a cough. 'Have you seen the cathedral at Chartres?'

'I'm planning to go there soon. The stained glass there must be magnificent.'

'Near the modern city of Chartres there apparently used to be some kind of folk religion centred on female deity worship. I heard that, in that locality, Christianity incorporated such goddess worship into its own worship of the Holy Mother and was widely received.'

Beside the strange beings which supported the scrolled pillar, was a series of carvings of human faces wearing idiotic expressions. One could not tell whether they were male or female faces, but in the centre of each hollow face had been carved deep, dark holes which served as eyes.

That was not the only sculpture bearing such hollow eyes. All of the sculptures in every corner of the room seemed to be staring at Tanaka through similar deep, dark holes. The faces of Adam and Eve which stood by the window were gazing at Tanaka from under the leaves of a fig tree which symbolized Heaven. The expression on their faces, like that of the weird creatures playing the flute and of the idiots which stood beside them, suggested that they, too, were confronting the heavy burden of their own destiny. The same could be said of the sculpture entitled *The Flight of the Holy Mother and Christ to Egypt* which had been reconstructed from the original in Autun cathedral. To Tanaka, the face of Mary and that of Joseph – even that of the donkey which bore them – all seemed to be struggling with their own inescapable destiny. The statue of St

Martin which had been carried down from a monastery in the Pyrenees had suffered severe damage to the lower half, but again the contorted face suggested one who had been buffeted by fate. There were other carvings of nameless people in the pillars of the same monastery which had been made merely to support the weight of the great stones with their heads. But in each case the eyes were fixed on a single spot. Their gaze appeared eternally transfixed. Those faces could neither laugh nor weep, rejoice nor grieve. With fixed facial expression, they merely accepted their heavy burden, symbolized by the stone. Over the centuries, as they were buffeted by the elements, those faces must have continued to gaze out on their fixed destiny through those dark, hollowed-out eyes. For some reason or other, Tanaka found himself recalling the stone walls of the prison at Vincennes. Sade had endured the pressure of those walls for fifteen years.

'There's something suffocating about it, isn't there?' Tanaka sighed involuntarily. 'There's something unbearably stifling about looking at these faces and their eyes.'

'Is that what you feel?' Sakisaka turned round and wiped the sweat from his face with his palm. 'Yes, this room's really stifling, isn't it?'

'I feel a strong sense of predetermination in each of these carvings.'

'That's right. Look at the face of this king. This is King David ... it's the face of one who knows only the destiny of a king. Joseph, too ... he has only the one fixed destiny. And Mary cannot escape her destiny as the Holy Mother.'

'Is that because the sculpture is medieval?'

'Rather than medieval, I prefer to see it as belonging to the first period of European history. After that came the second period of European history. When I came here every day, I used to feel it was just I who was suffocating – or that I was suffocating because my lungs were unhealthy and infected. But it isn't true, is it?' Sakisaka continued to wipe away the sweat as he muttered to himself. 'I see now that it was Europe which caused me to contract this suffocating disease.'

Sakisaka's words were somewhat exaggerated. This notion that his TB was somehow connected with the fundamental weight and oppression of European culture was interesting but slightly extravagant. To Tanaka, it seemed as though Sakisaka were desperately attempting to attach some significance, some symbolic value, to his illness. The emaciated figure who stood before him, his hand held to his mouth to cover his hacking cough, was that of a defeated man. In short, his period of study abroad had failed. That was the truth of the situation.

I must not end up like that. Looking at Sakisaka's dirty camel-coloured scarf, Tanaka sought to encourage himself. I'm also going to have to be really careful.

Tanaka followed Sakisaka into the next room. Here too were displayed sculptures from the old monasteries and cathedrals of the Haute Garonne and Corrèze regions. In each of those faces there also lurked the loneliness of those who live with a fixed destiny. Every statue merely stared straight ahead through dark, hollowed-out eyes. Just like those in the previous room, the facial expression on every statue was fixed and immutable. Tanaka felt that he was just walking round and round in a room with no exit.

Suddenly, just as Tanaka was stepping into the third gallery, the room was illuminated by a single streak of light. At first Tanaka thought it was the evening sun shining in through the misty window. But the light had not come from the window. The faint flash of light emanated from the statue of the angel which stood on the left side of the room. There was a faint smile on the angel's face and her large wings were outspread. With her right hand slightly raised, the angel was looking up at an angle, smiling at somebody. The white streak of light had come from the plaster and from that smile.

'Ah! That's beautiful. That's really beautiful,' he exclaimed.

With this statue they seemed to have come to an end of the succession of dark, hollow eyes and fixed facial expressions. Tanaka drank in that smile and white streak of light as though he had left the claustrophobic, dark room and emerged into the dawning sky and fresh air.

'*The Angel of Reims*,' Sakisaka informed him. 'This work marks the end of the medieval era. It's as though the world of the Old Testament became the world of the New Testament at this point. This can be seen as the second period of European history.'

'It's beautiful. Really beautiful,' Tanaka repeated.

'Whenever I come to this statue, I always think of the sky at sunset.'

'Isn't it more like a morning scene? The morning after a long night?'

Sakisaka shook his head emphatically. 'No. It's an evening sunset. It's a momentary flash of light in the evening sky. Look, after this sunset European art crashed to the ground. At least that's true of the formative arts. This sculpture of the angel was completed at the beginning of the fifteenth century ... I believe that there was a brief moment during the early part of the century when the spiritual element of the medieval age was fused with the human element of the Renaissance era to form this flash of evening light. You can tell by looking at this smiling angel and comparing it with the post-baroque sculptures over here that that light soon vanished, to be replaced by the third period of European history.'

It was just as Sakisaka had said. In the next room, containing sculptures from the sixteenth century and later, even an amateur like Tanaka, who was sadly lacking in knowledge of the formative arts, could sense the exaggeration and ostentation. It was as though the creators of these sculptures had renounced the spirituality evident in the earlier works, allowing a vulgar quality to permeate their art.

'Whilst you're in France, you have to experience that fact for yourself.' Perhaps Sakisaka's temperature had risen, for his eyes were clouded. 'No. In choosing to study abroad, one can't help confronting this fundamental reality. Look at me. I may be lazy, but I am an architect of sorts. Before leaving Japan and coming here, that thought had never occurred to me. But during the two years I have spent here walking those stone streets under the dark Paris sky, I have begun to realize for myself that I am part of a long tradition of art and artists. That realization is very different from the time when I was still in Japan studying from books and photographs. I was hoping if possible to spend the next ten, even twenty, years experiencing for myself that momentary artistic reality which is like the glow of evening sunset. But now I am broken by this disease and have to return home.'

'I'm sure you'll recover and be able to come again.' Although Tanaka tried to console him, he was aware how empty these words must sound to Sakisaka.

'No, I'll not be back. I've had enough. But Tanaka-san, we may be only foreign students, yet just by entering an insignificant little museum like this, we can stand in the great flow of European

119

history spanning all those centuries. I just didn't want to be like so many Japanese students who come here to study and become architects just by stealing one tiny fragment of that great flow and using their natural talent to make imitations of it. I felt that, unless I as a Japanese could confront the actuality of that great flow, then my whole motivation for coming here would have been made meaningless. What are you going to do? Are you going to ignore the flow and return home unaffected by the experience?'

Tanaka accepted Sakisaka's challenge in silence.

'You claim you don't want to ignore that great flow whilst living here. But there lies the real pain which is all part of the experience of studying abroad. You have to put up with that suffocating pressure you just mentioned – today, tomorrow, every day. In the end, you'll get sick like me. In order to enter that great flow, we foreign students have to pay some sort of a price. I've paid for it with my health.'

On the day Sakisaka was to enter hospital, it began to snow. Leaving most of his luggage in his room to be shipped on to Japan at a subsequent date and with Tanaka carrying the bag containing those articles of everyday use that he would need, the patient was seized by the occasional violent fit of coughing as the two men set out for the hospital on the boulevard Jourdan.

The snow falling from the heavily clouded sky became lighter. But every time Sakisaka coughed, the driver turned round with a look of repugnance and muttered, 'You must be sick.'

'No, he's all right. We're just going to the hospital to have a check-up.' It was Tanaka who spoke on behalf of Sakisaka.

'If it's flu, you should try hot water and rum,' the driver continued. 'That's the way all the French treat their colds.'

Sakisaka pushed his face to the window and stared out at the powder snow enveloping the place du Louvre. Aware that he would probably never see those buildings again, the trees lining the avenues and the faces of the people there, he appeared intent on impressing the scene on his mind's eye. The snow had begun to settle on the grey museums in both the place du Louvre and the place de la Concorde. The cars and trucks in the streets sent up plumes of snow as they drove past, though the ruts formed by their wheels soon turned to slush.

'That reminds me ... it was snowing like this when I arrived in Paris.' Sakisaka held his cheeks in his gloved hand and smiled wanly as he spoke.

By the time they reached the hospital, the powdery flakes of snow had turned into large flakes. In the short time it took them to walk from the car to the entrance, the snow fell in great white balls from the lapels of their overcoats. As they entered the waiting-room, they were confronted by the smell of cresol and the dank heat from the steam heater. A nurse appeared and handed them a form which had to be completed upon entry.

The ward for TB patients was on the fourth floor. Sakisaka was assigned to a four-bed room and, as they carefully opened the door, the gaze of the white patients stretched out on their beds was focused on Sakisaka and Tanaka.

'Bon jour,' Tanaka greeted them, but there was no response. Placing his case underneath a bed in one of the corners, Sakisaka took out his striped pyjamas and surreptitiously changed into them. The other patients in the room watched this operation in silence.

The door opened and a French doctor appeared, accompanied by the same nurse they had met at reception. He picked up the X-ray photograph that Sakisaka had brought with him and asked his Japanese patient to undo the buttons of his pyjamas. He then took out his stethoscope. Sakisaka's exposed chest was flat and pale and the area around his collar-bone was dreadfully depressed. Sensing the contemptuous gaze of the other patients focused on Sakisaka, Tanaka placed himself as a screen between them and the doctor.

The doctor continued to grill Sakisaka about his symptoms: his temperature, coughing, phlegm. ... He then asked the nurse to prepare a scalpel, pipette and some absorbent cotton. Making a small incision in the architect's ear with the scalpel, the doctor took a sample of blood in the pipette.

'And you are. . . ?' Placing a sample of the patient's blood on a glass slide, the doctor was addressing Tanaka.

'I'm just a Japanese who happened to be living with him.'

'Oh, so you're a friend. Would you mind stepping out into the corridor a second?'

Whilst the nurse was explaining the sheet that described the daily hospital routine and rules about noise she had given Sakisaka,

Tanaka followed the doctor into the corridor. The effects of the steam heater could be clearly felt. The room straight ahead must be the toilet, since Tanaka saw a young girl wearing a gown and carrying a urine glass opening the squeaky door.

Holding Sakisaka's X-ray up to the light in the ceiling, the doctor stared at it for a while. Tanaka could make out the ribs on either side, but had no idea what was wrong with the lungs.

'You see the two cavities here?' The doctor was fingering the area around Sakisaka's collar-bone – the same area which Sakisaka had been so careful to conceal with his hands just a short while before. The doctor's fingers were covered in a faint blond down. At the top of the negative they could see a whitish cloud with ill-defined boundaries. Those two whitish areas – they were more than just cavities – must be the two parts which had been eaten away by the TB bacteria.

'They are fairly recent cavities. Your friend is completely exhausted. And he hasn't been getting enough nourishment.' The doctor spoke as though Sakisaka's illness were entirely Tanaka's fault. Fidgeting nervously with his glasses, Tanaka recalled the angry words the architect had had to say three days earlier in the museum off the Trocadéro. 'You claim you don't want to ignore the great flow. . . . But there lies the real pain and hardship which is all part of the experience of studying abroad. . . . In order to enter that great flow, we foreign students have to pay some sort of a price. I've paid for it with my health.' Aware that those cavities were the sacrifice Sakisaka had paid in order to enter the great flow, Tanaka looked intently at that white area which floated in the middle of the X-ray like an inauspicious cloud.

'It will take at least three years to fix those cavities.'

'He said another doctor told him two years.'

'That's if we operate.' The French doctor shrugged his shoulders as though his self-esteem had been wounded. 'We need to remove the upper and middle lobes of the lungs. But in order to do that, we'd have to remove five ribs.'

Sakisaka must have been totally oblivious to such ramifications.

'Would he be able to manage that financially?'

'No.' Tanaka shook his head sadly. 'After all, he's only a self-supporting foreign student.'

'In which case he would do better to return to Japan and have it treated there. I'm sure he's got family over there and, all in all, that would be much more convenient for everyone concerned.'

As though a decision had already been made, the doctor set off down the warm corridor with the X-ray under his right arm.

When Tanaka returned to the room, Sakisaka was waiting for him, sitting up on the bed. 'What did you talk about? It looks pretty bad. Right?'

'No. Not as bad as all that.' Tanaka blinked as he spoke. 'He said it wasn't that bad.' Obviously he could not possibly tell Sakisaka about the operation which would require the removal of five ribs.

'I'm sure if you stay here for a while, it will get better.'

'Please feel free to go home.' Sakisaka spoke with an air of restraint. 'If the snow gets any worse, you'll be in real trouble.'

The world outside the window was now totally white. It seemed that the snow was accompanied by a thick fog, since the windows looked a milky white colour and the rooms and chimneys of the nearby ward seemed no more than shadowy silhouettes.

'I'll come again tomorrow. If there's anything you want me to bring . . .'

'No. I know how busy you are. So don't feel you have to come. I feel bad putting you out like this just because we happened to be staying in the same hotel.'

'Try to get used to hospital life as quickly as possible.' Aware of the fixed gaze of those around them, Tanaka continued in a hushed voice. 'You're bound to feel a bit miserable today.'

After a couple more comments Tanaka took the patient's hand and said goodbye. When Tanaka emerged from the hospital, large flakes of snow were dancing about even more wildly than before. Blown by the wind, the snow seemed to buffet his entire being. When he was back in the boulevard, various cars were scattering snow in all directions as they raced past, but there were no vacant taxis. Looking back at the hospital, Tanaka could still make out several dimly lit windows. He tried to locate Sakisaka's room but was unable to determine which one it was. As he walked through the snow to the Métro station, he occasionally stopped to wipe his glasses with the edge of his scarf. The road seemed interminably long under its blanket of snow and he felt he might never reach the station. Tanaka found himself wondering what he would be doing in Paris in another year – or even a year and a half. The mere thought of ending up like Sakisaka, coughing and confined to a hospital ward in this foreign country, was more than he could bear. He would have to finish his period of study in France in no more than a year and a half. After all, what point was there in jeopardizing his position in the university just to remain in this country? He was as yet far from bold enough to reject the life he knew in Japan merely for the purpose of experiencing life amidst that great flow of which Sakisaka had spoken.

Tanaka was overcome by an awareness of his lack of ambition, of his lack of pride. Raising his hand every now and then to protect his nose and mouth from the snowflakes, he could not help admitting that he was totally unqualified to study literature. This was an extremely painful realization. He had to confess that he had as much social ambition as the next man. He was painfully aware that his decision to study literature was essentially no different from the ambition of his former classmates to rise to the position of manager or director of their respective companies and banks. Yet the true man of letters was one like Sade who for years on end was incarcerated in Vincennes prison. Those who really desire to 'live' in the fullest sense of the word had to accept the price and end up, like Sakisaka, emaciated, with their lungs half eaten away.

Tanaka was oppressed by the realization that all he was trying to do was to manipulate literature for his own ends without paying the ultimate price by going to hospital or prison. If he were honest with himself, there was no denying that fact.

At the entrance to the Métro a crowd of people, thrown into confusion by the sudden squalls of snow, were vainly seeking taxis. Their coats and hats were completely white as they looked with surprise at the approaching Tanaka.

Removing his steamed-up glasses to wipe them, Tanaka noticed a Japanese man in a beret amongst the crowd waiting for taxis. It was Ono, the same Ono whom Tanaka had seen drinking with Manabe in the Montparnasse café some time previously.

'Ono-san.'

'Hey.' It was clear from the confused look in his eyes as he looked at Tanaka that Ono had been pretending not to see him. Ono, the Professor of H University, must still have resented the bad manners Tanaka had evidenced on that occasion.

'It's hopeless for taxis.' Tanaka was trying to ingratiate himself with Ono. 'I've walked the whole length of this road but I haven't seen one.'

'I think you're right.' Ono put his hand to his beret and clicked his tongue in irritation. 'French drivers are all the same. They're lazy. By the way, where've you been, looking like a snowman?'

'Sakisaka had to go to hospital and so I went with him.'

'Hey. Sakisaka-kun had to go into hospital, eh? I hear he has some kind of chest infection. You and I had better watch out.' Ono seemed totally indifferent to Sakisaka's illness and contented himself with such comments. 'That man's hopeless. Even though we are all studying in Paris, Sakisaka-kun has totally ignored the rest of us Japanese.'

'It must be because he's so weak.'

'But he's always assuming airs, like some intolerable prig.' Ono's criticism was clearly intended as a sarcastic jab at Tanaka's attitude in the Montparnasse café. 'Nothing can be done about it now. I'll wait a bit longer before giving up.'

'Where have you come from?'

'I've just been to the Seuil publishing company where I met M. Cayrol. We were negotiating rights for the book I'm planning to translate.' As he continued, the trace of a smile could be detected on the lips of the portly professor. 'I'm planning to have Suganuma-kun from your university help with the translation. I hear he's coming here in about three weeks. Is that right?'

'Eh? Suganuma?' In response, Tanaka merely parroted Ono's words. So Suganuma would be arriving in about three weeks! The news came as a thunderbolt to Tanaka. It was only to be expected that Assistant Professor Imai had failed to inform him of this latest development. But nobody from the university had bothered to contact Tanaka! All he had heard was that vague hint from his wife Kikue that Suganuma would be coming to France 'sometime in the near future'.

'What? You mean you hadn't heard?'

'Well, I've heard something to the effect that he was coming. . . .' Tanaka felt his face twitch and, in an attempt to disguise it, he remarked, 'I had no idea he'd be coming so soon.'

'I received an airmail letter from Suganuma-kun. How strange that you have heard nothing. You're from the same university after all!' Ono was scrutinizing the expression on Tanaka's face and was clearly teasing him. 'Suganuma's coming here is really going to help me. I plan to do all kinds of translation projects with him.'

A bus, its roof covered with snow, finally came into sight. Very slowly it pulled up in front of them.

After Ono and the others had boarded it, the bus disappeared once more into the blanket of greyish snow. But for a few minutes after that Tanaka remained motionless in the middle of the road. Why had the university authorities failed to tell him that Suganuma was coming to France? Why had Assistant Professor Imai said nothing about it? Tanaka had not even received a note from Suganuma himself informing him that he was about to go to France. Given that he himself was a lecturer and Suganuma a mere assistant, the fact that he was about to come without one word of greeting or forewarning could be interpreted only as a deliberate attempt to slight Tanaka.

In an effort to relieve his growing sense of anger and unease, Tanaka decided to go to the Bibliothèque Nationale instead of returning to the rue Hamelin. The library was usually crammed with students, but today, presumably as a result of the snow, there were only a few readers. They were all huddled around the steam heater in the corner, reading and taking notes in almost total silence. Tanaka sat down on one of the chairs and began heating his hands and feet which were numb from the cold. The boots he had bought just before leaving Japan had not been repaired since his arrival in Paris, as a result of which melted snow had dripped through on to his socks. The dripping wet boots and socks were most uncomfortable.

When he had managed to restore some warmth to his body, he approached material box number 2438, filled out a call-slip and handed it to the librarian on duty. That box contained the manuscript of Maurice Heine, who was studying Sade along with Ruby. It had been from this box that Tanaka had learnt that one of the descendants of Laure de Lauris, one of the many women in Sade's life, had been a personal friend of Marcel Proust. The mere fact that he was currently living in the same building in which Proust had breathed his last caused Tanaka to feel a more special affinity with this de Lauris than with the other women with whom Sade was intimately connected. She was born into a famous family from the South of France which could trace its ancestry back to the thirteenth century. The affair between Sade and this daughter of the nobility had flourished during the period of his engagement to the Montreuil daughter. During this period Sade had been intimate not only with his future wife, but with this de Lauris and with one other woman.

Since starting to pay regular visits to the library, Tanaka had begun to assume that this period had a great influence on the development of Sade's view of women. Obviously this was not a hypothesis that had been broached by either Ruby or Heine. But Tanaka came to believe that at the root of Sade's obsessive hatred for young women lay the memory of his rejection by de Lauris in his own past.

With his head resting on his hands, Tanaka sat for a long time reading the copy of the manuscript by Maurice Heine. As was the case with Ruby, the handwriting of this virtually unknown scholar, Maurice Heine, was clumsy and hard to read. But as he sat wading through each word crammed on to the page, Tanaka forgot all about Ono's earlier sarcastic grin and about Suganuma. As he read, the passionate breath of this unknown scholar, who showed utter contempt for the opinions of others in devoting half his life to the study of Sade, was fused into those small, densely packed words. With the aid of Heine, Tanaka would be able to return to Japan and write his doctoral dissertation.

Since his eyes were tired, Tanaka raised his glasses with his finger and looked at the window. The snow did not appear to have stopped, for all he could see outside was a vast grey void. Three or four students sitting in front of him were staring in Tanaka's direction and whispering to each other. He nonchalantly followed their gaze and noticed a tall, thin girl talking with one of the librarians. Her profile reminded him of the numerous photographs he had seen of Simone de Beauvoir. She wore a modest overcoat and had a silk scarf wrapped round her neck. The librarian led her into a special reading-room and the main room became silent once more. The image of Ruby's contorted, ugly face flashed before Tanaka's eyes.

'In France there are hundreds of people who know nothing about Sade and yet continue to discuss him. Take Simone de Beauvoir for a start. That woman knows nothing about Sade. But she's nevertheless used him to amass a fortune.'

6

That afternoon Tanaka moved his chair up to the window and, pencil in hand, busied himself writing a letter in French. He and Sakisaka had not spent much time together despite the fact that they were residents of the same hotel; and yet, with Sakisaka now in hospital, Tanaka felt strangely lonely. He was also oppressed by a painful sense that he had already experienced numerous depressing winters in Paris. It may well have been that he had inherited Sakisaka's penchant for living in isolation. When in Japan, Tanaka had not realized that the Paris winter could be so depressing an experience. It was almost more than he could bear. Every morning when he opened his eyes and looked out of the window fitted with net curtains, he was greeted by a grey, cloudy sky. The only colour in the scene outside the window was the black smoke emerging from the chimney opposite; and, when he returned to the hotel in the evening, he noticed the smoke billowing forth inexorably, creating a grey film on the window-pane. In an attempt to overcome his loneliness in having no one to speak to and his anxiety created by the knowledge of Suganuma's impending arrival, Tanaka diligently applied himself to his work. Every morning, waking at about eight, he would immediately wash and nibble on a loaf of bread by way of breakfast. It took only a couple of days for those long loaves of French bread to grow hard and dry. Sometimes he would wash down chunks of hardened baguette with water from the tap. He would then take the Métro from the avenue Kléber to Richelieu and go to the Bibliothèque Nationale. When he was feeling especially tired, he would sometimes order a cup of strong coffee at a nearby café. Apart from Wednesday and Friday afternoons, when he went to hear Professor Bady's lectures at the Sorbonne, he would stay in the library until six o'clock every evening. Then, as everyone in the reading-room started to get ready to return home, Tanaka too would put his notebooks and dictionary in his Japanese wrapping-cloth and brave the penetrating chill outside. Afterwards he would head for the student cafeteria near the Sorbonne and, having queued up with all the young students, would carry his bowl of meat and potato soup on an aluminium tray to a corner and eat his dinner alone. The garrulous French students hardly spoke to this melancholy Japanese man. Returning to his hotel room, he would often collapse on to his bed for a while and stare at the ceiling with its damp patches. He would then get up and write to his family and friends in Japan. The times when he would set about his pile of dirty washing, leaving them to dry on top of the rather inefficient steam heater, seemed especially pathetic. He wondered what his wife Kikue and his students would say if they could see him doing his washing until all hours of the night. Of course in his letters to Japan he never once alluded to this unsavoury aspect of his new life. On those thin sheets of airmail paper he always had to assume the role of the student of foreign literature, the lecturer in the French department. But, every now and then he would pause in the knowledge that his life as a foreign student was more aptly encapsulated in the row of long underwear and socks laid out to dry on the steam heater late at night in his solitary hotel room.

Yet, when he looked out on the grey sky and patches of black smoke he could see from the hotel window, he also realized that this was the same Parisian winter sky that Sade would have seen from his window in the Vincennes prison, rattling in the wind. Were there really women who could fundamentally change a man's view of the female sex? To Tanaka, who had never known any woman apart from his wife, the relationship between Sade and Laure de Lauris which he was currently studying in the Bibliothèque Nationale was fascinating. It was clear that Sade's actual appearance, which had always seemed to be shrouded behind some thin veil during Tanaka's years of study in Japan, had assumed a rather more vivid reality in his imagination since his arrival in Paris. Sade had first fallen for de Lauris's charms while he was engaged to Renée-Pélagie. For all that, several letters written by Sade to de Lauris between the beginning of 1763 and April of that same year were still extant. Recently Tanaka had been busying himself in the Bibliothèque Nationale transcribing those letters. As he copied the letters, in which the full passion of the southern Frenchman appeared to be faithfully recorded, Tanaka felt a sense of shame that he had never once experienced similar feelings of passion for a woman. It was only after his rejection by de Lauris that Sade began to be promiscuous with various women. There could be no doubt that de Lauris left an indelible scar on Sade for the rest of his life. And yet neither Ruby nor Heine had focused upon her. When Tanaka realized that this was a totally undeveloped area of research for him to exploit, his heart leapt as he worked.

Anne-Prospère, the younger sister of Sade's wife Renée-Pélagie, was another strange woman. Sade had also begun an affair with his sister-in-law whilst he was engaged. The affair had continued for more than half of Sade's life. This woman was Sade's constant companion, rather than his wife. When Sade escaped from the police and fled to Italy, again it was this woman who had never left his side. But this area of study had also been left virtually untouched by both Ruby and Heine. Tanaka resolved to write to Sade's descendant, François de Sade. Maybe he would have the same kind of welcome he had received from Ruby. But that did nothing to detract from the necessity of adopting such a positive approach.

This time he would have to be extremely careful not to wound the other party's self-respect in his letter. For Tanaka was aware that this François de Sade, ashamed of the infamy of his great-grandfather, the Marquis, was in possession of a considerable number of documents about his ancestor which he kept hidden away. Emphasizing Sade's reputation as a great man of letters, Tanaka went to some pains to stress that he had not embarked upon this course of study through mere caprice. On rereading his letter Tanaka was appalled at his childish French; but he had no inclination to rewrite it. Learning from Ruby's book that François de Sade lived in Rouen, he wrote a fair copy.

Letter in hand, he went outside. A veil of mist had descended. There were no signs of life on the slope leading from the rue Hamelin to the avenue Kléber. The bare horse-chestnut trees in the little park on the street-corner appeared to shiver in the breeze, and a single sheet of old newspaper had been caught up on the wet bench. Tanaka wondered what it was about Paris that had seemed so enticing to him in the past. He felt that the Paris he was now experiencing was a painfully oppressive and dismal town.

Having posted the letter at the post office, Tanaka had little desire to return to the hotel now that Sakisaka was no longer there. But at the same time there was something equally depressing about the thought of lining up with his aluminium tray in the student cafeteria. His mind started to wander to the Japanese restaurant he had heard about some time previously, apparently the only one in the city. He was aware that the prices there would be astronomical. But the very thought of the smell of *miso* soup and fried fish which he had not eaten for so long was enough to bring tears to his eyes. He was overcome by an overwhelming feeling of nostalgia. He boarded the bus in the mist of the avenue Kléber and alighted in the place d'Auteuil. He was sure that that was where the Botanya was situated. He had heard that the second floor had been made into a *pension* and that many Japanese visitors lodged there during their stay in Paris. Most of the shops he could make out through the mist were closed; there was just one solitary café with its lights still on. He stopped to ask for directions to the Botanya and started to follow the road down the hill as directed.

There were several groups of Japanese patrons dining at the Botanya. There were even a few Westerners amongst them who appeared to be struggling with their chopsticks.

Apart from *sukiyaki* and *tempura,* the menu did not look particularly appealing. But there was always *sashimi*. There was also *sake*. With his wallet in mind, Tanaka asked the French waitress for *sukiyaki* and *sake*. Realizing just how long it was since he had last eaten such food, he literally licked the corners of his mouth. When his meal arrived, he leant over his dish and almost dipped his nose into the food as he began to eat. When he finally paused for breath, he became aware of the wretched state of his clothes in comparison with those of the other Japanese.

'What a fog.' Opening the door brusquely, four or five men walked in arrogantly. The young man in front, who had turned up the collar of his overcoat, glanced around the restaurant and, on noticing Tanaka, looked away. Tanaka had seen that face somewhere before. He had been one of the men drinking with Ono and the novelist Manabe in the café in Montparnasse. He was one of the young artists.

'Hello.' But as he greeted Tanaka in a high-pitched, almost feminine voice, he turned to those behind him. Manabe was with them.

'Hey ... what are you doing ... in a place like this?' There was a note of surprise in his voice as Manabe addressed Tanaka. But that was all he said before making for some empty chairs in the corner. From the relaxed way in which they joked with the waitress who brought their menus, it appeared that they were frequent visitors to the place. Their arrogant manner in this Japanese restaurant was clearly a reaction to the inferiority complex with which they were forced to live elsewhere.

As he ate, Tanaka surreptitiously listened to their conversation. They seemed to have just come from a farewell party for Manabe who was about to return to Japan. Apparently the consul-general had also attended, as several names which sounded like those of embassy personnel kept cropping up in the conversation.

'Hey, Tanaka-kun.' Manabe was leaning his large frame against the wall as he drank. He looked pale. 'I hear that Sakisaka's sick. Chest infection, isn't it?'

'Yes.' Tanaka hurriedly swallowed the rice he had just eaten before continuing. 'He's in hospital.'

'Poor thing. I kept on telling myself I should go and see him. . . . But there was just no time. I'm going back to Japan the day after tomorrow. Please look me up when you're back in Japan.'

Tanaka bowed and thanked him. Manabe's words manifested all the conciliatory overtones of one about to leave directed at one who is to stay. But nevertheless, in view of their earlier confrontation, the mere fact that he bothered to address him in front of the whole group was pleasing to Tanaka.

The artists began drinking, totally oblivious of Tanaka's presence. But Tanaka could still hear everything they said.

'Have any of you been to visit Sakisaka?'

In reply to Manabe's question one of the young artists began to make excuses. It was clearly all for Tanaka's benefit.

'I'm sure he wouldn't want us to. He doesn't seem to like us Japanese.'

'He has practically nothing to do with us. If he doesn't want to see us, why should we be so anxious to visit him?' It was another artist wearing thick-framed glasses who spoke. He almost spat out the words. 'Sakisaka despises us.'

'Despises us? Why should he despise us?'

There followed a long discussion amongst the artists in which their contempt for Sakisaka was manifest. They were speaking in hushed voices; but Tanaka, seated at the next table, could not help overhearing them. Conversely, the artists must have been fully aware that Tanaka was listening to everything they said.

'Don't you agree, Tanaka-san?' One of the young artists was laughing as he addressed Tanaka.

'Um.... What?'

'Don't you feel that Sakisaka has this weird inferiority complex about anything Western?'

When he raised his eyes and looked at those around him, Tanaka noticed the novelist leaning against the wall staring at him. His blurred eyes suggested that he had drunk too much. Tanaka had no wish to become embroiled in another verbal battle. He recalled the intensity of the argument in the Montparnasse café and was loath to become the object of ridicule of his fellow countrymen once more.

'But he's really determined ...' – he was searching for a non-commital reply – '... in his effort to come to terms with this country.'

'Yes, that's what he thinks. He's like a sumo wrestler.' It was the youth with the thick glasses who spoke. 'But with sumo, you have to match men of the same build who agree to abide by the same rules. There's a fundamental difference between the French and us Japanese. As a student of French literature, perhaps you don't agree.... No, hang on a second. I think we learn a valuable lesson just by coming here and recognizing the existence of something which is fundamentally different from us. So I don't think there's any need for us to end up staying here indefinitely.'

'But....' Tanaka's hands had started sweating as he adjusted his glasses. 'Sakisaka was determined not to pass judgement on this country until he had taken in what he had seen. Perhaps that explains his sumo-like approach?'

'But what's the upshot? He's been forced to his knees and ends up with some lung infection. Right? Isn't that a bit too much of a kamikaze approach?'

'There's no need to describe it like that.' Tanaka had completely forgotten his earlier self-restraint and there was tension in his voice. 'Do you really think that in the space of a year or two you can really come to terms with the fundamental differences between the French and the Japanese? Wasn't it exactly that kind of attitude Sakisaka hated?'

'So this is just an introduction, is it, these one or two years spent studying abroad? But aren't you deluding yourself just as much if you think you can really come to terms with French culture by living here ten, even twenty years? Take Todo-san. He's been here for twelve years. He used to be quite a talented artist around Montmartre. But now he's reduced to acting as interpreter for the various singers and designers who come from Japan. There are hundreds of failed artists like him here in Paris – not only Japanese, but also Americans and Brazilians.'

Tanaka knew without being told by the man wearing the thick-rimmed spectacles that Paris was swarming with those who found themselves broken spiritually as well as physically as a result of staying too long. He had yet to meet the artist Todo. But the miserable image of Kohara with whom he had spoken at length the other day came immediately to mind.

'Sakisaka doesn't think like that.' It was Manabe who had suddenly interrupted. 'I met the artist Todo. But he's had it. He poses as a genius. But his paintings are terrible. Tanaka, do you remember Kohara I introduced you to the other day?'

'Yes.'

'It's people like that who arouse my curiosity as a novelist. But when it comes to everyday life, there's nothing more miserable. Tanaka-kun, have you ever stopped to wonder why these men here became so wretched?'

Tanaka stared at the dish on the table in silence. The remaining beef had turned dark red and was stuck to the bottom of the dish. For some unknown reason, that beef reminded him of Sakisaka's X-ray which he had been shown the other day in the hospital. Maybe the light-grey cavities he had seen on that photograph reminded him of the frothy liquid left on the dish.

'Whilst here, they come into contact with the best that art can offer. In Paris, you can see for yourself paintings and sculptures produced by the rarest of talents. They are inspired by such works . . . but such works gradually dry them up.'

In contrast to their previous meeting, this time Manabe spoke softly. The young artists also listened in silence.

'Everyone would like to create a first-rate piece of art, right? But included amongst us are those who, try as they might, can only produce second-rate work. He can spend the rest of his life trying, but a second-rate artist will never create a first-rate work of art.

There is a sense of destiny involved here. It's a depressing thought, but the second-rate artist has to come to terms with that fact sooner or later. Paris is the sort of town that is painfully honest in revealing to us, during even the shortest of visits, the exact extent of our ability. It's only the most dull-witted among us who can come here and still not recognize the limits of their ability and true destiny. There are swarms of such dull-witted people around Montparnasse and Montmartre. But ... they'll pay the price for their presumption – for having posed as first-rate artists.'

Manabe raised his drunken head and spat out his words with remorse. It was as though, during his stay in Paris, he had been forced to accept that he was no more than a second-rate writer. For a second the sorrow of that realization flashed across his blurred eyes. The only one to detect it was Tanaka; the young artists who were convinced that Manabe was directing his sarcasm at Sakisaka just stared at the two of them with intense curiosity.

'I don't want to have to face such a fate. At any rate, I don't want to become like Todo or Kohara. That's why I'm going back. I suppose I'm only a third-rate writer in comparison with some of the French novelists – just like you said that night in Montparnasse. No, I'm not being sarcastic or putting myself down. I've been thinking about that during my stay in Paris. But I'd still like to say the same to Sakisaka. I feel really sorry for him getting sick like that. But perhaps his illness is a blessing in disguise.'

Tanaka understood exactly what Manabe was trying to say. But there is a difference between understanding and agreeing. He lowered his gaze to the cigarette he had allowed to go out.

'I suppose Sakisaka-kun will be returning to Japan for treatment, won't he? When he recovers I suppose he'll find work in Japan as an architect. Over there, he'll lead the kind of life the artists over here would describe as a "failure". Even if he were to become a first-rate architect in Japan, his works would probably still be considered no more than third rate over here. But which is better, to overestimate one's ability and end up miserable over here or to accept one's limitations as a third-rate artist and to live one's life accordingly?'

Tanaka thought of the hospital. He recalled Sakisaka sitting in the taxi on the way to the hospital on that snowy day, his face pressed up against the window drinking in the views of the snow-covered place du Louvre and the place de la Concorde.

'But Sakisaka will be plagued by a sense of disappointment for the rest of his life.'

'Of course.' Manabe suddenly raised his voice, causing the guests at the nearby tables to look up in surprise. 'You sound like a spoilt child! Third-rate artists have to live out the rest of their solitary lives in the knowledge that they are not first-rate artists. That's obvious.'

'I see.' Tanaka nodded and apologized dutifully. 'That was my mistake. I take it back.'

The young artists began to smile gently at the cornered Tanaka. But Manabe seemed to pour contempt on them as he continued. 'Tanaka-kun, don't take offence. This lot don't understand a thing. Thanks for your apology ... but I just wonder how much you students of foreign literature really understand the loneliness of the second-rate artist. I really wonder.'

'Hmm, I wonder.' Tanaka merely threw Manabe's words back at him in a sullen manner. 'We had the same discussion the other day, didn't we?'

'But say you translate Valéry. If you do, you start convincing yourself that you, like Valéry, have become a first-rate artist. "Camus said this. Sartre said that." Before you know it, you start speaking as if you are in exact agreement. I get that feeling every time I read essays written by students of foreign literature. But you lot are not Camus. You're not Valéry. You students are not as smart as these first-rate artists.'

'I agree.'

'No, don't just tell me you agree to shut me up. Tanaka-kun, you don't understand. You have yet to experience the desolate realization that you are no more than a mina bird. If we are third rate, then you, too, are third rate.'

'Because I am third rate, I busy myself reading first-rate writers. That's the role of the student of foreign literature as far as I'm concerned.'

'Oh, really? I see. When you have accepted that as your cruel destiny, perhaps you and I will be able to discuss this at greater length.' Manabe blinked and spoke in a deliberate tone.

Tanaka was painfully aware that everything Manabe had just said about students of foreign literature was equally applicable to Manabe himself. In Paris Manabe, like Sakisaka, must have looked at first-rate works of art and suffered in his own way. He must have been brought face to face with his own limitations. The writer looked mortified and continued to drink in silence.

Tanaka visited the hospital on the day Sakisaka was due to leave for Japan. It was a typically grey afternoon. Outside the hotel a blind man was playing some melancholy pieces on an accordion. Tanaka went to the boulevard Jourdan by bus. But when he arrived at the hospital, Sakisaka's bed was empty and the three other patients in the room sat in their pyjamas dangling their feet over the edge of their beds. They were chatting quietly.

'Messieurs.' Tanaka muttered this by way of greeting and the men stopped talking and looked round at him.

One of them, violently scratching the crop of chestnut-coloured hair on his chest, addressed Tanaka. 'He's having an examination right now. Another Japanese man came to visit him a short while ago.'

Tanaka had no idea who that might have been. He went out into the corridor with its smell of cresol, but there was no one who seemed to answer to that description. He sat down on a small chair and waited for the patient to return, whereupon one of the other patients was considerate enough to lend him a newspaper.

When Tanaka asked him about Sakisaka's condition, the patient smiled wanly and pointed to the side of Sakisaka's bed. Hanging from the bed was a chart with a red line which presumably mapped Sakisaka's temperature. The red line was interrupted in places by the occasional sharp bump. This was clear evidence that Sakisaka's intermittent fever showed no signs of abating. Tanaka blinked and placed the chart on his knee. He couldn't help wondering whether Sakisaka was well enough to spend over a day in a plane as he returned to Japan.

A pale-faced Sakisaka returned to the room, his gown thrown over his shoulders. Breathing heavily, he exclaimed, 'Hey. You've come again today? I've just been to thank the doctor who's been looking after me, and on the way I had to pop in for a quick examination.'

'Can I do anything?'

'No. Everything's fine. I asked Kohara-san to get me a ticket and Todo is seeing to the necessary formalities at the embassy. They

137

make their living from helping Japanese out like that.'

'Apparently you had another Japanese visitor before me.'

'It was probably Todo-san. Don't you know him?'

It seemed that this Todo was the same failed artist whom Manabe had so maligned in the Botanya the other night. Tanaka was curious to meet him.

'About the luggage I told you I've left in the hotel, could you ask them to ship it to Japan by sea mail?'

Tanaka replied that he was only too happy to oblige. Removing some clothes from the case under the bed, the architect stared at them for a while.

Changing into these clothes, he walked to each of the other three beds in the room, shook hands with their occupants and left the room. There was a distinct note of sadness in the smiles on the faces of the other patients as they wished 'Bon voyage' and 'Ayez courage' to the Japanese patient about to return to his homeland.

As Tanaka went out into the hushed corridor carrying Sakisaka's bag, another Japanese man was walking towards him. There was something arrogant about his gait. He was wearing a duffle-coat, so popular among students at the Sorbonne, but he must have been forty-five or six. Tanaka realized that this was the Todo of whom Manabe and the other artists had spoken.

'Sakisaka-kun. I've sorted out everything to do with your visa at the embassy. Here's your passport. Everything you asked me to do is taken care of.'

Sakisaka thanked him and took out a white envelope from his pocket. 'It's not much. But please take it as a token of my appreciation.'

'What? You needn't have bothered.' But as he spoke, Todo extended a large hand and took the envelope. The dirt was clearly visible under his fingernails. 'Really? In which case, thank you very much.'

When they stepped outside, the cold air assailed their cheeks and nostrils. The Parisian winter was different from winter in Japan in its lack of blue sky; but the air was still dry.

'You still have two hours before your flight.' Todo had thrust his hands deep in his pockets as he walked. 'What do you want to do?'

'Todo-san, I want to form one final lasting impression of Paris.' Sakisaka had buried his chin in his camel-coloured scarf as he pleaded weakly with his friend. 'I don't mind if it's the Louvre or the Seine.'

'I suppose everyone's the same right before they go home. I understand just how you feel. Truly I understand. To me, Paris is just like Tokyo, but when you're about to leave the country I'm sure that desire must be stronger than ever.'

Todo stood in the middle of the road and laughed so loudly that the passing French women could only stop and stare.

They caught a taxi and Sakisaka sat down in the corner and carefully arranged the hem of his coat on his knees. He appeared even thinner than he had in the hotel. His face was grey. The period in the hospital did not seem to have made much visible improvement to his health. As the taxi moved off, Sakisaka pushed his face against the window, just as he had on the way to the hospital. He was clearly intent on remembering every detail of this Paris scenery: the street-cleaners sweeping up the leaves which had fallen from the horse-chestnut trees, the patrons reading their newspapers in the cafés ... everything as far as the eye could see.

'Sakisaka-kun, I have a favour to ask.' Todo chose to ignore the architect's sensibilities. 'Will you listen to me?'

'What is it?'

'Have you any contacts with any publishers in Tokyo?'

'Well, I do have some. But there's only a limited number of firms willing to publish the kind of articles we architects write.'

'It doesn't matter. If any of them need a hand with bookbinding, please tell them about me.'

Sakisaka looked uneasy. Tanaka sensed that he wished to be left in peace. They could see the place de Denfert out of the left-hand window. A newspaper-seller was arranging copies of *Paris Match* and *France Soir* on his stall. A flock of pigeons flew up from the church of St Potan and disappeared into the grey sky. Each of these must have revived memories of his period of study in Paris. Not surprisingly Sakisaka was intent on immersing himself in such thoughts in silence.

'Sakisaka-kun, please see what you can do.'

'Very well, I'll ask them ... but I have no idea what they'll say.'

'Please remember that I have to work to live. Perhaps you could help me sell my paintings?'

Tanaka stared at Todo's fingers as he took out an old pipe from the pocket of his overcoat and filled it with tobacco. Not only were his fingernails filthy but his hands were covered in paint.

'How long have you been living in Paris?' Tanaka spoke merely in order to leave Sakisaka in peace. 'I hear you've been here quite some time.'

'Me? I've been here about twelve years. I must have been one of the first Japanese to visit France after the war. At that time there was no peace treaty or anything. Japan was a defeated nation and so there was no embassy. It was only after I had been here for two years that they created what was called an overseas consular agency.'

'Do you have no wish to return to Japan?'

'Not really. Not in the immediate future. My wife has given up the idea. People like Kono and Furui came after me. Do you know either of them?'

'Yes. They're famous in Japan. They must be among the most active mainstream artists around. They are always on the radio and television.' Tanaka spoke with deliberation and there was a hint of sarcasm in his smile as he stared at Todo. Just as he had expected, Todo's face contorted with a look of ugly jealousy.

'Yes, radio and television ... they're all the same. Japanese journalists are so easily taken in. All you have to do is something just slightly out of the ordinary and they'll come running after you. Kono's paintings are just imitations of Luo, but the critics love that. That's what's so nice about the place.'

'How about your paintings?'

'My paintings? See for yourself. I shouldn't say this about myself, but the other day Morisot came to my studio and pronounced my work *formidable*. He said that next time he would come with a Swedish art dealer.'

The taxi was passing slowly along the Anatole France bank of the river. The bank itself stretched on for miles, and they had presumably named this section of the bank after the author of 'Thais, the Dancing Girl', since he was so fond of walking along the side of the river.

They could make out the cathedral of Notre-Dame, which seemed to rise up out of the river into the mist. There was now only a limited number of second-hand bookstores along the river-bank. In the old days this area was famous as a place where any number of rare books could be found, but now it was hard to find decent books there at all. Sakisaka went on staring out of the window, his chin in his scarf, and Todo continued maligning those Japanese artists who had returned to Japan. There was something unattractive about that face, contorted with jealousy. It was the face of a defeated man, the face of a man who had destroyed himself by living in Paris too long. It was just as the novelist Manabe had said. His self-respect would not allow him to return to Japan; and yet he had become blind to his limitations and, in his anxiety, had ended up floundering like a piece of driftwood. Tanaka wondered how many such people there were in Paris. Perhaps the same thing would have happened to Sakisaka. Perhaps the fact that he had been forced to return home because of sickness was indeed a blessing in disguise.

'It's nearly time. Shall we make for the airport?'

As they made for Orly airport, Tanaka found himself recalling the night of his arrival in Paris. What a miserable, rainy night it had been! He remembered how he had sat shaking timidly in the bus bound for the city, unable to speak a word of French! In another year or so he too would probably pass along the same road to the airport on his way back to Japan. Or would he, like Sakisaka, become so captivated by the charm of the place that he ended up deciding to stay?

At the airport a Customs official took one look at Sakisaka carrying his suitcase and a small parcel and asked him to open up the parcel. This was the signal for Todo to become embroiled in a heated discussion with him. Listening to Todo's clumsy, ungrammatical French, it was easy to imagine how he had spent the past ten or more years in Paris ignoring his basic studies.

'The French have become more and more stingy. Even Customs officials solicit tips these days.' Todo shouted out in Japanese, which was unintelligible to the official, 'I've been here over ten years, so I know what's what around here. I'll teach him to start fooling around with me!'

There were three or four Japanese standing in the lobby. Amongst them Tanaka could make out Ono talking to a tall French youth wearing a beret. Before Tanaka could hide behind a pillar, Ono caught sight of him and said, 'You're late. We've been here over twenty minutes.' For some reason Ono had raised his hand as he shouted, 'We've just heard that the plane's going to be a bit late arriving.'

'Have you come to meet someone?'

'What! Haven't you heard?' The way Ono blinked suggested disappointment. 'You're kidding! Didn't you know that Suganuma is arriving today? He's from your university, after all!'

7

Noticing the sudden change in Tanaka's manner, Ono stopped short in embarrassment. He looked round awkwardly, only to spot Sakisaka walking towards the lobby with Todo carrying his Boston bag. Ono looked even more perturbed.

'Hey! So you're leaving today, are you, Sakisaka-kun?' Then, lowering his voice, he continued, 'So he really has got to go home. Poor man! He's so ill he's got to go home, has he?' But his voice lacked sincerity.

Sakisaka for his part stopped short in confusion. For a moment he looked around him, unable to grasp what this group was doing at the airport. He was unaware of Suganuma's impending arrival.

'Well, how are you feeling?' Ono hurried to ease the tension. 'I'm really sorry I haven't been to see you even once since you entered the hospital. I kept planning to go, but every day seems to have been filled with meaningless chores.'

'That's quite all right. I know how busy you must be.' Sakisaka smiled wanly and smothered a couple of dry coughs in his scarf.

'We've come here for another reason. But what good timing! This way, we'll be able to see you off too – if you'll excuse the expression. What time's your flight? What! Really? Well, you'll have to go through Customs fairly soon.'

Sakisaka nodded in agreement and relieved Todo of the bulging Boston bag. The small bag looked really heavy in Sakisaka's emaciated hand.

'Well, I'll be going.' Sakisaka looked up at Tanaka and spoke in a whisper. His grey face was slightly swollen. 'Tanaka-kun, don't end up like me.'

'Sakisaka-kun.' It was Todo, who had been standing to one side, who spoke. 'When you get home, please don't forget what I asked you in the taxi. It doesn't matter which publisher. If you hear of any bookbinding jobs, please ask them to contact me over here.'

Sakisaka shrugged his shoulders around which hung the Boston bag and dragged his feet down the staircase to the Customs area. Half-way down he paused, took a deep breath and looked back at the group. After that, he did not look round again before disappearing from sight.

That was that. In a sense it was inevitable. But somehow, given that Sakisaka was leaving for Japan and the rest were staying behind in Paris, it was all too anticlimactic and brief.

'I don't suppose he'll come back.' Ono was staring at the stairs and mumbling to himself.

It was Todo, standing next to Ono, who responded.

'But if you're the sort of person who gets sick wherever you go, you shouldn't come to a place like Paris. I never get sick, wherever I go.' Todo yawned and, rubbing his shoulders, stared out at the setting sun shining on the airport.

A young French girl wearing a hat and surrounded by five or six men was casting an occasional glance in their direction.

'Ono-san, you're still waiting for someone, aren't you? Or shall we go home?'

The two of them seemed to have totally forgotten about Sakisaka who had left them only moments before. Two people may come together while they are in Paris, but as soon as one of them has to leave, then it is as though they had never met in the first place. That was because both of them looked on themselves as tourists in Paris and were living their lives accordingly. In the distance they could hear the piercing roar of an aircraft engine.

'Tanaka-san, what are you going to do?'

'Actually ... I've got some things to see to right now.' Tanaka tried not to look at Ono as he spoke to Todo. Ono remained silent. 'Well. Sorry to leave you. I'll be seeing you around.'

'I see. You're going, are you?' Ono touched his beret perfunctorily as he said goodbye to them.

They passed through Dijon in the early afternoon. As the train reduced speed somewhat, they could make out the long fence of a factory and the whitish plaster of a house. The blinds on the

143

window had been drawn and two or three shirts and handkerchiefs were hanging from the curtain-rail. This was the rural town where Edouard Estaunié was born and where Baudelaire had lived for some time. As he wiped the dirty window, Tanaka recalled that the philosopher Maurice Blondel had also been born there. On the seat opposite sat a middle-aged Frenchman reading the paper. Every now and then he would stop to chew a Camembert sandwich placed in a bag on the seat beside him. The other four seats in the compartment were empty, but a sign reading *Occupée* had been placed on each of these. For some time now a woman of about thirty wearing a mock fur coat had been leaning on the window in the corridor outside smoking a cigarette. Unlike the Japanese trains Tanaka was used to, this train had only the one corridor down one side of the compartment. Standing a little way away from her stood a short soldier. From the way he glanced furtively in her direction, it was clear that he was looking for a chance to start a conversation.

'It was so sudden....' Tanaka was staring vacantly out of the window. 'I wonder why I decided to leave Paris so suddenly like that.'

Obviously the excuse for this trip was to take a look at Marseille, the scene of Sade's infamous 'Bonbon incident'. Yet if that had been the only motivation, there was no reason for rushing into it like that. He could equally well have waited until spring, which was a much more convenient season for touring France. Especially since his spontaneous departure from Paris entailed missing some of Professor Bady's Sorbonne lectures which he had been attending so dutifully, there was no need to take off right then, just before the spring vacation.

Of course Tanaka was well aware why he had taken off like that. He was reluctant to meet Suganuma. He hated to admit it, but even though Suganuma had just arrived in Paris, Tanaka felt no obligation to take the initiative and go to see him. Given that he was Suganuma's senior at the university and had preceded him to France, Tanaka was very offended by the way in which Suganuma had chosen to come to Paris without so much as a word of warning. Moreover, he had no idea why he had been snubbed in this way by both Suganuma and Assistant Professor Imai. The more he thought of possible reasons, the more intense did his vague sense of uneasiness become. When he tried to picture the displeasure he was bound to feel when Suganuma tried to explain the situation, his melancholy merely increased. Sooner or later he would presumably have to meet him. But he was trying to put off that day as long as he possibly could.

The conductor, carrying a bell, arrived to take reservations for the restaurant car. For lunch it would be better to buy some sandwiches at Lyon. The wintry fields appeared endless under the leaden sky. Apparently it had snowed a couple of days earlier, for every now and then they would pass piles of snow blackened by smoke from the passing trains.

I bet he'll get along perfectly well in Paris too. Tanaka could picture Suganuma's swarthy, compact appearance and could well imagine the kind of life-style his junior would lead in Paris. He would visit some of the Japanese journalists assigned to Paris. This was important in order to keep up the constant stream of articles he would be sending back to Japan. He would already be on friendly terms with the French literature specialists like Ono and some of the other artists. And, having decided on a research project that would bring positive results, he would already be busily at work. Obviously there would be no respite in the stream of letters he sent back to Assistant Professor Imai.

But so what? Pushing up his glasses with his finger, Tanaka inwardly tried to laugh such a life-style to scorn. What on earth's the point of coming all this way just to carry on like that? Yet Tanaka himself was the first to realize that such an attitude of scorn reflected on himself. If the truth be known, he wished that he too were able to spend his time abroad living the kind of life-style he was now imagining would be Suganuma's. He wished that he too could use his experience studying abroad in preparation for greater success upon his return home. If not, there was no accounting for the feelings of self-pride and happiness he had experienced upon his arrival in Paris. Yet, for some reason or other, in his case it seemed as though he was losing sight of such feelings with every passing day. It was as though it had been on that rainy night when he had landed in Paris that he had first started to slip out of gear. And yet he had no idea what it was that had caused the gears to start slipping.

The man reading the paper was staring at him from behind his newspaper. When their eyes met, he abruptly averted his gaze.

Tanaka stared at his own reflection in the window. He looked tired. His cheekbones were sunken and his forehead ran with sweat. He had definitely lost weight since his arrival in France. His life-style was not that irregular; it was just tiring to live in that city of stone houses and stone streets. Tanaka closed his eyes and told himself that he must not end up like Sakisaka.

About half an hour later he took his bag down from the luggage-rack and pulled out his notebook. He looked at the documents about the 'Bonbon incident' that Sade had perpetrated in Marseille. Of course he knew virtually everything there was to know about this incident; but he wanted to arrange everything clearly in his mind before arriving in Marseille. He looked at his watch. It was 2.30. They should be in Lyon in another twenty minutes.

The incident had occurred in June of 1772. In the middle of that month Sade had left his château in La Coste for Marseille. Accompanied by his manservant, Armand, his plan was to raise some money there. On 25th June Armand contacted one Marianne Laverne in Marseille. She was a prostitute from a brothel called the Nicholas in the town of Aubagne. Receiving directions to the Nicholas, Armand had visited the brothel that day and informed three of the prostitutes there – Marianette, Marianne and Rose – that his master would be visiting them the following day.

On the following day Sade was taken to the Nicholas by Armand. On seeing the outside of the building, he must have thought that the brothel was too conspicuous, for he ordered the women to report to the house of the prostitute Mariette located in the nearby rue des Capucins by ten o'clock that morning. When the women appeared at ten o'clock, Sade drew a wad of money from his wallet, held it in his hand and declared his intention to choose as his first partner the woman who could guess the amount accurately. It was Marianne who guessed correctly. Having sent the other women out of the room, the Marquis ordered his servant, Armand, and Marianne to lie down on the bed. Then, while beating Marianne with a whip, he ordered Armand to arouse him. When this was over, he told Armand to leave the room, took out a gold-rimmed container and offered the woman one of the sweets inside. Marianne dutifully obeyed. But on placing one of the sweets in her mouth, she is said to have remarked that it tasted like fennel. Sade

146

explained to her that what she could taste was some kind of stomach medicine and made her eat seven or eight of the sweets. When she had finished, he asked her whether she wanted to engage in some kind of sexual deviation with either himself or with his servant. But not surprisingly, since the punishment for homo-sexuality and adultery in those days was death, the woman refused.

At that point Sade took a strange object from his pocket. It was a sheepskin whip. On the tip of the whip was a blood-stained, bent nail.

Sade ordered the woman to beat him with that whip. Reluctant-ly, Marianne beat him two or three times. But when she refused to continue, he ordered her to go and buy a broom. She left the room and ordered her maid, Lemaire, who was busy working in the kitchen, to carry out that order. With this broom, which the maid managed to pick up for one sou, Marianne began beating Sade more forcefully than before. It was at this stage she was seized by a violent stomach-ache and had to leave the room in agony.

Sade led the second woman, Mariette, into the room, and made her strip and kneel at the end of the bed. Having beaten her with the broom, he ordered her to beat him in a similar manner. As the beating continued, Sade recorded the number of blows he had received by carving notches with a knife on the mantelpiece. The number recorded was some eight hundred! Immediately afterwards Sade lay down on the bed with both the woman and Armand.

When he had finished with Mariette, it was Rose's turn. Having been forced to make love with Armand, she too was beaten by Sade. The next victim was Marianette. But catching sight of the blood-stained whip which was thrown down on the bed when she entered the room, she rushed out screaming.

The Marquis caught up with her, called Marianne who, for some time now, had been suffering from a severe stomach-ache in the kitchen and had the maid bring in some coffee. Whereupon he ordered both Marianne and Marianette to eat the sweets. Of course Marianne refused, but Marianette helped herself – only to spit one out as soon as she began to eat it. Sade then put his head close to Marianne's buttocks and savoured the smell.

The women began crying and tried to escape. Eventually, having threatened them severely, Sade handed a sum of money to each woman and allowed them to return home.

That evening Armand returned to the Nicholas and invited the women again. Not surprisingly his entreaties were refused. On his way back he found a prostitute, Marguerite Coste, an inhabitant of the rue Saint-Ferréol-le-Vieux, and solicited her services. On hearing his servant's report, the Marquis visited her at her home and urged her to perform various perverted sexual practices. But Marguerite refused on the grounds that she would not indulge in sexual deviation. At that point she was enticed to eat Sade's famous sweets and apparently consumed a considerable number.

On 30th June an investigation was ordered by the Marseille district court. The incident had come to light as a result of her severe stomach-pains and the black liquid mixed with blood that Marguerite had been coughing up since the 27th. Mariette and the other three women had subsequently been subjected to cross-examination. The unusual nature of the case attracted widespread public interest. Especially because the case involved the capital offences of homosexuality and sodomy, news of the incident spread rapidly.

On 4th July a summons for the arrest of Sade and his servant was issued. Informed of the imminent danger, Sade left La Coste with his sister-in-law Anne-Prospère and Armand and headed for Italy. By this time, the relationship between Sade and his sister-in-law had already changed from that of brother and sister and developed into that between a man and his lover.

Raising his eyes from his copy of the chronology of Sade's life, Tanaka noticed the golden rays of the afternoon sun which rained down on to the meadows like sheaves of corn. On the far side of the meadow some moist grey clouds could be seen floating by. There was a town beneath the clouds, sprawled out like an animal. It was Lyon. Whether because of tiredness or the noise of the train, he was less enthralled by the chronology of Sade's life than usual. He rubbed his tired eyes with his finger and tried to reflect on the two aspects of this incident which have been considered most significant. Tanaka was obviously aware of the emphasis placed by Simone de Beauvoir on the fact that this 'Bonbon incident' of Marseille manifested masochism, homosexuality, voyeurism and other acts of sexual deviation in addition to the inevitable 'Sadism'. Sade was basically the sort of man who was determined to observe himself detachedly even in the heights of passion. De Beauvoir had expressed her opinion that the objectivity with which Sade had examined his own actions was actually an example of 'the sense of unhappiness that weighed heavily upon Sade'. The act of having himself beaten by a woman and then calmly recording the number of blows with knife marks on the mantelpiece was suggestive of the detachment he evidenced consistently, and on such occasions one could detect the other Sade, coolly contemplating his own beaten body and his aroused passions. Nevertheless, in his desire to scrutinize his own physical being, it must have needed considerable effort on his part to keep alive sexual desires which were liable to dissipate like a burnt-out candle. It was de Beauvoir's contention that it was as a result of such efforts that, in addition to sadism, Sade had resorted to a constant round of masochism, homosexuality, sodomy, exhibitionism and various other acts of sexual deviation. It was possible for Tanaka, who had steeped himself in such interpretations of the Marseille incident, to abandon himself to the rolling of the train and recall each individual detail of the incident just as though he were reviewing a chart of mathematical formulae he had committed to memory. It was like those times when in the train as a junior high-school student on the way to an exam he would think up a problem for himself and then try to solve it.

At the same time Tanaka sensed the unfathomable distance which existed between the contents of these essays and himself. The various aspects of the Marseille incident failed to take root in his heart.

Leaning against the window, Tanaka began to ask himself what possible relationship there could be between the Marseille incident and himself. What possible connection could exist between his own life and the details of this incident in Sade's life?

It was almost as if the monotonous noise of the train were provoking him with such questions. Tanaka stood up, opened the door and went out into the corridor. The woman in the fur coat whom he had seen earlier smoking there was now standing outside the toilet, laughing and joking with the soldier. As Tanaka stood in the toilet, it occurred to him that, unlike that soldier, not once in his own life had he become involved with a woman he had met by chance. The woman's piercing voice penetrated the door of the toilet and he could hear every word she said. What possible connection could there be between Sade, who had never abandoned himself even when engaged in the dark acts of the flesh, and Tanaka, who knew nothing of such acts? But more than that, he wondered why Sade had remained so callous.

When Tanaka had washed his hands and gone outside again, the soldier and the woman glanced at him. The soldier's eye was somewhat bloodshot. Whilst Tanaka had been in the toilet, they had obviously been kissing.

Even after Tanaka returned to his seat, he could find nothing to counteract his feeling of emptiness. His future was clearly tied up with the foreign literature with which he was constantly grappling; but he persisted in maintaining a proper distance between the object of his studies and his own way of life.

'I just don't understand why you are studying Sade.' He could clearly recall the searing pain he had felt on hearing those words that afternoon in the house behind St Sulpice: and how could he forget Gilbert Ruby's wily little eyes as he spoke?

The small hotel in which Tanaka decided to spend the night was by the harbour. The harbour was full of yellowish-brown boats which looked like junks. There were also white boats leaving the pier bound for the Château d'If of *The Count of Monte Cristo* fame. Even with the blinds drawn, the shouts of men carrying their loads down by the harbour flooded into his room along with the rays of the evening sun. The hotel was surrounded by other cheap hotels and small seafood restaurants; and from these Tanaka chose the one that appeared to offer the cheapest food and satisfied himself with a bowl of bouillabaisse for his dinner. He was the only guest in the restaurant, whose grimy walls were alive with cockroaches. In a corner stood a basket full of oysters and cockle-shells, and every now and then a couple of dockers from the harbour would enter and ask the portly proprietress to crack open some of the oysters. Holding the shells up to their mouths, they would then drink the juice and leave.

Staring at the stains on the ceiling, Tanaka could hear from somewhere in the hotel the sound of somebody slamming a door and using the toilet. He suddenly found himself wondering how Suganuma would spend such an evening. No doubt he would treat himself to the opera or some such entertainment. Even an employee from one of the Japanese companies who had just arrived in France would not be so stupid as to come all the way to Marseille just to spend an evening sprawled out on a rickety bed in some cheap hotel. At the very least he would go out to a local bar and amuse himself with some French woman. Tanaka recalled the two women he had spotted hanging around by the harbour. He could tell from a glance that they were prostitutes. Why was he unable to act like Suganuma or any other Japanese? He had no idea. It seemed as though, during the long, dreary Paris winter, he had become more reserved and isolated than before. He rose from his bed and took up the two or three picture postcards he had purchased earlier from the tobacconist's next to the hotel. As he stood there staring at them, he felt utterly miserable. The pictures on the postcards were poor reproductions: one showed that famous landmark in Marseille, Notre-Dame cathedral, the other the white remains of the prison at the Château d'If.

He took up his pen and began a letter to his wife, Kikue. He could hear the shrill voice of a woman coming from the next room. Listening to her laugh, Tanaka was reminded of the woman of about thirty he had seen earlier, cigarette in mouth, leaning against the railing in the corridor of the train. He also recalled the bloodshot eyes of the short soldier looking round at him as he had emerged from the toilet.

'I'm in Marseille and doing fine. How's Keiichi?' Having written that much, Tanaka suddenly sensed the face of the baby he had not seen for such a long time looking down at him. It was all he could do not to weep, so strong was his urge to see his baby again. Strangely enough, his wife appeared to have receded into some vague and distant existence; but the face of his young child, that tender young body, appeared painfully vivid before his eyes. Repositioning his glasses with his finger, Tanaka recalled their small house in Setagaya. The fence and the stripes cast by the sun's rays. The house with the nappies and shirts hanging up to dry. The asphalt road running right in front of the house. The bicycle store with its old bicycles for sale on the corner of the road. The haberdashery next to that; and beside it the small lending library. He could see each of the stores on the road leading to the Odakyu line station. He felt a sudden urge to return home – to return home and embrace his child. The sound of a siren could be heard through the blinds. This was Marseille. He was here, caught up in the salty smell of the Marseille night.

Tanaka doubted his own qualifications as a student of literature. He felt more like a perfectly ordinary citizen. Why had someone like himself become involved in the study of Sade? Tanaka wondered whether he wouldn't have done better to pick on some more down-to-earth writer – someone less flamboyant, less ambitious.

'On my way back, I hope to spend some time in a place called La Coste, a place so small it's not even marked on the map. That was where Sade had his château. Please continue with the investment trust. No matter what my father might say, I insist that you do not buy any shares without my permission.'

From the room next door, once more he heard the shrill sound of a woman laughing and the whispered voice of a man rebuking her.

Pen in hand, Tanaka tried to imagine the two of them frolicking around in the room next door. On coming to his senses, he blushed and, in an effort to block out the sound of their voices, covered his ears with his hands. To Tanaka, who had spent no time with any woman since his arrival in Paris, even the sound of a woman's laughter was enough to arouse him.

He took out the notebook he had been studying in the train and began to read. Every day he had been going to the Bibliothèque Nationale and laboriously working on a biography of Sade. This was no more than a draft of the paper he would be presenting to his university, but his overall plan and the bare essentials he had by now virtually decided upon.

It appears there are two main catalysts for the sadism that appears in the works of Sade. Firstly it seems that the misogynist approach to life he evidenced from his childhood was nurtured by his hatred of his mother. Distanced from his father, a diplomat, and raised through the efforts of his mother, Sade developed a degree of love and respect for his father which stood in stark contrast to the Oedipus complex experienced by most men. Such feelings of proximity towards his father developed into an attitude of contempt towards his mother. There are frequent references in the works of Sade to the tyrannical struggle between mother and son; and, to borrow Sade's words: 'The male is the only complete form of human; woman is no more than a "deformation" of man.'

152

Tanaka had written that section within a couple of weeks of his arrival in Paris, long before Sakisaka became ill.

Another unique facet of the sadism in the works of Sade was his hatred of young women. As a result of his betrayal by Laure de Lauris, Sade is believed to have been profoundly imbued with a sense of the hypocrisy of young women. He was ultimately to expand this experience into a complete philosophy. In the Christian tradition the virgin is the symbol of purity. For example, the reason why purity is demanded of nuns and the reason why the Virgin Mary is praised stem from the Christian concept of purity. As a result of this betrayal, Sade came to nurture a suspicion of all young women. On the surface, they feign purity with their white and spotless bodies. But those bodies exist purely for the purpose of arousing men. Not only do young girls portray the image of the spotless God, they also represent the power of Satan luring men to sin. But women, feigning ignorance of that fact, adorn themselves with all the feminine virtues. Sade felt a deep sense of resentment towards this contradiction and towards the hypocrisy of young women. In peeling away this mask, he was also peeling away the image of the Christian God. Sade sought to peel away the image of this spotless and orderly creation and replace it with the unconditional energy of Nature.

Tanaka stopped reading with a sigh. Just as had happened in the train, this article of his failed to strike a responsive chord within him and drifted from his mind like sand slipping through his fingers. The words seemed no more than a string of letters that bore absolutely no connection with his own life. It was exactly the sort of thing that the best students write in school exams. Memorized merely so that they can be regurgitated on the answer paper, such ideas were like leaves blowing in the wind. As soon as the answer paper had been handed in, they vanished from the mind. He wondered just which of these thoughts bore any connection with his own inner being. Taking up his fountain-pen, he began drawing a rough line down the side of those false words.

'He was ultimately to expand this experience into a complete philosophy.' He could not argue with that. Even he could do it. It was the next line – 'In the Christian tradition the virgin is the symbol of purity. For example, the reason why purity is demanded of nuns and the reason why the Virgin Mary is praised stem from the Christian concept of purity' – that appeared to belong to a separate and totally unconnected world. And yet it was precisely because Sade had suffered and shed his blood so profusely in that different world that he had 'felt a deep sense of resentment towards . . . the hypocrisy of young women'.

Tanaka drew a thick line against the words 'young women' and 'hypocrisy'. Presumably he could not divorce himself totally from the word 'hypocrisy'. But the concepts of 'hatred of young women' and 'peeling away the image of God' would remain foreign to a Japanese like Tanaka for the rest of his life. Although he was responsible for writing those words, somehow they did not belong to him. It was worse than an auditor filling in the tax information of his clients in the accounts ledger. Yet, were he not to write such things, he would never succeed as a foreign literature specialist. Tanaka fell back on to his bed and stared at the stains on the ceiling.

When he awoke the following morning, a fine drizzle was falling. He could see through the hotel window that the fishing-boats which occupied every available space along the quay were all wet. A fisherman in black oilskins was emptying a box full of fish from one of those boats. People carried umbrellas as they passed by on their way to work. Tanaka boarded a bus in front of the hotel and set off for his destination. He had learnt from his study of the research of Maurice Heine that the little rue des Capucins which Sade had visited during his stay in Marseille in 1772 still existed, between the towns of Aubagne and Feuillan, and that part of the house in which the incident occurred was still intact.

He found the street in question quite easily. Presumably because of the wholesale greengrocer's at the entrance to the street, the wet surface was littered with cabbage leaves and rotten fruit. Several trucks were parked in the street. In front of them several men sporting tattoos on their arms stood around smoking. From the way their arms were folded, clearly they were waiting for work. Tanaka looked carefully at the houses on either side of the street and stopped outside Aubagne No. 50.

The building that stood before him was wet from the rain. There was a small window in the wall, which was so dilapidated it was as if it was afflicted by some skin disease. The window blinds were down. Beneath the window hung a sign that read *Jewellers*, but it was hard to believe that this filthy house was involved in the jewel trade. It was probably more like a pawnbroker's. And yet, if Heine's research were not mistaken, it was to this house that Sade had led the women on that early summer's day. Tanaka looked up at the window and glanced up and down the street. The men were still standing there talking, leaning on their trucks with their arms folded. There must be some kind of factory in the vicinity, for Tanaka could hear the grating sound of an electric saw cutting wood. He steeled himself and pushed open the door. As he did so, he was struck by a smell coming from inside, but he couldn't tell whether it was from the ground or the cement. The staircase leading to the second floor appeared to be the original and there were several places where the surface was badly worn. Evidently these dents had been made by the shoes of those who had climbed up and down. Tanaka was afflicted by exactly the same throbbing feeling he had experienced on his visit to Arcueil. He wanted to grope around and lick those hollows in the stone upon which Sade and the women must have trampled. This was the most positive, the most honest of all his emotions concerning Sade. It was much more closely connected with his real self than any of those comments about Christianity and the image of the young woman to be found in his notebook. Tanaka leant against the wall and began wondering what it was about those hollows in the stone which aroused in him that numbing sensation.

8

That evening he arrived in Avignon. There was a group of people, men and women, the collars of their winter coats turned up against the cold, who were picking up the taxis lined close to the pavement and disappearing in all directions. They had left Marseille in the rain, yet the square in front of the station was covered in a fine layer of powder snow. The sky was dark, but not as dark as the old castle wall which stretched out along the far side of the square.

There was hardly anyone to be seen, and Tanaka started to picture the lively place Avignon must be when the sun was shining. As he repositioned his glasses once more, he found himself for a while staring vacantly out over the square which was illuminated by the light from the street lamps.

In the middle of the castle wall there was a great gate and, beyond that, Tanaka could vaguely make out the red neon signs of a cinema and a café. With his bag in one hand and his camera hanging from his left shoulder, he began to walk through the powder snow. His old shoes left dirty marks on the pavement. The snow seemed to be easing a little.

He planned to spend the night in Avignon and the following morning to head for the village of La Coste where Sade's château stood. He had no idea what he would do if the buses stopped running because of the snow. He knew the French were so lazy that it took only a light shower or wind for the taxis to stop running.

He had no particular hotel in mind, but there was a building diagonally opposite the cinema with a sign that read *Hotel du Midi*. A couple of stars were painted on the sign over the door. Tanaka was aware that all French hotels had such stars painted over the entrance: one could gauge both the quality and the price range of the hotel from the number of stars. As he pushed open the door, he could see a number of couples having supper with their children.

One of the men stood up and informed Tanaka that the only room available was one with a private shower.

Tanaka left his bag at the reception desk and went out once more into the dancing snow. He knew that, if he went straight down the road, he would come to the famous castle of the Pope at Avignon. Since he would be leaving for La Coste early the following morning, this would be his only chance to look around the town. As he walked through the snow, he found himself quietly humming the melody of the children's song he had learnt long before – 'Le Pont d'Avignon', which appeared in every French textbook. He had first learnt the song from his teacher at the crammer for university students. Later on, his graduate students had sung this song at the farewell party they had organized for him at the small restaurant in front of the campus. Tanaka suddenly recalled the smiling face of

Nozaka Kazuko who had been in that group.

As he passed along the road, his cheeks were buffeted by the cold wind. This was the famous mistral that visited the South of France from time to time. The wind and greyish snow formed a thin curtain, on the far side of which he could make out the castle wall and a few towers which appeared to rise up like shadows.

Tanaka tried to convince himself that he would never be able to make his trip the following day. His shoes were now sodden from the snow and his glasses had misted up. It was rather disappointing, especially because he had come all this way, but there was nothing for it but to return to the hotel. When he reached the cinema, he caught sight of a poster with the photograph of a woman he had seen somewhere before. It was the face of Marie Bell, a now almost totally forgotten actress. Above this was a sign indicating that the film currently showing was a really old film called *Un carnet du bal*.

Tanaka stopped and stared at the yellowing photograph. Marie Bell, her hair arranged in a rather outmoded fashion, was looking down on him, her face enveloped in a beaming smile. It made Tanaka recall his own appearance as a pupil at the crammer some eighteen years previously. He remembered a military instructor who, sword in hand, used to shout at the pupils there.

Practically nothing was to be seen in the street and, in view of the ban on American and British films then in force, the cinemas could show only the occasional old French film. Consequently one could see films like *Our Friends, The Squadron of Foreigners* and *White Virgin Land* so frequently one could almost remember them by heart. He recalled the cinema called the Koonza in Shinjuku with its great damp patches on the walls. That cinema concentrated on films like this. The films themselves were covered in scratches and the sound was often poor. And yet to Tanaka, then a nineteen-year-old student, it was only when he was watching such films that he felt a sense of release from the stifling student life.

Looking at his watch, Tanaka saw that it was six o'clock. Calculating that he still had two hours before dinner, he bought a ticket. The smell of the toilet pervaded the whole place. When he opened the door, the light of the attendant's torch came slowly towards him. The sound of a baby crying could be heard coming from a corner of the small cinema.

Advertisements were being shown as he sat down. *Un peu de Vitapointe, beaucoup de beauté*. When the lights came on, a plump woman walked down the aisle selling sweets and chocolate from the basket she was carrying. There were only a few people in the cinema, most of them women who seemed to have dropped in during the course of shopping. With their children on their laps, they greedily licked chocolate ice-creams. And from the broken door on the far side the same smell of the toilet came wafting in.

Tanaka found himself wondering whether to send a postcard to Nozaka Kazuko on these lines:

In the middle of nowhere in France I came across this film which reminded me of one I saw eighteen years ago. Perhaps you don't know the film, but possibly it influenced me enough to change the whole course of my life. I never dreamt I would see such a film in a remote cinema like this filled with the smell from the toilet and the sound of a baby crying.

When he awoke the following morning and opened the window, Tanaka could see patches of blue sky between the dark clouds. The sunlight reflected off the snow was dazzling and he could hear the sound of someone busily raking snow in the street below. The snow had fallen all night long and was piled deep on the roofs and at the foot of the telegraph-poles. A couple of men were busy pushing the snow to one side in front of the cinema. One of the men was digging the signboard with the photograph of Marie Bell out of the snowdrifts. Some children were snowballing. Head in his hands, Tanaka stood at the window for a long time looking at the scene below.

'I want to know about buses to La Coste....' No sooner had Tanaka broached the subject with the woman behind the desk than she shook her head and said that he would probably be unable to get there even by taxi. She eventually agreed to telephone, and was told by the taximan that he would go as far as possible, but that he would need a generous tip.

'What more can you expect with snow like this?' The woman's husband now stood beside her, shrugged his shoulders and pointed out of the window as he spoke. 'And even if you do go to La Coste, there's nothing to see there anyway.'

'What kind of place is it?'

'It's just a small village in the mountains.'

'You can still see the remains of the château, can't you?'

'Was there a château there? I forget now.' He looked at his wife. 'I've never heard of it.'

Even the people of Avignon had not heard of Sade, nor did they know of the remains of his château in La Coste. Just as Ruby had told him, in a couple more years the château would no doubt disappear for good.

The taxi began to pass along the freshly swept road. After they left the town, the scenery to left and right was one vast expanse of white. The road, lined with bald poplars on either side, stretched out in front of them like a great scar. Feeling the cold in his legs, Tanaka put his coat over his knees. A wooden signpost with the legend *Ten kilometres to Châteauneuf* emerged at an angle out of the snow. With the sun reflected off the snow, Tanaka felt a pain in his eyes.

Several trucks and cars had obviously passed by that morning, for the road was just passable. But as they drove past, the trees on either side of the road shook and occasionally great balls of snow fell to the ground with a thud, sending a plume of snow flying in all directions.

'This is getting a bit tricky.' The driver held a cigarette-end between his teeth as he turned round to Tanaka. 'There's no chance of our getting through to La Coste.'

'Can't you do anything?' Tanaka adjusted his glasses and implored, 'Please try to get me there.'

A sign that read *Saumane* stood at a fork in the road. The road for Saumane seemed to stretch endlessly across the white farmland. Tanaka recalled that one section of Saumane, like La Coste, had belonged to the Sade family for generations. But the family had not owned any building in Saumane: they had merely collected rent on some land there.

As they passed by a sign on the left side of the road that read *Goult*, the driver stopped the taxi and opened the window. 'Monsieur, I'm right out of cigarettes,' he said. Then, with a sly smile, he pointed out a white hill on the other side of the farm. 'Well, that's La Coste over there.'

Tanaka was immediately aware that this demand for a cigarette

159

was another way of asking for a generous tip. He held up a five hundred franc note.

'That won't even cover the cost of the petrol!' The driver leered at Tanaka with a look of contempt in his eyes. 'If I had stayed in Avignon, I could have picked up a lot of good fares today too.'

It was not until Tanaka agreed to add an extra thousand francs to his original offer that the taxi once more set off in the direction of La Coste.

'We may well skid. I've really taken on a rough job here.' The driver continued complaining. 'If I mess up the car, I won't even be able to go back.'

But by now Tanaka was paying no attention to the driver. Attempting to overcome the urge to relieve himself which had developed as a result of the cold he had been feeling in his legs, he opened his notebook on top of the coat that lay across his lap. He tried to clarify for himself certain aspects of Sade's life in the château at La Coste.

This château was just one of the places in which Sade had secretly been able to realize his fantasies. Afterwards, every time he was confronted with the criticisms and censure of the people, the Marquis was in the habit of stealing away like a mouse to this small château in the Provence region of France. Provided he lay low there and did not attempt to venture forth, he was assured of a brief respite. That happened on several occasions during the course of his life. It was here that, shortly after his marriage, he had invited the actress Beauvoisin and several members of the local aristocracy and enjoyed some plays and ballet.

It was probably in this château that, in 1776, shortly after the Arcueil and Marseille incidents, Sade had engaged in the Trillet incident. This incident had come to light following a scandal involving Trillet, the daughter of a weaver, whom he had brought from Montpelier, two manservants and a maid called Cavanis. It had also been in this château that Sade had engaged in various acts of dissipation with girls from both Vienna and Lyon.

The château had been destroyed in September 1790. The effects of the French Revolution had spread as far as La Coste and on 17th September the local population had swarmed into the château, looted the furniture and private possessions and then made off. Receiving news of this in Paris, Sade had thundered, 'La Coste, of which I have such beautiful memories, no longer exists. This is the ultimate in despair.'

The hill drew closer and closer to Tanaka. He was overjoyed at having braved the snow to come this far and excited to be looking out over the same scenery at which Sade would have gazed every day. Had it been possible, Tanaka would have liked to get out of the taxi, pick up a stone from the ground and hold it to his cheek. He paused several times to reposition his glasses with his finger and gazed at the ruined village which lay huddled between the mountains. The houses in the village which had been built from crude stones looked like stone huts. They lay scattered on the hillside and, on the peak, stood the ruins of part of a castle. The towers and walls had disappeared and all that remained standing was just a small section of either side of the castle. It was completely destroyed, yet there was no denying that the château had existed. Its ruins lay white with snow under the greyish sky which stretched forth into the distance.

'I can't go any further. Ce n'est pas possible.' The driver shrugged his shoulders as he changed gear into neutral. 'C'est pas possible. The road is not asphalt and so the wheels are just slipping.'

Despite Tanaka's offer of a larger tip, this time the driver just shook his head defiantly.

'I've come all the way from Japan. I've got to see that castle. Can't you do anything?'

'There's nothing for it but to walk.'

'Can't you even go another hundred metres?'

'N'exagérez pas!'

When he got out of the taxi, the snow drove into his face from an angle. It must have been snow that had accumulated on the trees and then been blown off by the wind. The driver's obstinate refusal to continue was hardly surprising. As Tanaka began to ascend the steep slope, the snow grew deeper and deeper. At first it covered only his ankles, but soon his feet sank in almost up to his knees. He struggled for breath with every step. It was almost impossible to go any further. He took out his handkerchief and wiped his glasses and the sweat from his forehead. In the distant village the sound of a dog barking broke the silence of the great white void. Once more dark clouds floated across the sky which had recently shown signs of clearing.

161

'I've come all this way. I've come all this way.' Repeating these words like a parrot, Tanaka rubbed his face with his handkerchief. He had come all the way to La Coste but could not get to the castle. The castle was still a long distance off. There was no way of approaching it.

'I just don't understand why you are studying Sade.... I have no idea why an Oriental like you should be studying Sade.' At that moment he heard a hoarse, melancholy voice. It was the voice of Ruby.

He then recalled the night in Marseille. At that time, as he had re-examined every word he had written in his notebook, he had been forced to admit that they scratched only the surface of his true feelings and failed to give adequate expression to them. Sade 'was ultimately to expand this experience into a complete philosophy'. In peeling away this mask of the young woman, 'he was also peeling away the image of the Christian God'. What did he mean by that? His words still sounded just like those to be found in an accounts ledger. No, they were worse than that. Tanaka realized it was not the snow which prevented him from climbing that hill. It was not the wind and swirling snow which barred his way. It was his own fault that the château at La Coste was so far away. Tanaka stopped, realizing that the reason he was unable to approach the castle was that he had been unable to grasp the true nature of Sade's identity. The wind and snow continued to lash his face and glasses.

'What are you going to do?' The driver was shouting from down below, his hands held to his mouth. Tanaka decided to return to Avignon. He turned his back on the white castle which stood on top of two hills and resolved not to go there ever again.

He did not know why he had chosen the place de la Bastille as the venue for meeting Suganuma. Perhaps his decision had been influenced by his unwillingness to allow Suganuma to see his room.

On his return to Paris, Tanaka had found a letter from Suganuma amongst the pile of mail which had accumulated in his absence. For a long time after he had read his other letters, he left that letter lying on his desk. It would doubtless include an explanation for Suganuma's failure to inform Tanaka of his trip to France – and the reason for Assistant Professor Imai's failure to write to him even once during his stay.

Repositioning his glasses, he sat for a while blinking and staring at that white envelope. There was a look of fear in his eyes. Then gingerly he picked up the envelope.

When he opened the letter, however, he saw that it contained none of the anticipated information. In immaculate handwriting Suganuma merely asked whether it would be convenient for him to visit Tanaka the following Sunday. It was all written with due courtesy.

Tanaka took out one of the postcards he had bought in Marseille and wrote that he would be busy that Sunday but would wait for him the following day at six o'clock in the place de la Bastille.

On the far side of the square he could see some street artists performing. They were gypsies who had attached a boxlike trailer to a truck and wandered the streets of Paris as well as the countryside. Even from his vantage-point, Tanaka could hear the music, with which they hoped to attract some spectators, mixing with the noise of buses and cars. He suddenly recalled with a wave of nostalgia the day, only one year previously, when he had taken his son to the summer festival at the shrine in Setagaya. On that occasion, too, the noise of traffic had mingled with the sound of the drums which the youths of the town were playing. But now they were playing a popular French melody:

> What did Aladdin say
> When he came to Peking?

A young man in a new black overcoat crossed the square from the street on the far side. It was Suganuma.

'Well, this really is "long time, no see".' Suganuma bowed slightly and looked straight into Tanaka's eyes. His face was pale. He looked confident, without a hint of timidity on his face. Rather, it was Tanaka who looked somewhat diffident.

'I called you a few times, but since you were travelling in the South of France . . .'

'It was clever of you to find my address.' For Tanaka, that was the height of sarcasm. But Suganuma chose to ignore it.

'So this is where the Bastille used to be, is it?' Suganuma had both hands deep inside the pockets of his new overcoat.

'Yes. Sade spent some time there.'

'Not only Sade. Voltaire and Mirabeau were held here too. Rimbaud was here as well – and if my memory serves me right, even Lange and Maurelle were brought here.'

Tanaka winced but said nothing for a moment. He pointed out Suganuma's mistake with a look of chagrin. 'Mirabeau wasn't here. He was at Vincennes. He was imprisoned with Sade.'

'Oh, really?' Suganuma did not seem interested in pursuing the point further, but continued: 'Well how's your work on Sade coming along?' He spoke just like an assistant professor grilling one of his students in his study.

'Oh, you know. Not too bad.' Tanaka adjusted his glasses and smiled faintly. 'That's why I went down to the South of France. But how are things at the university? Is everyone all right?'

'Yes.... That's what I've come to speak to you about today.'

The two of them had started walking and crossed the square. The sound of the voices of the street artists gradually grew louder. There was a shop selling candy-floss and waffles. They were pursued from both sides of the street by the voices of men who were busy trying their luck at one of the stalls.

'Is there some kind of festival going on?'

'No. In Paris....' For the first time Tanaka was speaking with an air of authority. 'You can see this all over the place in Paris. Since you've only just arrived, you probably haven't seen any of it yet.'

'You must be angry that I came here without even sending you a letter.' Out of the corner of his eye Suganuma was still looking at the men and women who were brandishing giant metal weights in front of a group of about ten onlookers as he spoke.

'I'm not particularly angry. But I did think it was pretty unfriendly of you.'

'There was something that made it difficult for me to write.'

'What was it? Come on, out with it!' Tanaka was trying his best to adopt a magnanimous tone. 'We mustn't worry about trifles.'

'It makes me feel better to hear you say that....'

Unaware that he was being driven into a trap, Tanaka forgot his feelings of jealousy and anger towards his fellow student both at Orly airport and during his recent trip and a sympathetic smile played about his small mouth.

'I've brought a letter from Mr Imai.' Suganuma took a long

envelope from the inside pocket of his overcoat and, looking Tanaka in the eyes, merely added, 'This is it.'

'Is it all right to read it here?' Tanaka suddenly felt his pulse race as he held the envelope. 'But why didn't Mr Imai write to me direct by air mail?'

'That letter is not so much from Assistant Professor Imai as from the school. It's an important letter. They asked me to hand it to you in person.'

They could hear the laughter of young couples who were enjoying themselves in dodgem cars. Some children licking ice-creams ran between them. Holding the letter firmly in both hands Tanaka read it slowly. When he had finished, he read it through again from the beginning. He could not believe it.

> What did Aladdin say
> When he came to Peking?

'So they're going to farm me out to the School of Liberal Arts, are they?'

'Apparently the French grades of the students in that department are really bad. So the university authorities decided, in conjunction with Assistant Professor Imai, to make you, as the professor in charge, into some kind of powerful lever over there.'

'What about Professor Ueda?'

'Hmm. . . . That's. . . .' Suganuma stared at the ground with a gloomy expression. His face looked grave and sincere. 'I don't really know anything about it. They just asked me to give this letter . . .'

'But what about my position in the department of French literature?' Tanaka was trying not to become over-excited but his voice was shrill. 'What did Mr Imai say about that?'

'Doesn't he mention that in his letter?'

'No, there's nothing here. That's why I'm asking you!' Tanaka had not intended to shout. 'I haven't said anything about wanting to stay in the French department. I'm just saying that, if I am to be sent over to the School of Liberal Arts, I should at least like to clear up some unfinished work in the French department. If they're not explicit on that point, how can I possibly be expected to write a reply?'

Suganuma took his hands out of his coat pocket and quietly

straightened himself in front of Tanaka. 'As a mere assistant, there is no way I can answer that question.'

'Maybe so, but. . . .' Tanaka's small eyes blinked behind his glasses. 'You must follow what I'm saying. Right?' He was almost pleading now. Suganuma was a mere assistant and his junior, but Tanaka was here entreating him and, judging from his expression, desperately trying to ascertain the real meaning behind the letter.

The title 'Professor in Charge, School of Liberal Arts' sounded good, but really it implied that he was being replaced as department lecturer. Professor Ueda would shortly be retiring and then his replacement, Assistant Professor Imai, was planning to join forces with 'his' student, Suganuma, and Motoba, who had been isolated in the economics and law departments, and create deep divisions in the department. Tanaka himself was one of Professor Ueda's students. Thus, as far as Assistant Professor Imai was concerned, he was just an obstruction.

Nevertheless, all hope was not yet lost. Nowhere in this letter was Tanaka specifically ordered to resign his position as lecturer in the French department. He was merely being asked to act as professor in charge of French in the College of Liberal Arts. Perhaps they wanted him to fill two positions. Were that the case, then the situation was totally different.

'I understand.' Tanaka looked up and put the letter back in the envelope. 'I'll write to Mr Imai right away. Well? Do you want to go out for something to eat?'

'Yes, I'd love to, but . . .' – Suganuma shook his head sadly – '. . . I've been invited out by Ono tonight. Apparently he's got some work he wants to talk about.'

Tanaka recalled what Ono had told him that snowy afternoon when he had bumped into him by the Métro station after going to visit Sakisaka. 'Oh yes. I heard about that. From Ono-san.' Tanaka tried to look disinterested. 'He said he's going to translate Cayrol's latest work. But I really wonder if Cayrol will sell in Japan.'

'The H publishing company is going to put out an anthology of world literature, right? They're going to include it in that.'

What was that? This was news to Tanaka. In Japan, H publishing company was showing considerable interest in trans- lations of French novels and criticism. If they were really planning to bring out a series on world literature, it was only to be expected that they would look to the main professors in all the major universities for editorial supervision. Not to be included in this volume as one of the translators was a mark of failure. In particular, it was hard for Tanaka to accept that he, a lecturer, had been overlooked, but Suganuma, a mere assistant, had become involved. 'Oh, really? I see they are still concentrating on contemporary works in Japan.' Feeling his face stiffen, Tanaka tried to give the impression that such a development was not relevant to a specialist of the eighteenth century like himself. 'In that case, it can't be helped. Let's get together and talk properly sometime.'

'Do you mind if I come and see you in your hotel?'

'Please do. Remember, I'm usually out at the university or in the Bibliothèque Nationale till evening. By the way, how are all the other graduate students doing? How about Nozaka-kun, for example?' He spoke with an air of nonchalance. But that was one of the things which Tanaka had been determined to ask about.

On hearing that question, Suganuma's pale face turned red. 'She left graduate school.'

'Left?'

'I meant to tell you about that, too. Actually, I'm engaged to Nozaka.'

Suganuma, dressed in his brand-new coat, crossed the square and disappeared down the entrance of the Métro. Tanaka sat down on one of the benches on the pavement and stayed there motionless for a long time. As before, the voices of the street artists shouting to the passers-by and the laughter of the audience bore down upon him from time to time like a wave.

Where should he make a start in an effort to collect his thoughts? With the events at his university? Or with the anthology of world literature? Depending on how he looked on it, his attitude towards such a venture changed considerably. The reason he was not being included in the list of translators was because , unlike Suganuma, he did not spend all his time devouring modern works but was involved in more scholarly pursuits. That's how he should look at it.

Given that this was a comprehensive anthology, no doubt some eighteenth-century works were to be included in the series. Someone must have translated something by Rousseau.

Maybe Hayakawa of M University. Or Saeki of F University. If such people were to be included, there was no reason whatsoever why Assistant Professor Imai should not have recommended Tanaka as well. Perhaps the reason he hadn't recommended him was because he was planning to farm him out to the School of Liberal Arts. In which case, was he to be deprived of his position as lecturer in the French department? And was Suganuma to take over from him on his return from France? Tanaka suddenly began frantically examining his self-doubt for some straw to which he could cling. He was aware that he was creating his own problems as a result of his suspicious nature. Perhaps Professor Imai had been in no position to influence decisions about the anthology. He could hardly attribute his exclusion from the list of translators entirely to the guile of Professor Imai. He decided to reread the letter. He should make no decision until after he had received Professor Imai's reply. Everything that he was currently contemplating was pure conjecture.

> What did Aladdin say
> When he came to Peking?

But there was one other unpleasant fact – about Nozaka Kazuko. Why did he find the thought of her marrying Suganuma so distasteful? He had never felt any particular attraction for that student. It was nothing to do with him whom she chose to marry.

Tanaka recalled the night of the first meeting of the French literature society at his university. After the meeting there had been a party for all those graduate students who had helped out in any way. On that occasion, too, he had spoken ill of Suganuma.

'I don't deny his ability. But what about his standing as a true scholar? He shouldn't be trying so hard to curry favour with the media.' He had noticed the face of Nozaka Kazuko smiling at him. Or to be more precise: not only had he noticed it . . . he was actually speaking with it in mind. He had chosen to interpret her smile as a sign of agreement with his opinion. Since they both lived in Setagaya, at the end of the meeting the two of them had shared a taxi from Shibuya to Kamimachi and, during the trip, he had offered her advice about her graduation thesis.

'You're going to work on Camus, are you? All the female

students like Camus.'

'You are always saying things like that, Tanaka-sensei.' Nozaka Kazuko's voice sounded excited as she rested her head in her hands. 'My face feels so hot. I must be really red. It's your fault, sensei … you kept on telling me to drink like that!'

The road from Kamimachi to Miyanosaka had frequent sharp bends and she had bumped against Tanaka. Then she had placed her delicate hand on his knee. Even Tanaka did not know why he had taken her hand at that moment. It was not something a coward like him tended to do. A sense of pride and fear of being shamed made him completely passive with women. But Nozaka Kazuko had not tried to remove the hand he was holding. When he had applied pressure with his fingers, her fingers had responded. Then the taxi had drawn close to her parents' house.

On the day of his departure for France Nozaka Kazuko had presumably come with some of the other students to see him off and, on meeting him in the lobby at Haneda airport, had handed him a box tied with a thin pink ribbon. He had opened the box in the plane and discovered that it contained a tie and a letter. In the letter she had written: 'Tanaka-sensei, look after yourself. Even in France, please don't forget us – especially me, your female student.' During the trip from Anchorage to Hamburg Tanaka had read and reread that letter, saturated as it was with the scent of perfume. He sensed a multitude of nuances in the phrase 'especially me, your female student' and tried to analyse them all.

So she was going to marry Suganuma.

Standing up from the bench, Tanaka tried juxtaposing the name 'Kazuko' with the surname 'Suganuma'. Suganuma Kazuko. It wasn't such a bad name. But it was an unfortunate one. The very thought of what the two newly weds would talk about on the day Suganuma became a lecturer or the day Tanaka was sent off to the School of Liberal Arts was anathema to him.

> What did Aladdin say
> When he arrived in Peking?

A white castle. The white castle on the hill at La Coste. The powder snow and bracing wind which had bitten into his forehead. The distant castle which had stood there in the snow defying all his attempts to approach closer. Tanaka sensed two people within his being. The first was the petty-bourgeois coward who was jealous of Suganuma and clung to his position at the university. The other was the Tanaka who, on that snowy day, had been so determined to reach the castle. At the moment, both of these Tanakas were being held at bay.

9

There was no subsequent meeting with Suganuma. Suganuma did call a couple of times, but, every time, Tanaka made some excuse to avoid having to meet him. And it was not only Suganuma: Tanaka wanted nothing to do with any of the Japanese in Paris.

There were times in the Métro or bus on the way to the Bibliothèque Nationale when he came across a fellow countryman wearing glasses and a suit that had clearly been tailored specifically for travel abroad. Even if these Japanese gave Tanaka a friendly look, he would just ignore them timidly and stare out of the window. In the case of Suganuma, the reason was obvious, but even Tanaka did not understand his wish to sever all relationships with his fellow Japanese. Perhaps like Sakisaka who had recently returned home, he had begun to feel a sense of spiritual degeneration in associating with the Japanese in Paris.

His trip to the South of France had lasted less than a week, but somehow since then he had been unable to throw off his feeling of tiredness. There was a stiffness in his back and shoulders and, on his way home from the university or Bibliothèque Nationale his legs often felt like lead as a result of his exhaustion. Even when he awoke in the morning he felt too lazy to get up and would often lie in bed for a while gazing at the window with its old, yellowish net curtains. He was relieved to discover that, if he dragged himself out of bed and drank a cup of coffee, such feelings of listlessness disappeared.

But there was one occasion when his back was strangely painful all day. He felt both a stiffness and a searing pain at his shoulder-blade which caused him pain every time he tried to breathe. He remembered Sakisaka and lay head down on his pillow for a while. Before leaving for France, he had had an X-ray taken in order to obtain his visa and had been told that there was nothing wrong with his lungs, so he was convinced that it was not TB. But what was the cause of this pain? As he lay in bed he wondered whether he had not perhaps pulled a muscle during his trip. He knew that he must not get sick during his stay abroad.

It so happened that that was the day when Professor Bady was due to lecture at the university, and, since he had yet to miss any of his lectures, except during his recent trip, he was reluctant to miss one now. Nevertheless, the thought of becoming really sick played on his timidity and was almost unbearable. To beguile these feelings of loneliness, he even had an urge to meet some of the Japanese he knew in Paris; and yet the thought of calling up Suganuma at such a time was intolerable. At the same time he was not sufficiently close to any of the other Japanese to be in a position to ring them up and ask them to visit him. As a result, Tanaka spent the whole day lying in bed.

Around lunchtime the pain at his back had virtually gone, but, to be on the safe side, he nevertheless resolved to stay indoors the whole day. Lying in bed and staring at the stains on the ceiling, Tanaka found his mind wandering to that night in Marseille.

Since his return from his trip, his notebook – the notebook he had kept for the rough draft of the doctoral thesis he would write on his return to Japan – had remained in the drawer of his desk. 'In the Christian tradition the virgin is the symbol of purity. In attacking the virgin, Sade was attacking Christianity.' Such ideas would probably pass muster at the colloquia and seminars he would have to attend on his return. And yet, since his trip, he had come to view the unfathomable abyss that existed between such ideas and himself as a problem with which he himself would have to grapple.

Tanaka wondered about the nature of the student of foreign literature. There were numerous such specialists in Japan. Had they too struggled with the same problem as was now confronting him? He thought of Kikuchi, who had translated Rousseau; Tozuka, who had written his thesis on Balzac; Wakabayashi, who was focusing solely on the study of Gide; and Tabata, who was studying Baudelaire. As Tanaka pictured the faces of these colleagues and fellow students, it occurred to him that not once had this fundamental problem cropped up in discussion between these men and himself when he was in Japan.

These colleagues and fellow students seemed totally unconcerned about this problem, as though they were incapable of discussing it. They were not so much ignoring it; it appeared rather that they were closing their eyes to this issue – for, unless one closed one's eyes, there could be no progress in the study of foreign literature. A street-seller passed by announcing his wares in a loud voice. He was selling cabbage and a regular visitor to these parts, and, as his southern accent disappeared into the distance, the place seemed to become even quieter than before.

Again Tanaka fell to wondering about the nature of the student of foreign literature. He wondered about the connection that existed between specialists of foreign literature like himself and the universities. Just as the novelist Manabe had argued in that café in Montparnasse, students of foreign literature never confront the concept of 'creativity' throughout their lives. They merely translate and discuss the creations of others. Their perspective is fundamentally different from that of the critic. For when it comes to the critic, he tends to use the creations of others as a pretext for discussing something he can call his own. In the case of foreign literature specialists, however, to borrow Manabe's words, they had to spend their lives performing the role of a mina bird.

There is, however, one technique that the foreign literature specialist employs to reveal more about himself. This he achieves in the writer he chooses as the focus of his studies. Thus, the student of French literature who chooses to devote half his life to the study of Valéry succeeds, in that very choice, in saying something about himself.

Such thoughts led Tanaka to wonder what he had achieved through his choice of Sade. He realized that that choice clearly reflected something about the workings of his own mind. He knew instinctively, however, that his decision had been based entirely on pragmatic considerations. For a start, the study of eighteenth-century French literature was relatively unexplored territory in Japan. Furthermore, amongst those who were working in that field, nobody had as yet chosen to focus on the works of Sade. There was a tendency amongst students of vernacular literature, on chancing upon some new data, not to pass that data on to anyone else in the field. It was a similar base desire to keep his discovery to himself, to become an authority in that field, which motivated Tanaka in his decision to focus on Sade.

Yet at the same time he realized that that was not the whole story. Slipping out of bed, Tanaka went off to the toilet. As he pulled the flush, the water was noisily sucked into the recesses of the bowl.

Choice does not determine everything. *Just as with all interpersonal relationships in our life, we are made to suffer by those things we have chosen and, in confronting our choices, we gradually discover ourselves*. It occurred to Tanaka that, as his study of Sade had progressed, so he had come to worry more and more about the total lack of any connection between Sade and himself.

Tanaka did not return to bed but sat at his desk in his pyjamas and, pencil in hand, wrote the words 'student of foreign literature' on a piece of paper. His characters sloped to the right and looked just like those of an elementary-school student. He left a slight space between the words 'student' and 'of foreign literature'. Tanaka stared for some time at that white space between the words.

That was it! A student of foreign literature was someone who had constantly to confront the sense of incompatability between foreign literature and himself. He had to confront a writer who was totally foreign to him in all senses of the word and experience to the full a sense of inferiority and the spiritual distance that existed between them. Not only that, he had to struggle constantly to overcome that distance. Tanaka was not Sade. He was not great like Sade. Tanaka and Sade were two totally different beings, in terms both of their private lives and of their spirituality. Perhaps that was why his decision to study Sade was worthwhile.

As his thoughts proceeded in that direction, Tanaka finally felt a sense of relief, threw the piece of paper into the waste-paper basket and lay down once more on his bed. Like a scolded child, he slept till dusk, till the setting sun cast its pale yellow rays on to the walls.

From that day on, Tanaka began paying regular visits to the museum at Trocadéro which had been introduced to him by Sakisaka. He felt as though he could finally understand the architect's desire to visit the museum with its collection of exact replicas of religious carvings drawn from cathedrals in all corners of the country. Realizing that Sakisaka must have confronted problems similar to those with which he was currently grappling, Tanaka recalled with increased affection the figure of the man who had served as his guide, his head buried in his scarf and coughing painfully.

'Just by entering an insignificant little museum like this, we can stand in the great flow of European history spanning all those centuries.' Tanaka's recollection of Sakisaka's words on that occasion was clear. 'I just didn't want to be like so many Japanese here and steal one tiny fragment of that great flow....'

But Tanaka's circumstances as he walked round the museum were somewhat different from those in which Sakisaka had found himself. It was just before closing-time and there was nobody else in the great hall except a uniformed official. Listening to the hollow echo of his old shoes in the bare room, Tanaka stood examining each of the sculptures until it grew dark. He knew practically nothing about such art and had no idea which of the sculptures was famous. But just by standing in front of such sculptures as that of the carved stone pillar from the rue Minerval or the reconstruction of the *The Flight of the Holy Mother and Christ to Egypt*, from the cathedral at Autun, he felt a sense of oppression as though a heavy lever were pressing against his chest. It was a feeling born from an awareness that, as a Japanese, he was unable fully to comprehend such sculpture. Had he been a Japanese art historian, he would probably have expounded learnedly on certain aspects of the statues, but such clarification seemed both unnecessary and unreliable to Tanaka in his present mood. He looked again on the faces, half-human, half-animal, of the creatures supporting the scrolled pillar in both hands, on Adam and Eve peering out from the shadow of the fig tree and on King David with his gaze fixed on that one spot immediately in front of him. Around all of these lay a great frozen void. Sakisaka had seen that void as indicative of the heaviness of the medieval era with its single-minded concentration on destiny. Rather than medieval, he had described it as the first period of European history. But Tanaka sensed that another facet of the stifling nature of these sculptures was the sense of oppression which European civilization inflicted upon those who were not directly connected with it.

Of course it was not that Tanaka remained totally unimpressed by these carvings. Like everyone else, he was able to sense the light of something ineffable which emanated from each of them. He felt the dignity of even the smallest statue. But, when he stopped to think about it, he could not help feeling a sense of the distance, both physical and spiritual, which existed between himself and the source of that beam of light. Of course it was easy enough to attribute that something to Christianity, to a religion that had failed to take root in Japan. And it was just because it was so easy that those students of foreign literature who resembled the Tanaka of yesterday were able to use such words lightly and without any sense of pain in their scholarly essays and papers. But Tanaka was no longer willing to deceive himself with such trite explanations. The scholar of foreign literature, he realized, was the person who kept before his eyes a great foreign spirit, constantly experiencing the sense of distance between himself and that spirit, and keenly aware of his own inferiority.

Tanaka felt that this museum was one of those places in which he should forge his weak spirit in his attempt to achieve a skilful fusion and sense of harmony between the two traditions of East and West.

When he left the museum, it was already dark outside. A thin film of mist hung over the place du Trocadéro and the blue light from the street lamps appeared blurred. In front of the entrance to the Métro an elderly woman selling baked chestnuts was involved in some kind of argument with a newspaper-seller. In the distance, the lights of the busy Champs-Elysées were dazzling, but in the opposite direction the darkness of night hung over the area between the place du Trocadéro and the Seine. Sitting down on an empty bench beside the museum, Tanaka started to nibble at the ham sandwich which passed for his dinner. He wondered what Suganuma would be doing at that moment.

Today, like every day, the various Japanese artists and visiting scholars would be sitting in the Montparnasse café sipping their Martinis and Cinzanos, speaking ill of all and sundry and gossiping about those who had returned to Japan. But he remained totally disinterested in their world. He wondered what Sakisaka would be thinking about. He had received no word from him ... nor had he, for his part, written to Sakisaka. But, with Sakisaka, that did not seem to matter.

His shoulders and back felt vaguely tired and, placing his hand to his mouth, he coughed gently. Ever since that trip, he had felt the occasional searing pain at his back.

'Monsieur.' Someone called out to him in the darkness. It was a beggar. Realizing that the man who had occupied the bench before him was Oriental, the beggar spoke hesitantly. 'Il fait froid.'

Tanaka stopped nibbling at his loaf of bread and nodded in agreement. 'Il fait froid à Paris.'

It was after 1 a.m. when he finally stopped studying. When he had finished, he felt particularly clear-headed and so he sat staring vacantly at his desk for a while. The heating in the hotel was switched off at midnight, and so, by one o'clock, the room was already quite cold. The faint light from his lamp cast a vague shadow in the corner of the room. The heater was covered with his socks and underwear, which he had put there to dry. There was a can of seaweed and a Japanese mug on the small bedside table. When he had first arrived in this hotel and been invited to Sakisaka's room, Tanaka had sensed that, even in Paris, there was a distinctive smell to the rooms occupied by the Japanese. As he sat alone at his desk, Tanaka was struck by the fact that this same distinctive smell had come to pervade his room too.

Somebody passed beneath his window. Wiping the glass with his hand, he looked outside and noticed a young couple walking with their hands round each other's waists. They looked so happy. They must be returning from some dance date. When the two lovers had disappeared, there was no one left in the rue Hamelin. The windows on this side looked out over the courtyard and, on the far side of the courtyard, stood a brown wall.

In order to calm down before turning in for the night, he would occasionally boil some water in his electric heater and drink it with sugar. As he lay down and closed his eyes, the first image that came to his mind was of the child he had left in Japan. He hardly ever pictured his wife; it was always the face of his baby that came floating up in his imagination. There were even times when, unable to endure the poignancy, he would switch on the light once more, open the drawer of his desk, take out the photograph of his son in his wife's arms and stare at it for a long time.

When he had finished thinking of his son, his attention would turn to the snow at La Coste and to the château perched on top of the snow-clad hill. Of course he had seen photographs of that castle in Japan. He had chanced upon it in the Western book section of Maruzen bookstore as he glanced through a collection of essays by Ruby. Ruby appeared to have enjoyed writing that book. The work even included a childlike poem called 'In Praise of Sade' as well as several recollections from his study of Sade. The first page of the book consisted of a photograph captioned 'La Coste in spring'. It was not a particularly professional photograph; more like those one expects to see in travel brochures. Nevertheless, shortly afterwards, Tanaka had sat in his office for a while staring at that popular picture with a sense of curiosity inspired by the fact that this was the house where Sade had actually lived. The photograph had been taken with a telephoto lens showing a field full of poppies in the foreground and the ruined castle perched on the hill in the distance. A couple of spring clouds floated like cotton wool in the sky above the castle. And on the side of the hill lay the sleepy village of La Coste. Actually the image of this castle was in sharp contrast to the image of Sade which Tanaka had formed in his mind's eye. He had imagined a darker, more tragic castle towering up in a grey sky as being more in accord with Sade's own life. This idea had been formed gradually as he had continued to read about the life and works of Sade during the course of his studies in Japan.

There must have been a whole host of men and women who had indulged in a series of deviant practices in the rooms of that castle, and such episodes occasionally found their way on to the pages of Sade's novels. This was the castle where Sade had spent several nights with actresses from Paris; the castle to which he had fled when hounded by the authorities; the castle he must have thought about tearfully during the long years of his confinement in prison. It was the castle which had been pillaged and plundered by the local villagers on the day of the Revolution. The image Tanaka had formed of this castle, which somehow encapsulated the events of Sade's whole life, in a way belied the peaceful and melancholy castle which appeared in the photograph. The picture was too serene, like the picture of a young girl. As a result, Tanaka had enjoyed reading that book, but had not been particularly moved either by Ruby's poem or by the picture of the castle.

Nevertheless, when he had gone to visit Ruby in person, the

latter had started criticizing Simone de Beauvoir, but then turned suddenly gentle as he suggested, 'You should go down to La Coste. . . . Some crazy man from Marseille bought the castle site . . . a middle-school teacher who knows nothing about Sade. Of all the stupid things to do, he's cutting up the stones from the ruins and selling them off to some architect. In a couple of years, there'll be nothing left of the castle.'

On hearing this final prediction Tanaka, for some reason or other, had felt a pleasant sensation akin to physical passion. Even now he had no idea why he had felt that way. But it was certainly true that, at that moment, he had felt it was strangely fitting, given the events of Sade's life, that the château at La Coste should disappear for good. He did not know where Sade's body had been taken following his death in the hospital at Charenton. His skull had been taken by some young medical student and used as a plaything before being lost for ever. Perhaps the pleasant physical sensation Tanaka had experienced was due to his realization that both the castle and its owner had suffered similar fates.

At any rate he had seen the white château on that snowy day. The snow had been whipped by the wind and driven into his face. Although the snow had come up to his knees, he had managed to climb part of the way up the slope. But the castle had seemed to stand on that distant hill and leer at his efforts. All that had remained staring down at him had been the crumbling walls and the remains of two towers. Tanaka had stood in the snow trying to imprint the silhouette of the castle on to his memory.

Although, following his return to Paris, the details of the castle had slipped his memory, his recollection of that white image remained as vivid as ever. The castle perched on top of that white hill had been grey like a poppy seed. At night, as he lay in bed and closed his eyes, it was that image which was resurrected in his mind's eye. He had ultimately been unable to reach the top of that hill. But he determined that, once the snow had thawed – no, as soon as he had rediscovered the true nature of the relationship that existed between Sade and himself – he would return to La Coste.

After a succession of such nights he received another telephone call from Suganuma. 'I haven't seen you for a long time.' As always, Suganuma spoke in that confident yet correct manner of his. 'How have you been?'

'Oh, not too bad.' Tanaka's reply did not sound particularly friendly. 'How about you?'

'Everything's going according to plan. I've managed to keep up with the schedule I drew up in Japan. So I'm happy about that.'

'Really. That's good to hear.'

'We don't seem to be able to meet even at the Sorbonne. So I decided to call you.'

'That's because I only attend Professor Bady's lectures. They're the only ones I'm interested in.' With that comment Tanaka wanted to insinuate that, unlike Suganuma, he did not have the time to try his hand at everything. The foreign specialist was not a Jack of all trades. He was not the sort of person to try translating Cayrol, Roblés and Aragon. He was too involved in his own immediate affairs to dabble like that.

'I should very much like to see you again. Are you really busy?'

'Yes. Right now, I am.'

'Oh, really.' There was a note of entreaty in Suganuma's voice. 'There's something I particularly want to talk to you about.'

'In which case, why don't you ask me over the phone?'

'It's something I can't very well talk about on the phone. It's not particularly good news for you. But I think it's better to tell you at least.'

Tanaka held the receiver in silence. Repositioning his glasses with his finger, he wondered why Suganuma kept bringing up subjects that would upset him. He had made a special effort to pull himself together, and yet here was Suganuma trying to draw him once more into all the nastiness of the personnel situation at their university. Didn't he realize that Tanaka was weak? Was he trying once more to stir up all his latest base instincts?

'Oh, really?' Tanaka paused for a while and then continued, 'In which case, let's get together then.'

10

The two men walked along the bank of the Seine in silence. Suganuma wore the same new overcoat he had worn on the previous occasion. In keeping with his meticulous personality, it appeared that he brushed it carefully every day, for the collar and sleeves shone beautifully. Noticing this, Tanaka felt extremely sensitive about his own worn-out clothes and dirty scarf. There was a nail sticking through the bottom of his shoe which every now and then pierced the sole of his foot painfully.

'Shall we go to some café?' Suganuma was trying to humour him as he called out from behind.

Tanaka shook his head stubbornly. 'This is fine.'

It was not a particularly cold day, but the air was biting and the leaden sky seemed to bear down heavily on the roofs of the Parisian houses. They came across a small abandoned pleasure-boat, from which much of the paint had peeled away, moored to a stake on the bank of the grey river.

'Can't they even give it a new coat of paint?' Tanaka placed both hands on the railing of the bridge and clicked his tongue. 'Well, tell me what it's all about.'

'It's a difficult subject to broach. Please hear me out without getting too upset.'

'You are always bringing up these awkward subjects.'

'It may seem presumptuous of me.... But I think you should spend more time with the Japanese.'

'The Japanese? Who do you mean by that? Who do you want me to spend more time with?'

'Nobody in particular. But you must know what I mean. What harm could there be in spending a bit more time with your fellow countrymen?'

'You mean people like Ono-san? And all those artists who get together every night in that café in Montparnasse?' Tanaka was putting up a bold front, trying to give Suganuma a piece of his mind. But actually he was feeling distinctly uneasy. He remembered how he had heard them speaking ill of Sakisaka in the Japanese restaurant in Auteuil. Now he was in exactly the same position.

'But then, when you get back to Japan ...' – Suganuma fixed his forlorn gaze on one point on the river as he spoke – '. . . you will lose out.'

'You mean as a scholar?'

'No, I mean in terms of human relationships.'

'You and I think very differently. You can spend your time

abroad as you see fit. But please don't start telling me what I should do.'

'I'm not doing that.' Suganuma looked up at Tanaka indignantly. 'To be quite honest with you, your reputation here is not good. Both Ono-san and Honma-san of M University, as well as the other foreign literature specialists, are talking about you behind your back. I hate hearing it. As a student from the same university – and your junior at that – I don't like them talking like that.'

Suganuma was struggling to control the excitement in his voice and occasionally the words stuck in his throat. Tanaka repositioned his glasses and stared at Suganuma through his narrow eyes. Did he really mean it? Why was he unable to take him seriously? It was clear that Suganuma was in his own way showing a genuine concern for Tanaka. But what was the point of coming half-way round the world just to keep up the same kind of intricate relationships one might expect in the sumo apprentice schools? That was what he found so hard to live with.

'Would you be good enough not to get involved, even when you do hear malicious gossip about me?'

'Don't you mind being ostracized by everybody?'

'Who do you mean by everybody?'

'The Japanese in Paris. In particular, those who are connected to the academic world.'

'They just don't understand me. All I want is to be left alone to study. I'll probably never come to this country again and so I just wish they'd let me do as I please. You too would be well advised not to mess up your life with such trivia.'

Tanaka recalled his sickness of a few days earlier. For all his customary independence, hadn't he been desperate to meet up with anyone Japanese on that occasion? He had even been tempted to ring Suganuma. But now, out of a sense of pride, he had insisted on giving expression to those thoughts he should have kept to himself.

'Is that how you feel?' Suganuma stared straight at him. 'Just as you wish. I'll do my best not to ring you from now on.'

'Yes. Please do.'

'All right. I'll be leaving, then.' He extracted his pigskin gloves from his coat pocket and slowly put them on. He bowed and crossed the road.

As he watched him leave, Tanaka felt a keen sense of solitariness.

He had just been rejected not only by Suganuma, but by Assistant Professor Imai and all the Japanese academics in Paris. It was almost as though this had been his destiny from the day of his arrival in Paris. He felt himself sliding inexorably down a slippery slope.

An extract from Tanaka's notebook

Modern scholars have divided the life of Sade into two periods – before and after 1778. That is done not simply for the sake of convenience: the year 1778 was a kind of watershed in his life. In 1778 Sade was thirty-eight and his life up to that point had been that of the practising libertine rather than of an artist. Beginning with the incidents at Arcueil and Marseille, in his relations with numerous actresses and prostitutes Sade had chosen the real world of action, not the world of the imagination. At that stage he was not yet a fully fledged artist or philosopher. Superficially at least up until 1778 Sade was not so different from the typical eighteenth-century libertine. If there were any difference, it was that Sade was more of a social straggler than the rest.

For example, the first thing one notices in examining the first half of his life is the clumsiness of his behaviour. For all his timidity and cowardice, even in the case of the Arcueil and Marseille incidents, he seems to have acted with a total indifference to the preparations for and consequences of the events themselves. He was foolishly lackadaisical in his efforts to protect himself and, throughout his life, like a moth that swoops into a fire, he kept falling into the traps of the very society and laws he professed to hate. Ultimately it was because of this attitude of nonchalance that he had to endure his years as a vagrant and in prison.

In all probability there were other libertines and young aristocrats beside Sade in the eighteenth century who indulged in equally scandalous conduct. For example, the deeds of the relative of prince Condé, the Marquis Charlier, have been recorded. And there must have been others.

On the face of it, it would appear that the young Sade, the libertine, eventually emerged from this life of active participation and developed into a philosopher and writer. This change came about after 1778 in prison, as the misery of life behind bars fashioned him into an imprisoned writer.

In the first place, it is no exaggeration to claim that this life as an imprisoned writer began with Sade's meditating upon his former life. In this regard, it is necessary once more to consider briefly not so much the external events of his earlier life but their inner reality.

It is easy for subsequent generations to place a spotlight on men like Sade. In this sense, for the modern man of letters, Sade has emerged as another mythological being rather like Don Juan. What I mean here by the term 'mythological being' is the kind of person that writers and philosophers of every age have been able to create through a projection of themselves.

A closer examination of the first half of Sade's life highlights the following specific question: what was the basis for Sade's misogynistic approach to life?

The deep hatred of women that lurked in Sade's heart was not directed solely at Madame Montreuil and Sade's wife Renée-Pélagie. It is equally evident in his depiction of women in his great works. For example, many of his protagonists achieve happiness through their seduction of young girls. Alternatively, as Simone de Beauvoir was so quick to perceive, these heroes feel a deep sense of animosity towards the female organs. It has been claimed by Beauvoir that 'Sade never once wrote in praise of those parts of the female anatomy which are so extolled in *The Arabian Nights*. But even when he does have a word of praise for the female sex, he is invariably referring to an emasculated woman – and descriptions tend to be given in the following terms: 'She was a well-built, beautiful woman of thirty-six. Her skin was a pure chestnut colour and her whole body was covered in hair, just like that of a man. Her genitals were dry and red and unusually large. . . .'

The source of this misogyny can be explained in part through an examination of Sade's relationship with Laure-Victoire-Adeline de Lauris. She was the first woman to deceive Sade by means of feminine weakness. It may not even be too much of an exaggeration to claim that it was through her that Sade was first to experience feminine hyprocrisy.

Nevertheless, there are those who hold that the seed of this misogyny was sown much earlier – during Sade's childhood – in the form of the feelings of abhorrence he nourished towards his mother. One exponent of such a view is Pierre Klossowski, author of an article entitled 'Fathers and Mothers in the Works of Sade'.

According to Klossowski, it was because the boy Donatien Alphonse was raised in the Condé Palace by his mother away from his diplomat father that, in contrast to the Oedipus complex common in many boys, he developed a sense of love and respect for his father and a corresponding hatred of his mother. Most men who manifest such homosexual tendencies at such an early age either become effeminate out of a sense of fear of their fathers or else turn their aggressive nature upon their fathers. But, in contrast to these norms, Sade merely secretly yearned for his father's strength.

It is clear that, with the emergence of Madame Montreuil, this misogyny intensified. To quote Lucy, she 'was not particularly tall and had a seductive smile and laugh'. Yet she was more domineering than most men. Not only that, but, as the personification of an abstract social morality and law, Sade saw her as a threat to his very existence. Thereafter his hatred of the maternal was augmented by his wife, Renée-Pélagie. As has already been noted, Renée was, almost literally, a maternal wife to Sade. And yet every time he looked at her, Sade must have felt a profound sense of the insipid nature of womanly virtues and of ennui. Moreover, as time progressed, this wife came to represent more and more of a burden to him. This is because, rather than arousing feelings of love in him, her unstinting devotion incited only a deep sense of gratitude. It should be clear that, when a man is able to feel no more than a deep sense of gratitude towards his wife, she inevitably becomes a great burden to him – both as a man and as a husband.

Moreover, Sade had no choice but to depend on this virtuous wife every time anything went wrong in his life and during his long periods of incarceration. This feeling of inferiority as a husband eventually combined with the sense of thankfulness he felt towards his wife and developed into a hatred of the maternal element in woman.

It was Klossowski's conclusion that Sade developed this hatred of the maternal into a contempt for and hatred of women in general. Sade occasionally depicts a battle between a despotic mother and her son in his works. And, according to the protagonist in *The Unhappiness of Virtue* who hates his tyrannical mother, 'The male is the only complete form of human; woman is a mere deformation of man.'

From the psychoanalytical viewpoint, it is extremely difficult to verify Klossowski's claim that Sade's misogyny was derived from the mother complex he experienced as a child, since we do not have much information about Sade's childhood years. It is also true, as Simone de Beauvoir has argued, that 'these relationships are beyond our grasp'. And yet there is much in Klossowski's hypothesis that appears pertinent when one scrutinizes the life and works of Sade.

The second issue raised by a closer inspection of the incidents of the first half of Sade's life is the fact that Sade was not merely a 'sadist'. For example, as revealed by the Marseille incident, it is clear that he also indulged in masochism (in asking Marianne to beat him), homosexuality (in his relationship with his servant, Armand), coprophilia (as evidenced in the incident in which he forced the women to eat the sweets and then examined them intimately – a tendency that is treated in great detail in *The Hundred and Twenty Days of Sodom*) and a predilection for group sexual encounters (in the way in which he invited both Armand and one of the women into his room).

As mentioned before, Sade was a libertine, a category that would appear to comprise two basic characteristics. The first of these is that, unlike other types of dissipated person, the libertine is not a passive seducer 'willing to succumb to the temptation of others', but rather a more positive Don Juan type figure who is actively engaged in the seduction of others. As such, he clings to the freedom of the self and his independence at all costs. At the same time the libertine is also a callous observer of man. Irrespective of the love and carnal desire with which he is involved, he is never transported outside the realms of his consciousness.

As already stated, sadism involves the loss of this freedom and independence, but the masochism manifested by the Marquis de Sade in the Marseille incident was clearly no departure from the libertine norm. There is evidence here of a different type of masochism from that usually implied by the term.

Masochism usually implies entry into the realm of selflessness by means of the beatings and insults of others. Many masochists have confessed that they were drawn into a kind of Nirvana and transported into the realms of ecstasy by becoming slaves to some other controlling force.

But a study of Sade's attitude during the Marseille incident reveals that Sade did not lose himself in a state of Nirvana and an ecstasy of self-intoxication. This becomes clear from the way in which, whilst receiving the blows from Mariette's broom, he calmly recorded the number of blows he had received by carving notches on the mantelpiece. There was a cold glint in his eyes. He never lost that other self who was able to sit back and watch with total indifference as he was beaten. According to de Beauvoir, author of *Must We Burn Sade?*, the distinguishing feature about Sade was 'his desire not to lose himself in the darkness [of passion], but to bring life to such passion'. At the same time, 'the curse that weighed upon Sade' was surely related to such detached observation.

This callous determination not to lose himself was connected with his efforts to prolong for as long as possible those carnal passions which are prone to dissipate like a burnt-up candle. To this end, Sade also resorted to homosexuality.

The sense of sin which surrounds homosexuality and adultery arouses a greater passion than is excited by normal sexual relations. It doubles the sense of passion. Sade was more aware of this fact than anyone else. He wrote: 'When one considers the sense of evil which represents the true fascination of profligate behaviour, the sense of sin is much greater in the case of homosexual love than that of heterosexual love. On such occasions, one's passions are intensified.'

According to Klossowski, it is possible to accredit Sade's homosexual tendencies to his childhood sense of yearning for his father. But, to Sade, this trait was no mere whim.

In particular, he attached more value to exhibitionism than to either masochism or homosexuality. During the Marseille incident Sade watched the affair between Armand and the women and also had Marianette watch his own affair with Armand. That was no private affair but a sexual feast designed to involve a number of people. This tendency was not limited to the Marseille incident: it is claimed that he evidenced a similar pleasure in such sexual deviation in 1765 when, with the actress Beauvoisin, he assembled various neighbouring lords at his La Coste château, and also in 1775 when he summoned the girls from Montpelier.

Simone de Beauvoir describes such incidents as 'a socialization of eroticism'. In other words, she sees in this an attempt by Sade to socialize his own obsessions not by engaging in private acts of love, but by assembling as many accomplices as possible. It was Sade's ideal to become the producer and originator of that carnal feast. The preservation of freedom and individuality in the midst of passion, the retention of his ability for dispassionate observation and the attempt to prolong those easily dissipated carnal desires through a consciousness of sin – these are the distinguishing features of Sade's sexual behaviour during the first half of his life.

Life within the Vincennes jail was extremely hard for Sade. He had to wait till the beginning of December, three months after his incarceration, before being allowed a twice-weekly walk. And even that was limited to one hour in the prison courtyard which measured no more than thirty paces and had to be undertaken under the constant scrutiny of the guards and jailers. Even though the prisoners might approach them, the guards remained as silent as stones.

After he had walked round and round the cold winter courtyard, a bell would ring and he would be returned to his cell. There were only two meals a day: one in the morning at eleven and the other at five o'clock in the evening. Breakfast consisted of a thin soup and one other dish and, in the evening, the prisoners were provided with one dish in addition to a meat course. They also received bread and one glass of wine a day. On Thursdays and Sundays a couple of apples were added to this fare.

Amongst the prisoners, the director of the Vincennes prison, Charles de Rougemont, had a reputation for being a haughty autocrat. Sade himself despised him as 'a toad in tight trousers and a waistcoat'. Relations between de Rougemont and Sade were full of even more hatred and enmity than had existed in the relationship between the Marquis and the warden of the fortress at Miolans, de Launay. In the words of the letter of Mistress Lucy, the time spent in the prison at Vincennes was 'just too terrible for words'.

A look at Sade's actions of the time reveal the extent of his irritation and impatience. He hated with all his heart the society which had confined him to this prison. In February 1781 he wrote to his wife: 'I am a libertine. I admit it. And I know exactly what kind of person this libertine is. And yet I did not practise everything I knew and probably shan't in the future either. I may be a libertine, but I am no criminal. I am no murderer.'

He also felt a deep sense of anger about the moral values upon which society was erected and towards Christianity, the basis of those moral values. Whenever he meditated on the concept of 'God', the same two doubts would always well up in Sade's mind.

The first of these doubts was related to the fact that, although God always desired Good, His creation, Nature, insisted on opposing that wish and pursuing Evil and the Fall. Since Sade's view of Nature is important, we shall pursue that in greater detail later, but, for the time being, it is important to note Sade's belief that the goodwill of God fails to concur with the laws of Nature in this world (destruction and Evil).

The second of these doubts concerns the question of why, if God is truly omniscient and omnipotent, He entrusted man with the freedom of choice. To give man the freedom to choose was to test man. Even if it were true that man was descended from God, man was now able to transgress the will of God and even experience the pains of Hell. God had granted man such freedom and was now regretting that decision. God was an inconstant and weak being. Such animosity ultimately developed into Sade's personal philosophy and permeated his novels; but during the years of incarceration, he was forced to direct such hatred at his fellow human beings.

For the incarcerated Sade, writing was neither a diversion nor a means to forget the time during the long days. At the time, Mirabeau was also held in the Vincennes prison and was attempting to allay his fears and pass the time by engaging in translation and writing essays. But Sade's view of 'writing' was somewhat different from that of Mirabeau. Through his writing, Sade desperately sought to create a new world, a more real world, distinct from that which was currently crushing him, and there to maintain his freedom. He wrote this to his wife: 'You were wrong. You constructed the phantom that arouses my desires and requires fulfilment.'

The Dialogue between a Priest and a Dying Man is the record of a conversation between a Catholic priest and a dying atheist about God and Christianity. Inevitably, the dying man is Sade's own philosophical mouthpiece. The priest turns to the dying man and encourages him to confess his sins before he can administer the last rites. But the dying man argues that the mistakes he has made during his lifetime were not so much 'sins that he had committed' but instances of a 'failure to recognize the omnipotence of Nature'.

He claims his eyes had been dazzled by the Christian creed and regrets his failure to make adequate use of the abilities with which Nature had provided him. This is because the laws of Nature demand of man both virtue and vice in equal proportions. In accordance with the philosophical ideals of St Thomas, the priest attempts to have him acknowledge the wisdom of God as the first principle in the laws of Nature, but the sick man retorts that it is crazy to seek reason and wisdom in the manipulator of the laws of Nature. He persists in rejecting both God and Christianity, arguing that 'There is not a single virtue that is not needed by Nature, and conversely, not a single crime that is not necessary to her. In the perfect equilibrium in which she keeps one and the other lies all her art.'

This conversation evidences Nature as it confronts the Christian God.

In this way Sade was able to overcome the society which was isolating him from the outside world and, by skilful use of his powers of imagination, he attempted to preserve his own freedom. At the same time, however, society did not brush aside this challenge with silent contempt. For example, in later years in the Bastille, Sade pasted together strips of paper about twelve centimetres in length. When he had made of this a scroll some twelve metres in length, he began to write. In the silence of his cell he would write like a man possessed from seven o'clock in the evening until ten o'clock. For a whole month the light in Sade's cell was never extinguished.

On 28th January Sade completed his great work, a work that may be compared to *The Decameron* and yet was the most diabolical work that man could create. Sade himself said of the piece that it was 'the foulest work ever created by man'.

We shall return to *The Hundred and Twenty Days of Sodom* later, but, on the day of the fall of the Bastille in July of the following year, this and several other manuscripts were seized by rioters who had stormed the Bastille and were never returned to Sade. This particular manuscript was discovered in the Bastille by a man called Arnoux de Saint Maximin and subsequently held in the home of the Villeneuve-Trans family for three generations. It was finally prepared for publication in a hundred and eighty sections by the Berlin psychiatrist Ivan Bloch, in an edition full of mistakes.

Afterwards the famous scholar of Sade and former editor of *Humanité*, Maurice Heine, acquired these manuscripts from the German Bloch and determining, after years of research, that it was indeed the work of Sade, published the definitive version. It is said that the structure of *The Hundred and Twenty Days of Sodom* is based on Marguerite de Navarre's work *Heptameron*. Sade's great work comprises a preface and four chapters, but of these Sade completed only the preface and first chapter. The final three chapters were left in the form of a plan and notes. It is the tale of four men, the Duke of Blangis, his younger brother Curval, and Durcet, who resort to murder, intimidation and wickedness to achieve genuine material freedom. The four men assemble forty-two men and women in a remote castle called the *forêt noir* and, following a banquet, engage in various forms of passion and brutality. Included amongst the forty-two visitors are the wives and daughters of the four protagonists. The wife of the Duke of Blangis is a powerful woman who has already married and subsequently killed four previous husbands for the sake of convenience. Later, eight youths and eight young girls are joined by some slaves and indulge in a carnal feast which lasts a hundred and twenty days. At the end of that time, thirty of them are butchered to death.

The plot appears to be very straightforward, but the work brings to mind three incidents of Sade's life: the incident in November 1765 when he invited the actress Beauvoisin, several eminent neighbours and his uncle, the priest Sade, to La Coste; the Marseille incident of 1772; and the scandalous incident six years later when he assembled the girls from Lyon and Valence. *The Hundred and Twenty Days of Sodom* and these incidents reveal that Sade's appetite was directed towards group activity rather than affairs between individuals. This implies that Sade's carnal pleasures transcended mere instinctive desires and developed into large social events. By means of these great carnal feasts, Sade was able to divide those present into two categories: 'participants' and 'bystanders'. Alternatively, one can categorize these as 'observers' and 'the observed'. But for the presence of spectators, the men and women concerned would lose all self-consciousness through the arousal of basic animal passions.

The awareness of being watched must have served to intoxicate the participants and would certainly have prevented a relaxation of their consciousness. Simone de Beauvoir, who recognizes as one of the characteristics of Sade's work 'a desire to experience lust without succumbing to depravity', considers the Marquis, with his depictions of group activity, a callous rationalist. It is de Beauvoir's claim that, 'If the debauchee coincided exactly with his movements and the victim with his emotions, freedom and consciousness would be lost in the rapture of the flesh. The victim would experience merely brute suffering and the debauchee merely convulsive pleasure. Thanks, however, to the assembled witnesses, a presence is maintained about them. It was through these perform-ances that Sade hoped to reach out to himself: and, in order to see himself, he must be seen.'

One should also take careful note of the fact that *The Hundred and Twenty Days of Sodom* was completed in less than a month. This was incredibly quick and one is compelled to admit that it was written by a man literally possessed. And this applies not merely to this work: immediately after its completion, Sade wrote to his wife informing her of his wish to employ specialists in both Portuguese and Spanish, thereby providing ample testimony to the fact that he had already begun work on his autobiographical novel, *Aline and Valcour*.

The same can be said of *The Unhappiness of Virtue*, which was completed in a mere fifteen days some two years later.

How is one to interpret such incredible speed and crazed energy? The six years Sade spent confined in the prison at Vincennes and, later, in the Bastille, fashioned Sade into a writer who had penetrated the dark secrets of man and moulded him into an enlightened philosopher capable of seeing through the workings of society. In other words it was during this period that he developed into an 'incarcerated writer'. It may be held that the incarcerated writer is different from the usual writer in two respects. Firstly, he has been separated from the world by means of the thick, cold walls of his cell. In his state of isolation, there is no way to communicate with the outside world. This world, to be found on the other side of those thick walls, punishes him, suppresses him and tries to crush him. Secondly, the incarcerated writer experiences a sense of anger and indignation towards society and the outside world. He is forced to curse its injustice, its hypocrisy, its customary morals and the various workings of this society and raise his fists to it in defiance.

And yet the incarcerated writer is furnished with only one weapon with which to pursue this struggle. His only weapon is his power of creativity. With this power he has to construct the true society of his dreams away from real society. It is by means of this imagined world that he seeks to transcend society and to work for its ultimate demise. Sade's initial recourse during his years in prison was to the relationship which inevitably develops between the powers of the imagination and the incarcerated writer. Thereafter his feelings of animosity towards society and his desire for revenge provided the stimulus both for his breathtaking speed and the possessed manner in which he wrote.

The conquering of real society by means of his own idealized society – it was this that gave birth to his decision to portray the group as a prototype of society. The feast in *The Hundred and Twenty Days of Sodom* was the exemplar of his envisioned society. Furthermore, for Sade, this imagined society had to be more powerful than actual society.

Since this imagined society was so powerful, Sade was unable to write short stories. The size of the world of both *The Hundred and Twenty Days of Sodom* and his great work *Justine* bear adequate testimony to the frantic yet earnest desire of Sade, the incarcerated writer, to overcome the real world outside and to stand in opposition to it. The emphasis that Sade placed on 'size' is clearly evidenced in *Justine* – in his description of the size of the protagonist's private parts and again in *The Hundred and Twenty Days of Sodom* in the sheer quantity of murders that occur. But again this portrayal of size is different from similar depictions in *The Story of Gargantua*. For behind such scenes can be discerned Sade's aspiration to transcend society as it is by increasing 'size'.

'Sade's powers of imagination stretched out infinitely beyond the walls of his prison,' wrote the contemporary French literary critic, d'Astorg. It was precisely the intensity of his power of imagination that was to serve as Sade's primary qualification as a writer and it was through this power that he was able to confront contemporary society.

11

That day, as he was taking notes from the records in the Bibliothèque Nationale, Tanaka was suddenly overcome by a feeling of giddiness. As he looked at the words on the page he began seeing double and, shortly afterwards, his dictionary fell to the floor with a thud. When he reopened his eyes, three or four people were looking at him.

'What happened? Are you all right?' One of the men in the group lifted him up as he spoke.

Tanaka was able to mutter a word of thanks, but the pain in his head was intense. He forced a smile and repositioned the glasses that had fallen down over his nose. Somebody picked up the dictionary.

'You should go home. You look really pale.'

Heeding this advice, Tanaka tied up his belongings in his wrapping-cloth. Everyone watched as he painstakingly secured the ends of the cloth.

His head throbbing, he went out into the corridor and leant against the wall for a while. He recalled the difficulty he had experienced in getting up that morning and the feeling of nausea he had endured ever since. But he had been subjected to such feelings on a number of occasions recently and, each time, had managed to pull himself out of bed and brew some coffee. Entering the toilet at the end of the corridor, he turned on the tap and stared at his face in the mirror. His face was pale, exactly as the student had just told him. Indeed, it was not just pale; his face was ashen, the colour of clay. The sweat on his forehead glistened and, placing a wet hand to his brow, he felt strangely feverish.

As he went outside it was already dusk. He felt a sharp pain at his back. But he had been troubled by this, too, for quite a while now. With every deep breath he felt a faint yet resounding pain behind his shoulder-blade.

He returned to the rue Hamelin and collapsed on to his bed. He had bought a thermometer at the pharmacist's on the way home and, placing it under his arm, he lay quite still for a while. The mercury rose to 38.2°C.

Tanaka convinced himself it was no more than a cold and felt a surge of relief. If he had got TB like Sakisaka, the temperature should be lower. The mercury would certainly not rise above 38°.

Nevertheless, allowing for the fact that he had occasionally succumbed to such fevers since coming to France, he had to admit that his whole body must be exhausted. Come to think of it, he had not been examined once by a doctor since his arrival. He did not know what he would do if he were to be seen by a doctor and given a diagnosis like Sakisaka's. Burying his head in his blanket, he recalled the image of the architect as he walked away from them at Orly airport, the weight of his bag causing one shoulder to drop. He realized that the same would happen to him were he to succumb to sickness. He certainly did not want that. If he were to become sick, that would be the end of everything. Not only his study in France but the position in the university which awaited him on his return would all be frustrated. And there was no way he could afford the expense of hospitalization and the medical examinations that would entail.

When he awoke the following day, he was still feverish and felt very lethargic. It was as though molten lead were attached to both his legs. He could not abide the thought of venturing outside and just curled up in his blanket. That afternoon he asked reception to call a doctor. A young man carrying a black leather case appeared and spent a long time pressing against Tanaka's chest with his fingers.

'Is it a cold?'

'I think so. But just in case, once you're feeling better, you should go to the hospital and have some X-rays taken.'

'Which part is bad enough to need an X-ray?'

'No, that's not what I mean. It's just that I can hear a faint murmuring in your chest.'

Tanaka raised his head in alarm and the doctor reassured him with a smile that such murmuring could be caused just as easily by a cold as by TB. One could not, however, be too careful and he therefore repeated his advice that Tanaka should go to the hospital and undergo a closer examination. After the doctor had left the room, Tanaka lay for a long time staring at the ceiling.

The following morning, perhaps owing to the white tablets which the doctor had prescribed for him, his fever had gone. He

194

was also no longer aware of the pain by his shoulder-blade. Feeling much better, Tanaka tried to relieve his nagging fear and to convince himself that there was nothing wrong with him. He felt as though he were a character in one of Molière's comedies. He was just a hypochondriac.

That day, instead of going to the Bibliothèque Nationale, Tanaka decided to clear his mind by taking the Métro to Charenton and enjoying a walk around there. Charenton was a Paris suburb he had been planning to visit for some time now. This was where the psychiatric hospital to which Sade had been transferred late in life, and where he had died, was located. Of course there would be nothing left of that hospital now. But the scenery of the place where the two rivers, the Seine and the Marne, divide, would not be so changed from Sade's day.

He took the same bus he had taken earlier on his way to Vincennes. Looking out of the window after a while, he could see the cold-looking Seine, the heavy sky that suggested the possibility of snow at any minute and the gloomy old houses along the river. Tanaka felt a severe chill in his legs. A sooty goods wagon stood on the railway lines that led along the banks of the Seine to Charenton. Patches of smoke rose from the small engine at the front of the train and seemed to hang over the Seine as though they had been torn off by hand. The dreary-looking walls and chimneys of a factory towered up through the smoke.

When he alighted from the bus on the quai de Bercy, his face was buffeted by the cold air. The cold here was unlike that in Japan in that it pierced right through the skin. He bought a small bun filled with currants from the baker's on the far side of the street and sat down on a bench to eat it. It was lucky his students back in Japan could not see him sitting there all alone like that.

Unlike the previous two days, he did not feel particularly tired. But he still nursed feelings of fear and uncertainty. He realized that, rather than remaining terrified and alone, the logical thing to do was to follow the doctor's advice and go to the hospital for an X-ray. But the thought of receiving the diagnosis made him determined to put it off even for one more day. Moreover, for the past twenty-four hours the prospect of impending illness had become very real to him. At the same time he was aware that, in a given situation, one tends to be far more afraid than the danger of the situation warrants. That's how it had been all along. He blinked and rolled the paper bag which had contained the bun into a ball. He tried to convince himself that if he were to have an X-ray, the feeling of cold and loneliness would immediately disappear.

But those feelings were real. What was it that caused such feelings? They were the result of his quarrel with Suganuma. They stemmed from the fact that he was unable to get along with Ono and the other foreign literature specialists in Paris. He felt that Assistant Professor Imai's attempt to have him farmed out to the School of Liberal Arts had also contributed to his current state of mind. He felt cold and lonely, totally alone in Paris. Like a stray dog.

Immediately he began admonishing himself for behaving like a spoilt child. What was so lonely about his situation? None of these feelings were from the heart. It was just an expression of the frustration of a cheap desire for worldly success.

Placing his hand on the railing that ran along the river-bank, Tanaka was forced to confess that he knew nothing of the loneliness of the student of literature. Yet a student of literature he was.

A bag containing bread could be seen against the black surface of the Marne, caught up against a stake. Some birds crossed the dark sky, and from a nearby belfry came the faint sound of a bell. Apparently Sade had looked at the Marne every day towards the end of his life. Stricken with gout and rheumatism, the seventy-year-old Sade had stared at this river from the window of his room in the psychiatric hospital. His eye must also have caught sight of those bleak horse-chestnuts. Tanaka contemplated the loneliness Sade must have felt as he sat in his hospital room, his frozen hands held up to the dying embers of the fire, realizing that his philosophy was now neither accepted nor rejected by anyone. Tanaka recalled the diary of the young doctor, Ramon, who had worked in that hospital as a trainee. Ramon described how the lonely Sade used to walk down the corridor, head bowed and dragging his feet, refusing even to acknowledge a friendly greeting. Now that he was in Charenton, Tanaka could picture that frozen figure.

As Tanaka crossed the bridge, the iron railing continued along the left bank. A group of Algerian pedlars were sitting on the bank smoking. Spotting Tanaka, they immediately opened their bags containing purses and magnets and held them in front of him.

Behind them lay a small graveyard. In the middle stood a plain cement statue of the Virgin Mother with her arms outstretched, surrounded on all sides by row after row of gravestones. There were both iron and stone crosses. A frail old woman dressed in black was making her way between the gravestones, careful with each step like a bird. She fingered a rosary as she walked. Somebody must have been buried there a couple of days earlier, for a small wreath of fading flowers wet from the rain and wrapped in silver paper lay pathetically where they had been thrown down on the damp, black earth. Tanaka glanced at the names on each of the crosses as he walked by. On every cross was written not only the name but the dates of birth and death of that person. On some had been carved words of remembrance from loved ones and, on others, verses from the Scriptures. There were even crosses to which a small photograph had been attached. As he glanced at the names like Madeleine, Alexandra and Jean, he noticed one grave on which the words Anne-Prospère and Renée were inscribed. Was it mere coincidence? Those were the exact names of Sade's wife and her sister. There was no reason why Sade's wife and sister-in-law should be buried there. And Tanaka knew that Sade himself had been buried in the graveyard belonging to the psychiatric hospital and that his remains had subsequently been disinterred. Tanaka bent down, dug up some of the dark black earth from the grave and wrapped it in a piece of paper. He squeezed it tightly and, as he did so, he could sense with his hand the texture of the soil mixed with sand. He did not know whether this was the same soil as that in which Sade had been buried and left to rot. But experiencing the same throb of excitement as when he had squatted down to touch the stone road at Arcueil and the staircase at the Marseille jewellers, he squeezed it tightly. Some black earth oozed out from between his fingers. The blackness of that soil went straight to his heart.

Handing in his out-patient's card at the reception desk he sat down in an empty chair in the waiting-room, as requested by the nurse. As he did so the other patients, who had been absorbed in their newspapers and magazines, looked up and stared at Tanaka with expressions of distaste. This was by no means the first time he had been subjected to such treatment since arriving in France, and

Tanaka just lowered his eyes and waited until they stopped looking at him and returned once more to whatever they were reading.

When he had visited Sakisaka, it had never occurred to him that he would one day be coming to the hospital like this. He had been convinced that, during the period of his study abroad, he would have nothing to do with the steam heater and the smell of disinfectant which pervaded this building. And yet here he was, not very long after Sakisaka's departure, sitting terrified, awaiting his turn.

In response to a signal from the nurse, one of the patients entered the adjoining room. There followed what seemed like an eternity. At this rate it would be nearly noon before his turn came. All the papers and magazines had been taken by the other patients, so Tanaka just sat there playing with his fingers and recalling the time in Japan when he had done the same with his baby son. As he did so, the face of the son he had left behind in Japan suddenly closed in on him. He had to stop, otherwise he would have started crying.

His son was two years old. Every day when Tanaka returned from work in Japan, he would go straight to the bed where the baby was sleeping without even stopping to change out of his suit or wash his hands – much to the chagrin of his wife. But as he stroked the baby, its cheeks, which were invariably covered with milk and egg-yolk, would form into a smile. And since he had come to Paris, the photograph he had taken just before his departure had never left his person.

Watching Tanaka toy with his fingers like that, the woman sitting next to him smiled and spoke. 'It's always like this. Always.' She began to complain about the long wait. 'I have a heart condition and come here once a week. It always takes the whole day. You must be a student?'

Tanaka's pride was hurt at being taken for a student. 'No, I'm a lecturer at a university in my own country.'

Hearing this, the woman seemed uncomfortable and looked away. Evidently she thought Tanaka was lying.

At last the woman's turn came and she entered the examination-room. Twenty minutes later the nurse finally called Tanaka's name.

'Please remove your jacket and shirt in the cubicle and be prepared to take everything off.'

Noticing with a look of disdain that Tanaka wore a camel-coloured vest underneath his shirt, as is the custom in Japan, the nurse muttered something to herself. The doctor sitting on the other side of the desk writing something on a medical card was a young man and, on looking up, he remarked with surprise, 'Hey! We've met somewhere before, haven't we?'

Now that he came to mention it, Tanaka realized that this was the same doctor who had discussed Sakisaka's symptoms with him.

'You're a friend of that Japanese man, aren't you? What was his name? I urged him to stay and undergo treatment here. . . . Doctors like me may forget the names and faces of former patients, but we never forgot their diagnosis. Have you heard from him?'

Tanaka shook his head and the doctor seemed disappointed. Then, taking out a new medical card and rubbing it with his hand, he continued, 'Well, what's the trouble?'

'I caught a cold. My local doctor told me he could hear a murmuring in my chest, so I came here.'

'Have you got a fever?'

'I did have for a couple of days.'

'Do you find you cough a lot? Do you often feel tired?'

Tanaka deliberately leant over to one side and said nothing about the occasional pain in his shoulder-blade nor about the dizziness he had experienced at the Bibliothèque Nationale. He was afraid to mention this and wanted the doctor to treat the symptoms he had experienced as lightly as possible.

When Tanaka had removed his shirt, the doctor placed the stethoscope to his ears, raised his eyebrows and asked him in a tone which suggested he was neither joking nor indulging in idle banter, 'You're really thin, aren't you! Are you eating properly?'

As the doctor applied the stethoscope to Tanaka's shoulder and back, the cold sensation of the ivory caused him to shudder and the doctor asked him whether he was cold.

Tanaka replied that he was not.

'In which case, breathe in. . . . Breathe out.'

The tip of the stethoscope, which had been moving around, suddenly came to a halt on Tanaka's shoulder-blade. It was like a watch that had stopped working. That was the exact spot where Tanaka felt the occasional searing pain when he breathed. The doctor scraped his chair as he turned towards his desk. Frowning, he began to write something on the medical card. Tanaka had no idea what he was writing. He just stared at the doctor's hands with their covering of brown hair. The heater rang out faintly.

'Is it bad? Am I...?'

'No.' Without answering Tanaka's question, the doctor took a handkerchief from his coat pocket, blew his nose and asked Tanaka to follow him.

The X-ray room was dark. By the time Tanaka's eyes had grown accustomed to the darkness, the doctor was wearing glasses which looked like swimming goggles and sitting on a small chair. Tanaka was made to stand in front of a photographic plate and adopt various poses.

The lights when they came on were dazzling. Tanaka folded his hands across his chest like a woman.

'It's right here on the left-hand side.' The doctor poked the area around his collar-bone with his hairy fingers and spoke in a perfunctory manner. 'I can see a shadow.'

Everything became dark in front of Tanaka as he repositioned his glasses. 'Is that the infected area?'

'I don't know yet. We'll take some pictures a week from now.' The doctor explained that X-rays were arranged on an appointment basis. 'Please put your clothes on again. I think everything will be all right. But you can't be too sure.'

Tanaka stared up at the doctor who still appeared nonchalant and sympathetic. As an indication that it was time to leave, the doctor turned round and began washing his hands with disinfectant.

The corridor was quiet and the waiting-room already deserted. The electric clock that hung on the white wall indicated that it was 12.20. Sitting down in a chair, Tanaka sheepishly touched the area the doctor had just been poking with those hairy fingers of his. He felt no pain or anything unusual there. But the doctor had said that there was some kind of a shadow.

Tanaka turned up the collar of his coat and walked along the boulevard Saint Michel. As always, the road was swarming with students from the Sorbonne who had clearly finished attending lectures for the day. Several grey clouds, laden with rain or snow, floated over the Panthéon. As was to be expected, the jardin du Luxembourg was also almost deserted. A couple of labourers were busy digging up dead grass with a shovel.

He no longer felt like going to the Bibliothèque Nationale. Even were he to go, he was feeling so confused that he couldn't possibly do any worthwhile study. He had lost any urge to climb those stairs, hand in his card to the official and borrow dictionaries and the paper envelope containing the records with which he was working.

'I've had enough.' A couple of students were deep in conversation as they passed him, but he could make out only these last few words. But these clung to the back of his mind like a piece of paper caught up in the wind and wrapped round a telegraph-wire.

He sat down on a park bench and held his head in his hands. So he really was sick. Strangely enough, however, the truth of the matter, which had so terrified him until the previous day, now seemed totally unrelated to the reality of his current situation. Even were he to be told that he had contracted TB, he wouldn't believe it.

From somewhere a siren rang out. In his university in Japan the lunch-break would just be finishing and afternoon lectures just beginning. Around the brazier in the assistant's office a group of students and junior assistants would be passing the time in idle chatter. Just before Sakisaka had left Paris, he had stared longingly at those statues in the museum in the place du Trocadéro and remarked, 'You claim you don't want to ignore that great flow whilst living here. But there lies the real pain that is all part of the experience of studying abroad. . . . In order to enter that great flow, we foreign students have to pay some sort of a price. I've paid for it with my health.'

Tanaka tried to convince himself that he had only just placed the tips of his toes into that great flow. His sickness was not what Sakisaka meant when he talked about 'payment'.

Three or four pigeons had come right up to him and were eating crumbs. With their feathers ruffled, they looked cold and lonely as they walked around his feet emitting a shrill chirping sound from the backs of their throats. A young boy being led by his nurse approached Tanaka in an attempt to see the pigeons. His cheeks were red and his hair a beautiful blond. The boy smiled just like the son he had left behind in Japan.

'Keiichi.' Tanaka pushed up his glasses. 'Your father's had enough. He's really had enough. What should he do?'

As though for the first time, Tanaka was racked by a wave of loneliness at the thought of being all alone in a foreign country. There was not one person on whom he could rely here in Paris. He wanted to see not only his child but his wife.

When finally he stood up from the bench, he kept his hands in his coat pockets and set out for the exit near Port Royal. His shoes felt as though they had been crammed full of stones.

'Tanaka-san.' Someone was addressing him from behind in Japanese. 'It's Tanaka-san, isn't it?'

When he turned round, he saw a tired-looking man in a faded beret smiling at him through the iron railings. It was Kohara, the man who had acted as a guide for the novelist Manabe that time. A shopping basket hung from his arm. 'You look really ill.' Kohara had pushed his hand through the railings and handed him a paper parcel. 'Please. Help yourself to one.'

The parcel was full of roast chestnuts. Placing a burnt chestnut on the palm of his hand, Tanaka had a sudden impulse to cling to this man.

'If you eat these, you'll be reminded of the stone pavements of Tokyo.' Kohara looked down at the roast chestnuts and continued in a serious tone, 'There used to be a shop on the edge of Hibiya Park that always sold chestnuts. That was some thirty years ago, but I remember how I would always buy some on my way back from the Imperial Theatre, put them in my pocket and warm my hands on them.'

'The Imperial Theatre has been turned into a cinema now.'

'Yes, so I hear.' Kohara's gaze was fixed on one spot in the sky as though he were looking at some distant object. 'That area must be totally different now. Over the years, I've grown old here in Paris without noticing it.'

'Will you never return to Japan?'

'I don't think I could. When you get like this, you can't return even if you want to.'

Tanaka recalled how, on their previous encounter, Kohara had described himself as no different from a man without nationality. Half of him was Japanese, the other half was not. He could still clearly remember his complaining about the fact that he could never become French.

'Oh, I completely forgot.' Kohara pointed to the basket he held in his right hand. 'My wife asked me to do some shopping.'

At a greengrocer's near the Métro exit Kohara picked up some cabbage and artichokes. He then moved on to a grocer's and bought a large bar of soap for washing clothes. With the basket over one arm and the cabbage in his hand, he proceeded to haggle furiously over the price. As he did so, all traces of the man who had once been posted to France by the Bank of Japan disappeared. He was now the bedraggled and shabby old Japanese man who had been subjected to years of ridicule by his French wife and children.

'Au revoir.' Kohara offered his parting greeting in French, though his bad accent belied the thirty years he had been living in Paris. Holding the basket clumsily, he disappeared into the swarm of people on the boulevard like a twig engulfed in a drain.

With no particular goal in mind, on leaving the Port Royal Tanaka continued walking away from Montparnasse. The nail he had yet to have repaired in his shoe was painful on the sole of his foot, and once or twice he considered taking a break at one of the street cafés. But in every café the sight of jovial young men and women was strangely depressing. His mind was more occupied by the image of the shabby-looking Kohara whom he had just left.

He recalled the complaints that Kohara had voiced in their previous encounter. The latter believed himself to be half Japanese, but was convinced that the other half could never become French.

Tanaka rubbed a long stone wall with one hand and realized that the same was true of himself. The student of foreign literature experienced exactly the same sentiments as Kohara. The Japanese could never understand the French; yet here he was studying French literature! Recalling that in the Marseille hotel he had assumed a more positive view of the student of foreign literature, Tanaka became aware of the depth of his present state of depression, both physical and mental. Even though he was aware that it was on just such days that he should go to that art museum by the Trocadéro and confront the 'great flow' of which Sakisaka had spoken, somehow his feet refused to proceed in that direction. He had no desire to add that sense of suffocation to his already depressed state of mind.

When he touched the photograph of his child which he carried in his pocket, his heart cried out, 'Keiichi, your father's had enough.

What should he do? Please tell me, even though I know you don't really understand what it is that I'm going through.'

He finally discovered a deserted café and sat down on one of the chairs on the pavement. Two or three glasses of wine felt warm in his throat and his face turned slightly red. He put his hand to his sweat-covered brow to check whether he had a temperature but was unable to tell. Until he received the results of the X-ray, it was difficult for him to make any plans. He had convinced himself that the results would be bad.

The wine had gone to Tanaka's head somewhat and he considered the situation. Within a week he would know for sure the state of his health, but the thought of having to return to Japan as Sakisaka had done was unendurable. It was quite likely he would have no second chance to visit France. He could not bear the thought of having to abandon his programme of study which had just begun to take definite shape. But more than that, he was intent on seeing to what extent he could stand up to that 'great flow'. After all, what else was the role of the student of foreign literature? He felt that it was this, rather than concern about his position in the university or disappointment at being overtaken by Suganuma, that was most important to him at the present stage.

The effects of the wine had been sudden, and they dissipated equally suddenly. He paid the bill as the street lights came on and set off again. But the cold seemed even more penetrating and he was assailed by even greater fears of sickness and an even more intense sense of gloom. He bought a ticket at a small cinema in the boulevard Raspail. Since he had not drunk too much, he did not care which film he saw. He just wanted to distract his mind from such insufferable thoughts for a couple of hours – or however long the film lasted.

The cinema was cold and almost empty, presumably because it was still only dusk. The plot of the film was hard to follow, but on it went, totally oblivious to Tanaka's feelings.

'That man's playing with his fate.'

'There's nothing we can do for him. If only he could be a bit smarter.'

Tanaka stared at the screen and listened to the French dialogue with a blank expression. When the film was over the lights came on and five or six people turned up the collars of their coats and went noisily outside. A girl selling ice-cream and chocolate was stifling yawns as she passed up and down between the empty seats. Once more the lights went out and the news came on the screen. There were stories about exercises being conducted by the French fleet and the construction of a dam on the Garonne. A new sluice was being opened and a large whirlpool, which appeared to have been taken with a high-speed film, poured over the dam and down the other side. 'This dam should bring a rich harvest to the areas around the Garonne.' The voice of the commentator was very professional.

Tanaka stared at the mountain behind the dam. It was only for a second, but, on top of that mountain, he could just make out the ruins of what looked like a medieval castle. The shape of the mountain was like that at La Coste. The way in which the castle had been reduced to ruins also reminded him of Sade's château. It was a white castle. The swirling wind blowing the powder snow into his face. The melancholy sound of a dog barking in that distant village piercing the silent white void, and the castle towering up amidst the snow on that distant hill seemingly resisting all his attempts to draw closer. The castle which had finally enabled Sade to realize his secret dreams now stood on that hill above the ruined village, mocking him. Above it, the grey sky seemed to stretch out indefinitely.

'I've no idea why you're interested in Sade. . . . I have no idea why an Oriental like you should be studying Sade.' He recalled Ruby's forehead glistening with beads of sweat and those small eyes glaring at him with a look of derision. The snow-drifts were growing deeper and he now sank in up to his knees. Yet, even though the tower and main walls may have disappeared and all but a small section of the two side walls had been destroyed, there was still no denying that the castle actually existed.

12

A young girl in a white raincoat was sitting at the table opposite. She had placed about half a dozen postcards on the table and was busy writing with a fountain-pen. The sun pouring through the window shone on her down-covered cheeks and her thin neck, around which she had wrapped a polka-dot scarf. The chestnut hair that protruded from the sides of her beret sparkled in the sun. For some reason Tanaka was reminded of Nozaka Kazuko.

From the café in the place Bellecour in Lyon Tanaka looked out on the people bathed in sunshine outside. In the square an old man with white hair was walking amongst the crowds holding a multicoloured balloon, and he was followed by a donkey with a bell around its neck pulling a cart full of children. As he watched, a baby let go of the balloon which his mother had just bought him and it floated off over the rooftops in the direction of the colline de Fourvière like a soft spring cloud. At this, the mothers who had been busy knitting stopped talking, smiled and cried out, 'Oh là là'.

It was a Sunday. A Sunday in an unknown town in a foreign land. That was not a particularly good feeling. It felt as though a sprig of parsley had caught on his tongue. Although he had left Paris that morning and arrived in Lyon shortly after noon, he felt surprisingly awake. He wondered why that should be.

The sky was not exactly blue, but there were patches of hazy blue sky appearing between the clouds. The shimmering rays of the sun were painful to his eyes and shone full on the wall of the post office and police station which connected the rue de la République and the rue Auguste Comte. Beyond that wall ran the Rhône, even faster than the Seine. Tanaka had just crossed the river to reach the square.

The patron of the café told him that he had chosen a good day to come. Seeing his bag, he asked him whether this was his first visit to Lyon and assumed that he had come to see the festival due to take place that evening. When Tanaka told him that that was not the reason for his trip, the owner informed him that, in that case, he was even more fortunate. For a start such balmy weather was rare during the Lyon winter. Until the end of March, this was a town of fog and mist, particularly bad for those suffering from asthma and arthritis. 'But today, being the festival, God must have performed one of His miracles.' So saying, the proprietor opened the bottle of beer he held between his legs, accepted Tanaka's tip with a smiling 'Merci' and withdrew to the interior of the café.

He had not come to Lyon to pursue his study of Sade. He had planned to go straight on to Avignon and from there to head for La Coste. Even he was not quite sure why that morning he had suddenly been moved to take the train and return to the castle. It may have had something to do with the fact that he would be hearing the results of his X-ray in a couple of days. He recalled the faint white cavity which had lurked in the middle of that black film of Sakisaka's X-ray. He was convinced that there would be something similar on his own negative and that the doctor would also order him to enter hospital. It was as though that very thought had inspired him to visit the castle while he could.

Just as before, the train had passed through Dijon and finally reached the outskirts of Lyon. Just at the moment they began to cross the iron bridge over the Rhône, he recalled a section of the novel *A Story of France* by Nagai Kafu which he had read with such pleasure as a student. He had read the section about 'the banks of the Rhône' so many times he could remember it word for word: 'Staring at the waters of the Rhône in Lyon from beneath the stone embankment, I threw myself down exhausted on the green grass that covered the sand of the beach by the river. I spent my days idly and yet I was extremely tired. I was mentally and physically exhausted.'

As he leant on the window of the train and stared out over this blackened place, the second largest city in France, that final line had been especially poignant to Tanaka. So Kafu had been mentally and physically exhausted, had he? That was just how Tanaka felt at this moment. He was tired of the Paris winter. He was tired of life in a foreign country. As the train had slowly pulled into the station at Lyon, he had taken down his hand luggage from the net overhead and alighted on the platform.

'I hear there are the remains of a Roman amphitheatre.' Tanaka addressed the same café owner. 'Can you get there by bus?'

'No, you can take the cable-car. If you go down to the cathedral of St Jean, you'll see it straight away.'

As this conversation proceeded, the young girl who was busy writing letters at the table opposite looked up. Returning her pen to her handbag, she smiled at Tanaka innocently and suddenly said, 'Monsieur, I am going that way too. Shall we go together part of the way?'

'C'est parfait.' The owner slapped Tanaka on the shoulder and winked. 'You're a really lucky man. First you come to Lyon on a rare beautiful day and then you manage to go for a walk with a young lady like that.'

Tanaka had not taken a walk with a young woman since his arrival in France. He was reserved by nature but, smiling shyly, followed the girl outside. She was apparently a student at the University of Grenoble. She explained that she had been born and bred in Lyon and that her family still lived there; but, having always wanted to study at the foot of the Alps, she had chosen to go away to college there.

'Are you Japanese? We have about ten Orientals at my university but no Japanese.' As they crossed the bridge, she removed the polka-dot scarf she wore under her white raincoat. They had walked only a short distance but the heat was enough to make them perspire slightly.

'This is the Saône.'

The Saône was dirtier and muddier than the Rhône which Tanaka had seen earlier. A stream of murky, yellowish water flowed into the muddy waters of the river from the drainage pipe which had been built on the river-bank. The girl explained that this was the oldest part of the town. 'When the Romans were here, they too lived on the colline de Fourvière. Apparently the aristocracy used to live in castles on top of the hill because the stores of the merchants were located around here.'

'Mademoiselle.' Tanaka rubbed his hands together and nodded obsequiously. 'You know Lyon really well, don't you?'

'Hardly surprising, seeing that I was brought up here. By the way, my name is Mademoiselle Madeleine Leange. But you can call me "Made". That's what they call me at home and at school.'

Just as she had said, the buildings around them looked as though they had been standing for a couple of centuries or more. Actually they could more accurately have been described as accumulations of stones bleached by the elements rather than buildings. The street was worn and uneven and marked with dark entrances which looked like caves on either side. Children and elderly women kept going in and out of them.

'Do you know something of the history of the Roman era?'

For some time now Tanaka had been looking in vain for an opportunity to let Madeleine know that he was a lecturer in a Japanese university. The fact that she should ask him that question believing him to be a typical foreign student was slightly disconcerting.

'The general, Hannibal of Carthage, came to Lyon and crossed the Saône on an elephant in order to wage war on the Romans there. Have you heard of Hannibal?'

Tanaka smiled wryly as he told her that he was aware of such basic facts. He wanted to tell her that his students were girls of about her age. He wanted her to know that he was a university lecturer. The image of Nozaka Kazuko taking copious notes came to mind. But because he failed to answer, she began to explain. She presumably spoke with the best of intentions, but she sounded as though she were describing something to a younger brother.

'Hannibal destroyed the Roman army in the second Punic war. He was later defeated by the general Scipio and committed suicide.'

'You must be a history graduate?'

'No.' Madeleine shook her head. 'I'm studying Law. But all French students have to study this kind of history.'

Surprised by the innocence of her voice, Tanaka looked at her once more. It was virtually impossible to tell the age of the French. This young woman in the beret and raincoat had earlier struck him as being about twenty-four or twenty-five but in reality she could not have been more than eighteen or nineteen. Otherwise she would not be speaking with such pride.

He was concerned that she had asked him nothing about his work in Japan, but he was pleased to be with this female student. During those dark days in Paris, not once had he enjoyed such an experience. His was the life of the ascetic, a constant round of commuting between his cheap hotel in the rue Hamelin and the Bibliothèque Nationale. As he sat eating all alone in the corner of those cheap restaurants and when he went to that cold art museum, he felt cornered and alone. Were he a young foreign student like Suganuma, there would no doubt be chances to relax like this, but he was far too shy to approach any of the female students even when he did go to the university. He was not only too shy, he was attempting to reject such a life-style for himself. But just this once, Tanaka thought. Even I must be allowed my Sundays.

It was a Sunday in a strange town. A day that tasted of parsley. Through the gaps in the clouds the sun shone down on the surface of the water and a flock of pigeons flew up from the cathedral of St Jean.

'I hear that today is the day of the Lyon festival.'

'Yes. It's quiet now during the day. But tonight there will be a fireworks display. There will also be music in the main square.' She stood still and looked up at him. 'Shall we go to the festival together? I was planning to go anyway.'

After leaving Madeleine, he followed her advice and climbed the colline de Fourvière. As he stepped out of the cable-car, he was confronted by a basilica reputedly of nineteenth-century origin. But the building, which had been modelled on the Eiffel Tower in Paris, was too conventional. The Roman amphitheatre, too, was smaller than expected, with the places where it had been repaired too conspicuous. There were still a couple of men working in the round amphitheatre, but Tanaka just sat down on a cold stone and experienced the joy of knowing that he would be meeting the girl again that evening.

It was not the famous relics which moved Tanaka most about the place. Strangely enough, as he looked down from that hill on the city of Lyon, he was moved almost to tears. He had no idea why.

The town looked for all the world like a great grey smudge. The factories emitted clouds of smoke and the houses with their reddish roofs seemed to enclose the two rivers, the Saône and the Rhône, as they reached into the distance. The roads were filled with diminutive people and trams. At various points church steeples were to be seen towering above the houses, streets and the scenes of everyday life there, pointing up into the grey sky. Straining his ears, Tanaka could just make out the faint sound of a bell caught up with the commotion of the town. From the edge of the town the great brown plains stretching forth into the distance looked sorrowful as they disappeared into the purple mist.

So this was Europe, was it? At that moment Tanaka himself would not have been able to explain clearly whether this was the real Europe: he would probably have been better able to answer that question when he had been in Japan. But now, come to think of it, that had all been an academic type of knowledge. He had not been here long, and yet, since his arrival in France, he had come to experience a different Europe from that which he had known before. And it was this newly experienced Europe which now stood before his eyes in the form of the city of Lyon. This grey and desolate-looking expanse of life. The sound of the cars and the bustle of the people. And, from the fissures in that cloudy sky, a stream of sunshine rained down on to the spires in the midst of that dreary life. Tanaka could not help feeling that Europe had remained like this for centuries. At the heart of that history was what Sakisaka had described as 'the great flow'. And the Sade of his studies, too, had ultimately been forced to accept that history and had lived within that great flow.

Once more Tanaka succumbed to a feeling of despair similar to that which had assailed him in Paris. He realized that within his being was incorporated none of the great flow of European history.

The hollowed-out stones continued up the colline de Fourvière and a nun using her umbrella as a walking-stick and a Catholic priest wearing the kind of coat usually worn by high-school students made their way up the slope. A basket containing a monkey had been left outside a dilapidated old house. On seeing Tanaka, the monkey clung to the metal netting and began to whimper, its body shaking. Tanaka stopped and stared at the filthy-looking animal. He did not know whether the monkey was mocking him or attempting to show some sign of affection. In order not to be late for his appointment with Madeleine, he ran to the place de la Victoire and, as he did so, reverted to the carefree attitude he had enjoyed that morning.

The square gradually filled with people. The leaves had fallen from the horse-chestnuts in the square and a group of men carrying musical instruments were busy with final preparations for the performance. There were paper lanterns hanging from the branches of the trees and a roar of approval rose up from the crowd when these were illuminated.

Madeleine was waiting for him outside the café. She was still wearing the same beret and kept both hands deep inside the pockets of her white raincoat as she stared at the crowd. Tanaka was struck by the similarity in appearance between her and Nozaka Kazuko as she had stood on the athletics ground on the day of the university festival. His heart was pounding like a young boy's, causing Madeleine to ask him whether he was feeling tired.

How old do I look? He repositioned his glasses which had slipped down over his nose owing to the sweat and tried to seem relaxed. I feel young even now.

Actually he was not in the least bit tired. The feelings of tiredness he had experienced in the Bibliothèque Nationale and the leaden sensation he had experienced every morning in Paris before his departure, now seemed like a dream. He began to convince himself that perhaps he was not sick after all. Perhaps it had all been a mistake.

The two of them walked together into the crowd of people in the square. Over the shoulders of the audience they could hear the strains of a Weber waltz. It was not a particularly professional performance but was nevertheless enjoyable. The performers – the trumpeters and the violinists – all looked serious as they played.

Madeleine told him all the performers were amateur. 'That's why they are so happy to be able to perform here today.'

'Ce n'est pas mal. Ce n'est pas mal.' Tanaka nodded in agreement and clapped his hands like an excited child every time there was a break in the music. 'This is such fun.'

The people leaving the square made for the rue de la République. The sound of cars mingled with that of the people. The light from the neon signs reflected off the street. That evening there was a competition for the best show-window decoration in the shops on the main street.

'Please don't let me out of your sight.' Every now and then Madeleine would stop in the middle of the congestion. 'Let's go towards the station. They have lots of stalls and attractions there.'

They heard a sound like bamboo splitting and then noticed the fireworks over the colline de Fourvière. The crowd stood still and watched, raising a chorus of 'Oh, là là' as the red sparks glistened for a second like confetti before disappearing. It was a paltry display of fireworks. Tanaka felt a sudden urge to allow these crowds the opportunity to compare the best fireworks of their respective countries.

'In my country we have fireworks which are much, much more beautiful.'

'Really?' Madeleine shrugged her shoulders incredulously. 'But the fireworks at Lyon are famous throughout the country.'

Tanaka was struck by the girl's charm. The smell of acetylene grew steadily stronger. The stalls were huddled together like a desert caravan and from them emerged the shrill voices of the sellers of candy-floss and sandwiches. There was a steady stream of sailors with their girl-friends taking turns to shoot cork bullets at the row of dolls lined up in the shooting-gallery. At another stall rings were being thrown for prizes. Next to that was a dodgem-car centre.

'Do you want a ride? What does one have to do?'

'You have to try and crash into as many cars as possible.' Madeleine laughed. 'It's really painful.'

'Let's have a go.' It was the first time since his arrival that he had done anything like that. He was reminded of the time he had visited the Korakuen amusement park in Tokyo with Keiichi and his wife, when Keiichi had taken a ride in one of the aeroplanes and had started to cry. Tanaka paid and the two of them got into a red car. With just a slight touch of the accelerator, the car began to move. Somebody coming in fast from the right kept bumping into them. Every time he hit them, the other driver shouted out gleefully and Madeleine clung to Tanaka's shoulder. It was a long time since he had laughed like that.

Another firework exploded in the sky. For a moment, as it did so, they could see the faint white basilica on top of the colline de Fourvière. Tanaka was glad he had left the train at Lyon. This was the most enjoyable day he had spent since his arrival in France. A magician wearing black trousers was carrying silver hoops in both hands and skilfully joining them together and then pulling them apart. A woman who had covered her hair with a cloth in gypsy style sat behind a large glass ball and was busy telling fortunes.

'Go on. Have your fortune told.'

'No.' Madeleine shook her head and continued stuffing roast chestnuts into her mouth. 'I'm Catholic. But feel free if you want to, monsieur.'

To keep her happy, Tanaka stretched out his hand before the diviner. The gypsy woman placed it on top of the glass ball and stared into the haze on the surface.

'You're a lucky man. Everything's going to go really well for you.'

'Really? I've come all the way from Japan,' Tanaka replied in high spirits. 'How about my health?'

'There's nothing wrong with you. Honestly. So please don't worry about it.'

Another firework broke the silence of the night sky. It flashed for a second and then disappeared. Tanaka felt sure that he was not sick after all. Despite all the walking he had done that day, he was not in the least tired. He was experiencing none of that dreaded feverish feeling he always felt in Paris. He could almost hear the doctor's words: 'That faint shadow we detected was all a mistake. There's nothing on the X-ray.'

They also watched a man who allowed himself to be tied up by members of the audience and then proceeded to extricate himself.

'Look, Madeleine, that's a smart fellow. He's having his wrists bound. That's what I call a great trick. In Japan we call that *tsutsunuke*.'

The café in front of the station was full of people happily drinking beer and coffee. Amongst them Madeleine discovered three or four groups of friends and walked about shaking hands and explaining how it was that she came to be showing a Japanese visitor around.

Somewhere a church clock struck ten. She told Tanaka that she had to be getting home. In France young girls had to be back by ten or they would be scolded by their parents. He nodded but could not hide his disappointment. He had been shamefully hoping that theirs might develop into a more intimate relationship. But the more he thought about it, the more crazy such an idea seemed. He put her on her bus at the now deserted place de la Victoire and, turning up the collar of his coat, repositioned his glasses before moving on. The wind caught the scraps of paper that had been left behind, causing them to dance. An old man went around extinguishing the lights in the lanterns that hung from the branches.

But for all that, he felt satisfied. He was really glad that he had alighted at Lyon.

`

Standing in the middle of a piece of cultivated land, Tanaka turned towards the East. The hill at La Coste lay in that direction. Some of the clouds in the sky which hung over the Lubéron plain beyond the horizon were white, others a more dreary greyish colour. There were no signs of life in the wintry fields and the tall poplars which bordered the ploughed fields in the distance seemed to shiver in the wind. Plumes of snow whipped up by the westerly wind seemed like white flames and, as Tanaka strode across the frozen surface, the soles of his shoes made a sound like that of grinding metal. It was bitterly cold, but there was something invigorating about breathing in that clean air.

Tanaka was overcome by a host of conflicting memories and sensations. He had returned to the castle at La Coste.

He stood still, took off his gloves and rubbed his red ears with his hands before setting off again. When he reached the line of poplars he had seen earlier in the distance, the road divided into two. One road led to La Coste, the other to Ménerbes. The hill was still covered in snow and, as before, he approached it slowly. He was still unable to see the castle from where he stood, but he could easily make out the brownish dots of the stone cottages on the side of the hill. They must be the houses at the extremity of the village of La Coste. They were situated some two hundred metres from the castle. One of the men from the village was slowly making his way up the snowy road. Tanaka felt that if that man could climb it, then so could he.

Looking at his watch, he discovered that it was almost noon. He had reached the outskirts of the town but not a sound was to be heard. The snow had been piled up on either side of the road and there were clear traces of wheels as well as footprints in the snow on the road. But the wooden doors of the houses remained closed, with nobody visible through the grime of the windows. Nor was there even any smoke coming from the chimneys. The houses were little more than piles of brownish stones carelessly piled on top of each other and seemed more wretched and desolate than any farmhouse Tanaka had ever seen before. These houses had probably looked just the same during Sade's lifetime. Tanaka stood still in the middle of the narrow lane and looked around him. He had no idea in which direction the man he had earlier seen climbing the hill had disappeared.

Suddenly he heard the sound of something slipping and then a great crash. The snow heaped up on one of the roofs had fallen to the ground. The sound reverberated through the great white void, to be followed by a silence even more complete than before.

When he reached the far side of the village, a great black dog rushed out and began to bark, its teeth bared. Tanaka readjusted his glasses in alarm and stepped backwards. Packing some snow into a ball, he threw it, but the dog merely screwed up its nose and prepared to pounce. But then a man in a beret opened the door of his house and began to scold the dog. He then challenged Tanaka.

'Where are you off to?'

'To the castle.'

'The castle! There's nothing there!'

'Will you give me a glass of wine? I'll pay you for it.' Tanaka was aware that, after drinking wine, he would start struggling for breath and that it would be even harder to climb the hill, but he wanted to talk a bit longer with this man.

He wanted to look inside one of the farmhouses of La Coste which had remained unchanged for some three centuries. He wondered whether Sade had visited these peasant homes. But the man merely went inside with his dog, then came out with an aluminium cup and looked on in silence as Tanaka drank the dry wine. Then, taking Tanaka's money in his heavy palm, he slammed the door brusquely without so much as saying goodbye.

Tanaka set off up the hill again. He was surrounded by one vast expanse of snow. Fortunately the snow was not as deep as on the previous occasion. The Lubéron plain stretched out grey and brown below him. In the distance he could just make out the houses of the town of Apt through the haze and fog. Then, finally, Tanaka was able to make out the crumbling walls of the castle.

The castle was over there. It stood above a steep precipice at the top of the hill. Of course neither the towers nor the roof remained and all that was left was one small section of the walls. But, from that moment on, the sight of that towering château was to remain imprinted on his memory. The wind bit at his cheeks and the trees shook as though about to crash down into the snow.

When he reached the snow-covered plateau, the wind was even more biting. Holding on to his glasses, he looked at the castle from this new angle. It was cruelly dilapidated. The wall to the left was more like a stone screen and appeared to offer no support whatsoever. From the remains of the main building it was impossible to determine the location of the original rooms. It was no more than a pile of snow-covered stones strewn about.

In comparison with that, the right-hand tower still maintained a semblance of its original shape, but, like a giant tree which had been felled by the wind, much of the main body had been torn away. Tanaka recalled the disappointment written over Ruby's face as he had told him of the imminent destruction of the castle.

He came across a well. This was the only part that retained its former appearance. The sides of the blackened well were overgrown with dead thorn-bushes and beside it lay a broken statue of what appeared to be a Greek goddess.

He was now inside the castle. Sade would have walked about where he was now standing. Here Sade must have frolicked with the actresses he had escorted from Paris. It was within the confines of this ruined château in which Tanaka now stood that Sade would have acted out his drama. On that day the local aristocracy had assembled in La Coste and filled the room with candlelight and the noise of music. It was in this same castle that Sade had beaten the five young women he had escorted from the countryside. It was here too that the young woman called Marie had given birth to her child.

As if turning the pages of a great tome suspended above his head, Tanaka could visualize the various incidents of the man's life.

The sun was finally coming out and the clouds hovering above him appeared brighter. There was even the occasional patch of the clear-blue winter sky of the South of France. Through a hole in the crumbling wall he could see the Lubéron plain, clearer and more vivid than before. The parched brown fields now gleamed in the sun and, threading its way through them, he could make out the Cavalon river, still enveloped in mist. Like a blind man groping in the dark, Tanaka passed his frozen hands over the remains of the walls and windows. He just wanted to touch and squeeze his lips against something that still retained a hint of the fragrance of Sade. He was the only Japanese ever to have come this far. He was convinced that in the future there would be a plethora of scholars of French literature absorbed in the study of Sade. But he was the first to have visited this castle. Consumed with such childish pride, he chuckled. As he did so, his eye was drawn to a slight stain on the opposite wall.

At first he had taken that stain for a shadow. But as he shuffled through the snow to take a closer look, he noticed a red dot there. It was a deep red, the colour of blood. He assumed that it must date back to some time, long since past, when the walls had been painted without the use of wallpaper.

As he stood amongst the ruined rooms and the snow, that red seemed strangely vivid. It reminded him of the lips of someone sated with pleasure. The red of lipstick painted on to a pair of thick lips. Those thick lips appeared to belong to Sade. Or to one of his victims. As Tanaka stood there in the snow among the ruins, that red spot seemed to be the sole testimony to the people who had once lived there. Tanaka placed his head against that spot, closed his eyes and remained motionless for a while. Even though the castle might perish, that red spot must never die. That red spot signified life.

Tanaka stood there for a long, long time. In the distance he could hear a dog barking.

It was time to be moving on. That dark city of Paris awaited him once more. The world of Suganuma, Ono and Assistant Professor Imai awaited him. No doubt he would continue to enjoy moments of nervous happiness and anger in their midst. But would that red colour – that redness which could never be erased – remain with him also? He wanted a red dot that could never be eradicated.

As he left the castle, he was struck by the whiteness of the snow. He felt something welling up in his throat and bent over to spit it out. His blood spattered on the fresh snow. This was followed by some warmish liquid which rose from his chest into his throat. Even more blood oozed out between the fingers with which he had covered his mouth, leaving stains on his clothes and dropping on to the snow. His blood-stained hands caught his spectacles, knocking them to the ground. He gazed vacantly at the snow and the blood. It was the same colour as that stain he had detected on the wall. Strangely enough, that was the first thought which came to him as he stood there.

13

That was the first time Tanaka had coughed up blood. Since his glasses had fallen off, both the whiteness of the snow and the red blood-stain appeared blurred as though they were some distant reality. In his mind the red spot on the wall merged into one with the blood-stain. The lips of the man exhausted with pleasure, the thick lips of Sade, the women beaten by Sade somewhere within the confines of this castle. That vivid red image which would survive despite the destruction of the castle some two hundred years previously. Tanaka quietly contemplated the fact that, even if, as Ruby had predicted, the castle were shortly to be destroyed, that red stain would survive for eternity. Suddenly Tanaka was able to comprehend the fact that he had coughed up blood for the first time in his life shortly after seeing that red spot.

Yet a voice within him seemed to be contradicting him. 'So what are you saying happened? That's got nothing to do with you. You're dreaming. That's not possible.'

The piercing wind whistled. He moved his gloved hands in front of his eyes. The fingers were damp from the snow and the blood. As he stared into the wind, it all seemed so unreal. 'Keiichi, what am I doing? What's happened to your father?' He knelt down on the snow like a dog and began to grope around for his glasses. Replacing them with trembling hands, he could see more clearly the snow-covered plain and the wind sending up small white plumes of snow in front of him. With one hand on his troubled chest, he began to retrace his steps. He was now afraid of coughing up more blood. He walked slowly across the snow, fear showing on his face every time he nearly fell. Occasionally he stopped to swallow saliva. His feet inside his snow-covered boots felt warm, as though immersed in hot water. In the distance another dog barked and the man who had earlier given him the wine stood in the doorway of his house staring at him. . . .

'Voilà.' A young nurse, her auburn hair tied up with a piece of white cloth, beat the blanket with her fist as though testing the softness of a mat. 'You've brought your pyjamas, haven't you?'

As he changed into his cheap pyjamas, Tanaka crouched down to avoid the intense stares of the surrounding patients. He had bought those pyjamas that very morning in a small back-street shop on his way to the hospital. There were multicoloured gowns on all the other beds and Tanaka felt ashamed he did not own one.

He buried himself under the bedclothes and took the thermometer the nurse held out him. But when he tried to place it under his armpit, she shook her head and said in a hushed voice, 'Not there. Please put it in behind.'

'Behind?' Tanaka could not understand the nurse's mumbled French.

Finally she blushed and explained resolutely, 'Please place it in your anus. That's how we do it in France. It's the most accurate method.'

This was the cue for a burst of stifled laughter from the other beds. Closing his eyes, Tanaka recalled Sakisaka, who had earlier entered this same hospital. The realization that Sakisaka had somehow endured this same sense of shame was a great source of strength to Tanaka. Opening his eyes again, he noticed the nurse still standing beside him holding what appeared to be a stop-watch.

'Voilá.' Moving his hand down to his buttocks, he inserted the thermometer. He was standing awkwardly, like a chicken. He found it hard to believe that the other foreign students had never experienced those feelings that had troubled both Sakisaka and him. Why did everything seem to go so well for them during the course of their studies abroad? They enjoyed Paris, their studies proceeded smoothly and, following their return home, a clear connection seemed to exist between their studies abroad and their subsequent lives. Yet in his case everything seemed to run counter to that pattern. He had not been particularly lazy. And yet his axe had struck a great rock and broken. Finally he had succumbed to sickness and been subjected to the giggling of the other patients in his ward. Nevertheless, he was still a student of foreign literature.

'Hmm. 37.2°.' The nurse muttered to herself, took a pen from her pocket and with her left hand carefully wrote the date and some red and blue marks. The red was his temperature, the blue apparently his pulse.

'We'll be doing a urine test later, so before going to the bathroom please come to the nurses' office.'

A young doctor opened the door and strode in. He appeared disinterested as he took out his stethoscope, applied it to Tanaka's bare chest and carried out a perfunctory examination. He made Tanaka cross his legs and tapped his kneecaps with a metal instrument. He then had the nurse assist him as he extracted a sample of blood from Tanaka's ear and smeared it on to a couple of slides with a pipette.

'Is that the last time you coughed up blood?'

'Yes, I had an injection to control the bleeding at the hospital in Avignon.'

But the doctor continued to stare at Tanaka with a look of suspicion. He had both hands in the pockets of his examination coat. When they had left, Tanaka laid his head on his pillow and continued to think of Sakisaka. It had been snowing the day he had entered hospital. He had held his head close to the window of the taxi in an effort not to miss even one building, one tree, as he left. The steam heater in the ward made a slight murmuring sound and provided almost too much heat. The man in the next bed was reading aloud from a tabloid newspaper. The youth in the bed opposite looked like a student and lay staring at Tanaka, the blanket pulled up around his chin. Tanaka raised his eyes in greeting and the young man asked him if he was Chinese. When Tanaka explained that he was Japanese, a look of disappointment came across his haggard face. Tanaka looked at his watch. It was 3 p.m. Apparently the time for the afternoon nap had finished, for the nurse came back carrying a large pot and distributed cakes and milk. One of the patients took one look inside the wax paper he had been given and yawned. 'What! Biscuits again?' he muttered.

The man who had been reading the paper was chewing away unenthusiastically at his biscuit. He looked over at Tanaka and asked him whether he had coughed up blood. When Tanaka replied in the affirmative, the man continued, 'You must have some cavities in the bone.'

'Yes, underneath the collar-bone. How about you?'

The man turned his back towards him and lifted up his pyjama top. Tanaka could make out a thick scar, like a small brown burn, on his side.

'Did they operate?'

'Yes. But they failed. They're going to try once more.'

The other patients were listening to this whispered conversation in silence.

'How many months have you been here?'

'It's not just a matter of months. I've been here a year and a half. One and a half years!'

Tanaka did not have the means to remain in hospital for six months, let alone a year. He realized that, like Sakisaka, he too would eventually have to return to Japan. But at that moment the very thought was anathema to him.

He remained with his head in the same position on his pillow until evening. He could hear the distant rumbling of the cars and buses on the far side of the darkening window. He closed his eyes and listened, trying to convince himself that he was not in Paris but back home in Japan. But it was no good. There was no denying that this was Paris. And he was lying all alone in this Paris hospital. At this moment people would be enjoying themselves under the blurred lights of those cafés in the boulevard Saint Michel, huddled around those heaters on the terraces. He wondered what had happened to his room in the hotel in the rue Hamelin. Would the supervisor have removed all of his luggage? Tanaka visualized that deserted room, the rays of light from the setting sun shining in weakly through the window. It reminded him of Sakisaka's room after he had returned home. The room had preserved something of that uniquely Japanese smell. Before long, some other foreign student would no doubt arrive full of trepidation, head for the same hotel and stare up with a similar sense of awe at that sign recording the death of Proust in that very same building.

Tanaka dozed off for a while. When he awoke, the windows were bathed in the blackness of night.

The nurse took temperatures at seven o'clock in the morning. The patients would then wash and eat breakfast. Apart from the one moment when the doctor popped his head around the door to ask how everyone was doing, they tended to sleep until noon. The period when all patients must remain absolutely quiet finished at four o'clock and, for the next couple of hours, the ward was the scene of much animated conversation. That was the only time when visitors were allowed into the ward. Realizing that he was unlikely to receive any visitors, Tanaka looked in the opposite direction as much as possible and contented himself with sleep and reading. Dinner was served as soon as all the visitors had left. At nine o'clock an elderly nurse went around each of the wards in turn and switched out the lights with a perfunctory 'Bonne nuit'.

The same routine was followed every day. Although Tanaka felt as though he had been in hospital for quite some time, in fact he had been there a mere two weeks. During the second week he was taken to the X-ray room and given a comprehensive examination by four or five doctors. With the recently developed chest X-rays spread out before them, the doctors quietly discussed the best course of treatment.

'I think we should try operating.' Presently the doctor who appeared to be the most senior in the group turned to Tanaka and announced their conclusions. 'Of course we'll have to keep you here on medication for about six months before that.'

'Actually,' Tanaka stammered, 'I can't afford to pay for that.'

The expressions of the doctors stiffened visibly. It might have been different before he had entered the hospital, but to start mentioning economic necessity after having spent a couple of weeks there was obviously considered selfish.

'Can't I possibly return to Japan?'

'What are you talking about? You wouldn't survive the trip back to Japan. What would you do if you started coughing up blood in the plane?'

Tanaka continued to plead with the doctors, but not one of them was able to give his consent. With the issue still unsettled, Tanaka left the examination-room.

Returning to the ward, he discovered on his bed a bundle of mail which had been forwarded by the hotel. Included in the bundle were some airmail letters from Japan. One was from his wife, the other an unexpected letter from Sakisaka.

Of course his wife knew nothing of his illness. He had yet to inform either his family or the university of his coughing up blood and subsequent hospitalization. Since entering the hospital, he had picked up his pen on a couple of occasions, but somehow he had found himself unable to write. For one thing he could not tell his wife of his current state of anguish. Moreover he was afraid that, in her panic, she would inform the university, thereby jeopardizing his position in the department and making his transfer to the College of Liberal Arts a certainty. His wife's letter included information about the shares she had sold during his absence, their son Keiichi and her dissatisfaction with his father, but as usual it seemed to represent little more than a rambling series of complaints. Tanaka found himself growing increasingly irritated as he skimmed the letter, stopping only to reread the part in which his wife informed him that Keiichi was now able to walk unaided. He then looked at the third page, on which his son had impishly drawn a series of lines in crayon.

'Is that a letter from your wife?' The man in the next bed took his eyes off the tabloid newspaper he had been reading and smiled pleasantly as he spoke to Tanaka. 'You must be really happy.'

'Yes.' Showing him the crayon drawing, Tanaka explained that his son was responsible for it. In fact nothing else about his wife's letter interested him. With her husband sick and alone in some foreign country, all she could write about was their shares and the daily routine. Her insensitivity angered him.

Sakisaka's letter was also written on airmail paper in tiny characters. Of course he too was totally unaware that Tanaka had succumbed to exactly the same disease as he had and was in the same hospital to which he had gone.

I imagine you are well. By now you have probably moved out of that hotel in the rue Hamelin (a hotel that holds nothing but dark memories for me now), but I shall mail this letter to that address anyway. I am sure you are now completely accustomed to the Paris winter. Your studies must be progressing smoothly too. Your studies are also vital, but please remember that your health is the most important thing. I should hate you of all people to experience the grief and loneliness of those, like me, who fall ill during the course of their studies abroad.

Nevertheless, whilst on the one hand continuing to pray for your health, I cannot help thinking about the contradictions involved in studying abroad. Since my return home, I find it even harder to fathom those students who return home fatter after their period of study abroad. Such people must have closed their eyes to what is most important during their stay abroad. There are just so many students who return home acclaiming the great progress they made in their studies whilst away! And yet how are they able to make progress like that? Why don't they end up tired and exhausted like me when they go over there? I am more inclined to empathize with those who claim that, during their stay abroad, they were unable to stand up to the great lava flow with which they came into contact. Since my return home, I have continually thought about that museum in the place du Trocadéro which we visited together. Those rows of stone carvings still lined up in those cold rooms. I termed it the 'great flow of European history'. I feel as though I can still recall vividly each and every one of those statues.

On occasion, I tried to convince myself that that flow and the Japanese flow were fundamentally the same, because, judging from outward appearances, there are clearly several points of similarity between the two. For example, you are probably acquainted with the Shakyamuni triptych in the golden hall of Hōryūji temple? The posture, eyes and fingers bear a striking resemblance to those of the statue of Christ and the angels in the cathedral at Moissac. And please try comparing the statue of Yakushi, the Buddha of Healing, at Hōryūji with the face of the wooden carving over the door in the cathedral at Chartres. Both in their appearance and the lines of their facial expression, they look just like twins, don't they? When you compare the statue of the Goddess of Mercy from the old Korean kingdom of Kudara with that of the Virgin Mary at Chartres, I am sure you will be surprised at the superficial similarity. Compare the expression on the face of the Maitreya Bodhisattva at the Chūgūji temple with that of Da Vinci's *St Anna*, the statue of Mary Magdalene in the art gallery at Cluny with the Bodhisattva Seishi in Hōryūji, the side profile of St Catherine in the art gallery at Saumur with that of the Bodhisattva Gekkō.

When I was depressed, I would visualize these expressions of the similarities between East and West and attempt to convince myself that that great lava flow did not actually exist. That way I felt much better. But for that, there would have been absolutely no point in my spending a couple of years before your arrival all alone in that cheap hotel, would there? But ultimately all I learnt in that hotel was the insuperable distance between the cathedral at Chartres and the Hōryūji temple, the unfathomable disparity between the statue of St Anna and the Maitreya Bodhisattva. From the outside they may appear similar, but the blood of those who created them was very different. I spent two years living with this uncomfortable realization. People will no doubt ask me if that is all I learnt. But there is a great difference between acquiring knowledge from a book and learning it experientially. At any rate, that is all I gained during my period of study in France.

We cannot receive blood from those of a different blood group. That is what I thought about on those lonely winter evenings in Paris....

225

There was a smudge of ink from Sakisaka's pen on the page around the word 'blood'. With one hand resting on the bed, Tanaka stared vacantly at that black stain. The shape of that smudge reminded him of the red spot he had seen on the wall of the château at La Coste. 'We cannot receive blood from those of a different blood group.' So the blood he had spat out at that snowy scene had been Japanese blood. Or maybe it had been blood he had coughed up through an inability to endure something Western which had flowed into his body. Tanaka continued with such incoherent thoughts until evening.

When the doctor arrived for his daily visit the following morning, he appeared unhappy about something. But he had finally granted Tanaka permission to return to Japan. 'However, that does not mean that the hospital has authorized this action,' the doctor repeated emphatically. 'We must not deprive you of your individual rights and so are willing to turn a blind eye to it. That's all. Actually, the other Japanese man who was here a short while ago made the same request and we were uncertain how to respond.'

'But please try to understand the feelings of a student studying abroad.' Tanaka was vehement in his attempt to justify himself. 'We come here from a distant country for the sake of our studies. There is nothing more depressing than to waste time getting medical treatment.'

The doctor folded his arms and shook his head wistfully. 'You have a whole lifetime ahead of you. You shouldn't be in such a hurry.' He continued by recommending that, at the very least, Tanaka should spend ten more days resting there. There was a pleading note in his voice. 'If you don't, you will end up coughing up blood again in the plane.'

But, as soon as the doctor left, Tanaka pressed his cheeks to the pillow and realized that this was the end of his period of studies in France. He recalled the rainy night of his arrival at Orly airport, the Paris he had seen from the bus on the way to Les Invalides – his very first views of Paris. On that occasion, damp from the rain, Paris had glistened the colour of pig-iron. It appeared dirty like the walls of a prison. He then thought of the Japan to which he would shortly be returning. He was disinclined to think of the university and of his future, but he wanted to think of his home in Setagaya.

226

The sunlight on the hedge and the nappies hanging out to dry on the washing-line. He could suddenly picture his son's face. It seemed so close. He would soon be seeing all this for himself again. He began to shed involuntary tears on to his pillow.

The following day he opened his trunk, took out his notebook and spread it out on his blankets. He had not looked at it for some time. He had been gripped by an urge to read his own account of Sade's experiences in the hospital at Charenton. Of course, unlike Tanaka, Sade had not entered the hospital as a result of illness, but rather, unable to endure life in prison, he had been assigned to the psychiatric hospital. There was nevertheless a time when he was relatively free to converse with the other patients, to walk about the wards and even to form his own small theatrical group within the hospital. The local dignitaries and literary scholars of Paris had even been invited to the performances put on in the hospital by this troupe. And yet from the end of 1813 Sade had been deprived once more of such liberties and been forced to endure more dark days. The memoirs of Dr Ramon, an intern in the hospital at the time, record Sade's loneliness in vivid detail:

> I often saw the Marquis de Sade dragging his feet down the corridors near his room, a blank expression on his face. I never saw him conversing with anyone. If one greeted him as one passed, he would bow politely yet coldly, thereby making us reluctant to address him. It was hard to believe that this was the author of *Justine* and of *Juliette*.

As Tanaka lay listening to the faint noise of the steam heater as he read, it was the following passage from the memoirs of Dr Ramon that held his attention.

> In later years, I was present at the cleaning of his grave and took Sade's skull in my hands. I later received a visit from the famous physiognomist, Dr Spritzheim, and, having received his assurance that it would be returned, was forced to lend him the skull. But before long, Dr Spritzheim, who was lecturing in both England and Germany, died and I never saw the skull again.

That was all it said and yet for a long time Tanaka stared at those few lines he had copied as a memo. Of course he had known about that even before entering the hospital, but at that stage it had not gripped him in quite the same way. Why was he so moved by the fate of a man who had lived his life with such passion, whose grave had been dug up and whose skull had been removed and subsequently lost?

Ruby attempted to trace the whereabouts of the skull in Spritzheim's possession, but apart from a rumour that it had been carried off to America, he was unsuccessful in this effort. In all probability, to this day the skull is decorating the home of some unwitting individual.

Tanaka closed his notebook, pulled the blanket up to his chin and, for the first time in his life, began to consider the nature of human fate. He was assailed by a realization that this was not unique to Sade; there was ultimately a certain cruelty about fate.

When he opened his eyes, there was someone standing beside him. It was Suganuma, his coat as always carefully brushed, who stood looking down on him, his arms folded in front of him.

'Oh, it's you.' Tanaka groped for his glasses which had fallen somewhere by his pillow, but Suganuma picked them up for him. There was a note of bitterness as he spoke.

'Why didn't you tell me? I didn't know anything about your going to hospital until I called the hotel this morning.'

'I thought we agreed not to trouble each other over trifles.'

'This is different. Don't you think you're standing too much on formality?' Suganuma seemed to be talking to himself as he continued. 'How could I ever show my face in the university again if . . .'

'There's nothing to worry about.' Tanaka contorted his face and continued with a touch of sarcasm, 'I'm sure the university will be delighted to hear about this. If I resign for medical reasons, then they'll have the perfect excuse to farm me out to the College of Liberal Arts.'

Suganuma looked miserable, like a dog that has just been thrashed, as he stared down at Tanaka.

'How are your studies coming on? All right?'

'Yes, thank you. I'm making some kind of progress. It was definitely worth coming here to study.'

'Good.' Tanaka forced a smile. 'I'm really jealous. You must be quite used to Paris by now.'

'Yes, in a way. I feel as though I've really immersed myself in Paris life.'

'You mustn't get sick like me. Of course there's not much likelihood of that in your case.'

'Yes, I'm sorry to have to say so, but I feel really healthy right now,' Suganuma continued innocently.

'Haven't you put on weight?'

'Yes, I'm really trying to organize my life systematically.'

'Studying systematically. Enjoying Paris systematically.' Tanaka was still smiling. 'I can almost see it now.'

'I bought this on my way over.' Suganuma removed a paper package from his coat and placed it on the bedstand.

'It's honey. I heard that it's good for restoring strength. And if there's anything else I can do for you ...'

'Actually ...' – Tanaka repositioned his glasses with his finger as he thought – 'there is just one thing. Would you be good enough to arrange my visa at the consulate when I go home?'

'Are you returning home?' Suganuma looked surprised.

'Yes, I've got to. I have no choice. I'm sure the university can't afford to pay my medical expenses over here.'

'Oh, really? Is there nothing we can do? I'd be happy to write a letter to Professor Imai.'

'No. There's no hope. You know that as well as I do.'

Suganuma continued to look down sadly and rubbed the floor with his well-polished shoes. As he watched him, Tanaka thought him underhand. He wondered what he would be thinking if he were in Suganuma's shoes. Half of him would be full of commiseration, but the other half would no doubt be consumed with a sense of superiority. When he had learnt of Sakisaka's sickness, he had felt sorry for him, but at the same time he had nursed a secret sense of one-upmanship.

'I don't know what to say. . . .' The look on Suganuma's face was full of guile. 'But please don't give up.'

'You just get on with your studies over here. I've had some time studying over here too.... By the way, how's Miss Nozaka? She never writes to me any more.'

After Suganuma had left, the nurse distributed the usual unappetizing dinner. Tanaka placed the aluminium tray holding a glass of wine and some meat that was as tough as leather on his knees and recalled the conversation he had just had with Suganuma. Come to think of it, even though his junior colleague had come all the way to visit him like that, there had been a barb of sarcasm in each of Tanaka's comments. He was disgusted with himself. Why did he have to be so perverse? Since coming to Paris he had developed into a sly old man. Repositioning his glasses, Tanaka chewed the tasteless meat.

Tanaka realized that, even after his own return to Japan, Suganuma would continue to study systematically and to enjoy Paris to the full. He would eventually return to Japan with his case full of presents for Nozaka Kazuko. He would marry her, become a lecturer instead of Tanaka and keep up a profitable correspondence with his acquaintances in Paris. One by one he would translate the new novels and prize-winning works and achieve recognition as a promising young scholar of foreign literature.

But just as one is bound to die if one is transfused with blood of a different group, so are those who are infused with a different mentality bound to be crushed. Whereas Suganuma was skilfully and adroitly closing his eyes to that fact, Tanaka had foolishly confronted that reality since his arrival in France. Moreover, having confronted it, he had not succeeded in conquering it but had merely been repulsed by it. Tanaka recalled with displeasure the words the writer Manabe had addressed to him in that Montparnasse café shortly after his arrival in Paris. 'What sort of relationship is there between you lot and the literature you read?'

His associates had continued to spout the same logic over and over again.

'You lot are just getting a free ride at someone else's expense.... You mimic the words of another human being like a mina bird and call it a translation.... But if that is really so, then I wish you'd reveal the pain and suffering of living like mina birds in your lives!'

A Japanese man of letters like Manabe had never paused to consider the destiny of a man like Tanaka. And if this were the burden to be borne not only by himself, but by all specialists of

230

foreign literature, then ...

'It's time for lights out. Shall we get ready for bed?' The man in the next bed extended his legs, white like those of a woman, from beneath the blankets and slipped on his slippers. The man, who apparently worked at the local post office, brushed his teeth and spat into the washstand erected in the corner of the room. As Tanaka awaited his turn, brush in hand, he rubbed the window which had misted over as a result of the steam from the heater. Outside, light snow had begun to fall.

'It's snowing!' In response to Tanaka's involuntary cry, all the other patients in the ward put on their gowns and gathered by the window. A faint light seeped into the ward through the window and the snow danced like countless small white elves. A thin layer of snow covered the roofs of the buildings. Only the sky beyond those roofs glistened with a reddish hue.

'You can see the reflection of the neon signs in Montparnasse,' someone remarked wistfully. 'Right now, the women must be hard at work.'

'You'll be back there one day. Don't worry.'

Tonight, like every other night, the Japanese students and artists would be huddled together in some warm café drinking and absorbed in heated discussion. Suganuma would be there, too, sitting silently in that carefully brushed overcoat of his. Tanaka could picture Ono turning to Suganuma and commenting between yawns, 'I hear Tanaka-kun is sick. Poor chap.' He realized he had been treated as little more than a pile of rubble, a stepping-stone.

Tanaka suddenly found his attention drifting to things totally unrelated to the snow and the reddish glow of the neon signs. So, as far as the other Japanese were concerned, his existence – and that of Sakisaka as well – and the fact that they had both been taken sick during the course of their stay in Paris were meaningless details of absolutely no value, were they? Or would their experiences serve rather as stepping-stones for the next generation of students of foreign literature? To Tanaka at that time everything appeared unclear.

'All right. It's lights out, everyone.' The elderly nurse who came round every night to switch off the lights popped her head round the door and, on seeing Tanaka, said to him, 'There's a phone call for you.'

Tanaka took the telephone in the nurses' office. The call was from the reception desk of the hotel in the rue Hamelin.

'Another Japanese student has just arrived and I am thinking of giving him your room. That's all right, isn't it?'

'Yes, that's fine.' He could vaguely hear the clerk speaking as he conveyed Tanaka's reply to the new Japanese student. He could almost picture that student, carrying the same heavy trunk and bundle bound in the Japanese wrapping-cloth as he had done on that first night. In a few moments that new student would be sitting down on the edge of the bed in the very room which Tanaka had previously occupied. His very first night in Paris. The copperplate sign in the hotel lobby, which read *Proust died here*, now damp from the snow. The new student would be looking out at the snow, thinking about his future life and studies in Paris with a mixture of anticipation and trepidation.

The night-time corridor in the ward was dark and long. Tanaka pushed up his glasses with his finger and tiptoed back to his bed. In his mind's eye he tried to imagine that new student.

'And you, too,' he muttered to himself.

NIGEL WATTS

BILLY BAYSWATER

After losing his job on a London building site, young Billy slips through the social security net. Retarded, disorientated and destitute, he is as vulnerable to deceit and abuse as he is responsive to the girl who shows him temporary kindness, and to the beauty he finds in the parks' trees and flowers. Delightful and devastating by turn, BILLY BAYSWATER draws a poignant, topical portrait of life for the homeless in the big city, at times the loneliest place on earth.

'A beautifully crafted imaginative expression of one very particular view of the world'
The Guardian

'A tremendous imaginative triumph and should be read by anyone who still thinks that all homeless people are bludgers'
Mary Hope in The Financial Times

'A swelling anger gathers force through the story, made all the more powerful because of an emotional counter to it, a glorious sense of humanity and of the city's beauty'
Judy Cooke in The Guardian

'This fine and careful novel about those who live on the margins of our society is an indictment of that society without saying a word against it'
Andrew Sinclair in The Times

'I believed in Billy. His fine, highly written story worked very well. It's very sad and true'
John Healy, author of THE GRASS ARENA

MAX EGREMONT

PAINTED LIVES

George Loftus, a young art restorer invited to the decaying country seat of Cragham to assess a number of family paintings, stumbles across the diaries of the dead wife of the house. The tableau that emerges, through these memoirs and the prudent confidences of a close family friend, is one of passive desperation beneath the façade of a charmed aristocratic marriage, and of former glories misremembered in the present.

'A superb novel, beautifully crafted, with an elegance that justifies its author as one of our leading novelists'
Geoffrey Bailey in the Daily Telegraph

'A sharply idiosyncratic work, the standard lament for lost, upper-class time, yet with a hard, scything edge . . . it is brilliantly done'
D. J. Taylor in The Spectator

'Egremont is a mellow and extremely funny writer and this is a novel to be savoured: superbly written and complete with a sparkling plot and a cast of cultivated eccentrics. Great acclaim, I hope, will now reward the author's efforts'
Janet Barron in The Literary Review

'Brilliant . . . there can be no doubt that in evoking the bleak northern country house of Cragham, and the power it exerts, he has come into his own, expressing his true voice – ironical, subtle and never less than sympathetic'
Hugh Montgomery-Massingberd in the Daily Telegraph

sceptre

CESARE PAVESE

AMONG WOMEN ONLY

A powerful depiction of self-estrangement set against the fashionable post-war society of Turin. Pavese portrays two very different women, one a successful dressmaker from Rome, the other a solitary victim of the fashion world which surrounds her. Behind the bustle of restaurants and casinos, of artists' studios and private parties, we sense the pervading melancholy and emptiness that Pavese saw reflected in the society around him. AMONG WOMEN ONLY is a masterpiece.

'A very great writer. Pavese, Camus and Forster are among the most liberal of the great writers of the century'
The Spectator

'A novelist of power and great intelligence'
The Listener

THE DEVIL IN THE HILLS

Cesare Pavese is now generally regarded as one of the most important writers of the century. This novel is among his best work. It is the story of a young married man, rich and self-indulgent, who has an elderly mistress, and whilst participating in the debauchery prevalent amongst his friends, nevertheless desires to lead a more useful life.

'Erotic, extraordinarily delicate and controlled'
The Guardian